## 20 Years A Soldier of Fortune

This story involves some of the most interesting and exciting times in the history of our nation. It includes the years immediately before and during the First World War, when Alaska was an untamed territory and gold mining was still the major industry, having lost little steam from the boom years at the turn of the century. Adventure and excitement were felt wherever one ventured, with opportunity unlimited in the Alaska Territory—and that is where the "Alaska Kid" (author Floyd Marsh himself) made it rich. Raised in the cotton fields of Oklahoma, he became the Horatio Alger of the Far North, soon becoming U.S. Commissioner in the Territory.

In addition to gold mining in Alaska, the story reveals interesting adventures of gold mining in the states of Arizona, California, Colorado and Idaho. Here are true first-hand accounts, not only of the last frontier of the gold-mining era, but of events that took place in the Prohibition years of the Roaring Twenties, revealing the corruption of enforcement officers as well as high officials.

You will read how "bootleggers" (liquor dealers), gamblers and sporting houses operated in our supposed law-abiding country. Less than ten per cent of the people in Portland (perhaps in the nation) knew what was going on in the underworld during the fabulous Twenties. While head of the Portland Police Vice Squad, Author Marsh was once transferred to the "sticks" (suburban uniform beat) for making a statement that he could clean up the city in two weeks if given the authority to do so.

In this story of "20 years as a soldier of fortune," Floyd Marsh has given the true facts of events both inside and outside the law—and he saw as much of the action as any enforcement man. The story is as he lived it—and saw it—and let the chips fall where they may!

# 20 Years
# A Soldier of Fortune

By

Floyd R. Marsh

**Binford & Mort**
*Thomas Binford, Publisher*
2536 S.E. Eleventh • Portland, Oregon 97202

*20 Years a Soldier of Fortune*

Copyright under international
Pan-American copyright conventions
Copyright © 1976 by Floyd R. Marsh.
All rights reserved including the right
to reproduce this book, or any portions
thereof, in any form except for the
inclusion of brief quotations in a review

*Printed in the United States of America*

First Edition
1976

**Library of Congress Cataloging in Publication Data**

Marsh, Floyd R. 1898-
   20 Years a Soldier of Fortune.

   Autobiography.
   Includes index.
   1. Gold mines and mining—Alaska—Personal narratives.
2. Gold mines and mining—The West—Personal narratives.
3. Alaska—History—1896-1959. 4. The West—History—1848-1950.
5. Marsh, Floyd R., 1898-   I. Title.
F909.M36       979.8'04'0924       76-864
ISBN 0-8323-0270-8
ISBN 0-8323-0269-4 pbk.

*This book is dedicated to
my wife "Bo"
and our sons,
Dr. Richard F. Marsh and
Dr. Dennis E. Marsh,
and our daughter, Kathi.*

# Contents

|  |  |  | Page |
|---|---|---|---|
| Chapter 1 | The Young Miner | | 1 |
| Chapter 2 | Mining Partners | | 8 |
| Chapter 3 | Two Boy Mining Company | | 15 |
| Chapter 4 | Join the Army | | 23 |
| Chapter 5 | Armistice Signed | | 35 |
| Chapter 6 | Arrival in Alaska | | 40 |
| Chapter 7 | Move on North | | 46 |
| Chapter 8 | An Alaska Sweetheart | | 61 |
| Chapter 9 | Appointed U.S. Commissioner | | 72 |
| Chapter 10 | Take Office as U.S. Commissioner | | 86 |
| Chapter 11 | The Jury Verdict | | 101 |
| Chapter 12 | The Mines Open | | 122 |
| Chapter 13 | Seattle Show Business | | 139 |
| Chapter 14 | Back to Gold Mining | | 143 |
| Chapter 15 | Trip to Phoenix | | 146 |
| Chapter 16 | Back to the Northwest | | 151 |
| Chapter 17 | Leave Salmon River Area | | 166 |
| Chapter 18 | Gold Mining, Boise Basin, Idaho | | 170 |
| Chapter 19 | Joined the Portland Police Department | | 177 |
| Chapter 20 | On the Vice Squad | | 180 |
| Chapter 21 | Mining in Arizona | | 194 |
| Chapter 22 | Building a Gold Dredge | | 200 |
| Chapter 23 | Start to Dredge Gold | | 218 |
| Index | | | 235 |

# List of Photographs

Floyd Marsh in 1914, opposite page 1
Sandy hills homestead, opposite page 1
Floyd Marsh in the Field Artillery, 30
Floyd Marsh in the Hospital Corps, 30
Wilbur Foster, 30
Anchorage, gold, 1917, 51
Fish caught in Mt. McKinley range, 51
Cabin on Yellow Creek, 51
Fanny Quigley and dogs, 55
Pack dogs, 55
Caribou, 55
Floyd Marsh, U.S. Commissioner, 75
Larry Cross, 75
Freight dog team, 75
Mail dog team, 82
Big River roadhouse 128
Floyd Marsh panning gold, 128
Mary Kirkenoff, 131
Widow Marsh and sons, 149
Copper mines, Santa Rita, N.M., 149
Floyd Marsh a police officer, 191
Floyd Marsh during vice squad days, 191
Floyd Marsh vacationing in Arizona, 191
Newspaper items of Marsh's
    Vice Squad activities, 192, 193
Bo and I at Mt. Hood, 205
Fred Reed, Bo and I, 205
A deer and I, 205
Front end of dredge, 210

Rear end of dredge, 210
Bo and I at the dredge, 215
Conveyor bucket line, 215
Fred Reed, superintendent, 215
Floyd Marsh in control house, 217
Bo and friends on bridge of dredge, 217
Camp at the dredge, 222
Fred Reed in front of office, 222
Gold bars from last clean-up, 222
Leona "Bo" Marsh, 232
Floyd Marsh, 232
Floyd Marsh, 40 years later, 234

# Acknowledgments

I have written this story from my memory and notes, and the people I would like to mention here are those who have had a great influence on my life—persons who made much of this story possible.

Strangely enough, one of these was the old miner that I met when I was fifteen years old. I knew him only as Tom at the "Little Mint" mine at Clifton, Arizona. From him I learned the first principles and techniques of mining, and these have had a bearing on my entire mining career. The little Dutch preacher at the mine, Herbert Lang, set me right on living. It seems that impressions on a young life are very lasting; in my own case, this certainly proved to be true.

Later on, I met other men who had a great impact on my life. One of these was Dr. Oliver Lemon, a captain in the Hospital Corps of the U.S. Army. He helped and guided me during my entire enlistment in the Army, most of which was spent in the Medical Corps. He gave me a sense of direction. A few years afterwards, Judge Cecil H. Clegg of Fairbanks, Alaska, played a major part in my Alaska adventures.

Fifty-two years ago (1924), a man by the name of Fred B. Reed became a business associate and adviser. Today Fred Reed is a very admired friend. He is the only man still living of the ones mentioned in these acknowledgments. Only a few days ago, when I mentioned I was writing this story, he remarked that it would be fantastic.

Early in life when I was bumming around the country, I met a man by the name of James W. Foley, writer for the former *Saturday Evening Post*. In addition to lecturing at local Y.M.C.A.'s around the country, he seemed to take an interest in this Wandering Boy. He gave me much wise advice on keeping out of trouble. He said we always have to live with our deeds, and bad ones might never be lived down. We kept in touch through letters until he passed away; at the time, I was still in Alaska.

On one occasion, Mr. Foley sent me a card with his picture and a poem on it. I kept these for many years before they became lost in the shuffle of life. I would like to repeat a roughly remembered version of that poem here, in memory of this fine man:

> It is not so far from right to wrong,
> The trail ain't hard to lose;
> There have been times I would almost
> Give my life to know which to choose.
>
> There ain't no signboards up,
> To keep you on the track:
> Wrong is sometimes whiter than snow,
> And right looks awful black.
>
> I've lost the trail sometimes myself,
> And may get lost again
> While traveling down life's
> Long, long path of sunshine and of rain.
>
> So when I see a man that looks
> As though he's gone astray,
> I want to put my hand in his
> And help him find the way.

# Introduction

At a little country store in the sand hills in the northwestern part of Oklahoma, where my father had taken up a homestead, I made a vow to myself that when I grew up I would not be *poor*. This came about when I asked my father for a nickel to buy some candy and he opened his pocketbook (called coin purse now, but seldom used) to show me that he didn't have a nickel. The purse was completely empty. This just about broke a little heart. I was only five years old at the time but I clearly remember that I thought I might have a five-year-old son some day. If so, and he asked me for a nickel, I was going to have one to give him. I think it was about that time I started to figure out a sure way to have that nickel.

On the homestead we lived mostly on wild rabbits and cornmeal mush. Occasionally we would have chicken (usually chicken and dumplings); Mother herself raised the chickens. We also had hogs, which we sold at the market to purchase clothes for the family. However, when one could be spared, Dad would butcher it and cure the meat in a smokehouse. After five years on the homestead, Dad called it quits, traded the homestead for a team of mules, and loaded the family—which now consisted of Mother and five boys—into a covered wagon and moved to Elk City, Oklahoma, where we began to raise cotton on a rented farm. It was in the cotton field that I realized what it was like to be poor.

An act of God moved us out of Oklahoma. It was soon after the 4th of July 1908, when our 140 acres of cotton was about 10 inches high, that a severe hail storm laid the cotton so flat the ground looked like a football field. Dad loaded the family into the same covered wagon that had brought us out of the sand hills and moved 20 miles south to Sayer, Oklahoma, where the cotton had not been hailed out; here we worked in the cotton fields the remaining summer. About this time Dad's health began to fail so he decided to seek healthier and greener pastures.

Dad got enough money together to charter a boxcar with another farmer by the name of Alfred Stewart. In the boxcar were loaded farm implements, two teams of mules each, household furniture, housekeeping items, and both families' possessions. With Claude (my oldest brother), now eleven years old, and the Stewart boy (Henry), about the same age, and Dad riding in the boxcar, they headed for Duncan, Arizona, where on a previous trip Dad had rented a medium-size farm while looking for a place to improve his health.

Mother and the four other boys followed by train. I will always remember that train trip. Mother had taken a basket of fried chicken and a large number of sandwiches on the train and we ate all the way from Oklahoma to Arizona. After two days and nights on the train we arrived at Lordsburg, New Mexico, where we changed trains for Duncan, Arizona. Mother evidently thought that we had had enough chicken and sandwiches because she took us into a Chinese restaurant for a meal. The five meals came to $1.05 and Mother told the cashier that she thought she had been robbed. If Mother were living today, she would certainly think there are a lot of robbers in the country.

In Arizona, we became involved in something as bad as cotton, and that was raising corn and trying to keep the Johnson grass down. However, corn produced more money for the hard work both involved. After a couple of years Dad had saved enough money for a down payment on a 30-acre farm in the Mormon Valley near Duncan. It was here that my youngest brother, Ted, was born. Hard work to produce a living for his large family, combined with the worry of keeping up payments on the newly purchased farm, contributed to the deterioration of Dad's health. He passed away January 30, 1914, from tuberculosis. I thought that life had more to offer than what I had seen, and I was going to find it. I hoped it would not be too late to help my mother and brothers—and this accounts for my early roaming years.

I really don't recall when the gold bug bit me, or when gold got into my blood. It could have been the adventure and excitement of looking for something of value. It certainly lured me first to California and then to Cripple Creek, Colorado. From there I served a hitch in the Army during World War I, and from there I went to Alaska, where I did find adventure, excitement and gold and even romance. After that I spent several years gold mining in some of the Western States.

On one memorable day between my gold-mining years (December 20, 1926), I joined the Portland Police Department, and after being assigned to the Vice Squad for some time, I was appointed head of the squad. I was also in charge of the Mayor's Secret Police. What I learned about the underworld and prohibition while performing these duties, I reluctantly reveal in this story. I think this is the first time this material has been put into print.

I brought to an end my adventure of gold mining by building a gold dredge on the Trinity River 40 miles west of Redding, California. It was both an exciting and profitable adventure, which is fully revealed in this story. Gold mining has been good to me. I have taken out over five million dollars' worth of gold (at today's prices). Although I do not have it now, I do have my health. I have had a wonderful life, and the greatest treasure of all, a wonderful family. I have that son I visualized when I was five years old (and he now has a family of his own)—and when he was five years old I did have that nickel for him.

Above: Floyd Marsh in 1914 at Duncan, Arizona, where he embarked on his "20 years as a soldier of fortune."

Below: Homestead in the sand hills of northwest Oklahoma, where the author lived as a boy. This picture of the house, built in 1901, was taken by the author in 1956. Shown is Claude Marsh, the author's brother.

# CHAPTER 1

## *The Young Miner*

The year 1914 was just an ordinary year on the Gila River—which ran through Mormon Flats near Duncan, Arizona—for a widow and her seven sons who had been left alone a year earlier by the death of the husband and father. Widow Marsh knew nothing about farming. She had been brought up the old-fashioned way to take care of the home, cook, and look after the children. The seven boys ranged in age from 17 years to the 2-year-old youngest. Claude, the oldest at 17, had been a hard worker on the farm; he was also a good manager who'd taken hold of things after the senior Marsh passed away.

Second in age at 15, I had been more of a rambler and had taken several trips over the country via empty boxcars. (There was no hitchiking in those days and I had no money.) The rest of the seven boys consisted of Virgil, 14; Arthur, 12; Joe, 9; Johnnie, 5; and Ted, 2. All except the two youngest pitched in and helped Claude make a living for the fatherless family. All but these two had been brought up in the cotton fields of Oklahoma and had moved to Arizona with their parents only a few years previously. Our farm crop consisted mostly of corn, which we harvested and sold. We also raised a few farm animals, such as milk cows, hogs, a few horses, and some chickens.

Though I had only partly completed high school, my feet began to itch to do some traveling. I told my mother that there were enough of the boys to run the 30-acre farm and that I should go to the mines at Clifton, Arizona, only 40 miles away, and work to supplement our meager farm income, as we practically lived off the farm the year around. I can recall going with my father to the gristmill where we had corn ground into cornmeal to make corn bread. Only once a week were we treated to biscuits made from flour. I put up such a sales talk to my mother that she finally told me I could go and try to get work in the mines.

I soon found a job in the big copper mine at Clifton, but it was not exactly what I was looking for. I had always been interested in minerals and the techniques of mining, and wanted to come in contact with something along this line. Instead, I was given a job of spotting ore cars along the tunnels on different levels. After a couple of weeks in Clifton I became acquainted with an old prospector whom I only knew as Tom. He did have a surname that I was never able to pronounce. Tom was a rugged old fellow about 50 years old. He told me that he had been in Alaska and a lot of mining camps in the western states. The tales old Tom told the few days after I met him instilled in me the desire of adventure and exploring for unfound riches.

Tom and four other miners were doing some exploratory work for a small mining company headed by a man named Ralph Higgins. It was a small mine carrying minerals of gold, silver, and lead, located about seven miles from Clifton up Frisco Creek. From what Tom had told me, it was just what I was looking to get some experience in actual mining and mineral knowledge. Tom took me to Mr. Higgins, who himself was a husky old miner about Tom's age.

Higgins was a rough-talking old fellow. He shook my hand with a ham-like hand that completely covered mine and remarked, "What the hell is a kid like you doing in a mining camp like Clifton?" I replied that I wanted to be a miner. He said, "Good for you," and further remarked that he wished more young men like myself would get interested in mining, as the old-timers like himself and Tom were about to phase out.

After warning me that mining wasn't easy, that it was a lot of hard work on the end of a pick and shovel, he said that I looked like I could do the work and that he would give me a try.

The next morning Tom and I, with two other miners of middle age, and a pack burro with supplies, hit the trail up

Frisco Creek to a small mine called "Little Mint," which included four cabins, a large cookhouse, with dining and lounging space, a blacksmith shop, and a large bath-house with a spring running through it like a creek. The seven miles up Frisco Creek seemed like a long journey to me. I was not used to the light mountain air and climbing a steep trail. While I was tired, I was excited and enthusiastic about my new adventure.

The next morning after breakfast—like you never get in the cities—the four of us who had come up from Clifton the previous day, and two miners who were already at the mine, started working in two of the three tunnels at the mine, which had several off-drifts, or side tunnels, off from the main tunnel. The face of the main tunnel was 5 feet wide by 8 feet high and followed the foot wall of the vein. We would pick and shovel the loose and soft material into an ore car that ran on a steel track. Then we would dump this material at the face of the tunnel.

During the day we would drill 1-inch holes 3 to 4 inches deep into the hard rock, then load them with dynamite, which we set off at the end of our day's shift, as it would take all night for the powder to clear out so we could work in the tunnel. A powder headache is something you would want to stay away from; it hangs on for a long time and is very painful.

As we had no machinery, all the drilling was done by hand. It was hard work, but I liked it. It was learning something about mining, and about different kinds of mineral ore, rocks, and formation from the old-timers at the "Little Mint," who seemed to know a lot about mining. Somehow, to my surprise, the old-timers had taken a liking to me, and I thought that they all were fine fellows, too. They were the most congenial bunch of men I had ever worked with.

In the evenings we would sit around a kerosene lamp and potbelly wood stove as it was chilly up in the mountains. The old-timers would unravel yarns of their experience in various mining camps, which seemed to be as interesting to them as they were to me. After a few weeks I felt like I had been in every mining camp in the West. It was surprising to learn the hardships and rough times these men had been through—all of which seemed to kindle their feelings for mankind.

Of course, there was no church at the "Little Mint," but we held services there every Sunday just the same. There was one old-timer, a little fellow of Dutch extraction from Kentucky by the name of Herbert Lang, who shaved and dressed up every Sunday and conducted services in the large dining room. Herbert said that people could worship the Lord regardless of where they were. He wasn't a bad preacher either.

Tom and I would take off every Sunday after our little service for some prospecting in the nearby rugged mountain. I learned a lot from Tom about minerals, formation, and prospecting in the six months that I was with him. In fact, I thought that I had learned enough to venture out alone on a prospecting trip, but the old-timers at the camp told me that this particular part of Arizona was too rugged to go out into alone. Besides, if a valuable mineral was found in the mountainous country that we were in, it would take a fortune to get machinery in to work it as the whole country was of very hard-rock formation. They advised me to go where there was placer gold mining. This is sometimes referred to as "instant money" because it doesn't take so much money to set up an operation.

It was now getting into the summer of 1915. I had been at the "Little Mint" since before the first of the year. I felt that I had accomplished a lot in the way of mining experience and in the identification of different minerals. I had also saved my wages while in the mountain, which I perhaps would not have done if I had remained in the mining town of Clifton. And the wages were good for 1915. I got $40 a month and board for an 8-hour day, which was much better than I received working on a farm in Mormon Flats, where the wages were $30 a month for a 10-hour day.

It was a few days before the fourth of July that I bid the old-timers goodbye at the "Little Mint" and headed out of the mountains to Clifton, where I caught the train to Duncan for a

## The Young Miner 5

visit with my mothers and brothers. I stayed only a few days at home as I was anxious to get to the California gold fields. I purchased a ticket on the train from Duncan to Lordsburg only 75 miles away. In order to save my money I rode empty boxcars to Sacramento, California.

At Sacramento I was advised that there was some dredge and placer mining on the Feather River near Marysville and Oroville, about 60 miles north. I took a bus to Marysville where I got a job on the night shift of a gold dredge a few miles out of town. It was a medium-sized dredge that employed a night crew of three men. The dredge was operated by a Mr. Schultz, a tough guy to work for, and he believed in telling you only once what to do. I managed to get along with him all right and he became more friendly as time went on. My job was cleaning the riffles of trash and moss that collected on them. It was an interesting job; I could see the gold in the riffles, which compensated to some extent for the long lonely hours I had to work. My shift was from 10 p.m. to 8 a.m. for $3.50 per day, but while the work was interesting, I was not gaining much in the way of mining technology.

I had been with the dredge about a month when I heard of something that sounded very good to me, and that was a placer mine at Oroville some 30 miles farther north. Placer mining is where sluice boxes, about 12 inches wide and the same inches in depth, are set up on a 1-inch to 1-foot decline with riffles in the bottom to catch the gold. Water is run through the sluice box as the gold-bearing gravel is shoveled into the box—which resembles a trough. The gold goes to the bottom and is caught in the riffles.

This job was what I had been looking for, as I had always heard that placer mining of this type was a poor man's way of mining, or at least a way to get started in mining. I told Schultz when I came to work on that evening shift that I would be leaving the next day. Somehow he seemed very much displeased and wanted me to stay on.

I was surprised that Schultz would be concerned about my leaving. However, the dredge master told me that Schultz liked me and hoped that I would stay on. He also told me that other fellows working the riffles had robbed them of gold nuggets and that Schultz had a new man on this particular job every few days. I asked the dredge master how Schultz knew the men were taking the gold, and all he would tell me was to say Schultz had a way. This taught me something I would always remember, and that is to pursue an honest course regardless of anything else. It was very tempting for me to reach down in the riffles and pick up the nuggets that I could plainly see, but on this occasion two thoughts entered my mind. One thought was that the gold was not mine, and the other thought was that there was someone watching, and that was the great "Supreme Being" above, who someday would be the Judge of all my actions.

Schultz never told me that he knew I had been honest with him, but he told me that he never had a better worker, and wanted me to come back. He gave me the names of some placer mines at Oroville with a note of introduction. I found Oroville a prosperous little town of placer gold mining, which is what I was looking for. I soon got a job shoveling gold-bearing gravel and sand into a sluice box. It was hard work, also wet and cold. However, we were paid good for the work—75 cents an hour—and only worked 8 hours a day. This was almost twice the money I was making at the dredge and I was working fewer hours. Also, I was learning something about gold placer mining. I had now worked here a little over a month. It was the first part of October, and the wet work was getting cold and miserable. I had begun to give some thought to moving on.

At the Oroville placer mine I met a likable kind of fellow by the name of Wilbur Foster, who was a few years older than myself. We struck up an acquaintance and friendship from the first few days we met. Perhaps it was because we had a common interest, and that was in mining. I had told Wilbur of my experience at the Little Mint mine in Arizona, and he seemed to be interested in the fact that I had some mining experience.

Wilbur told me that he had some mining claims at Cripple Creek, Colorado, with a cabin on them and also a tunnel on one of his claims. Wilbur also said that this was his second summer in the California placer mines, where he had come to replenish his grubstake for prospecting and mining on his own, as there was no place he had found that paid 75 cents an hour for labor. He had been at Oroville since midsummer and was ready to leave for Cripple Creek to spend the winter working his claims. The tunnel he had already started would be an ideal place to work in during the winter months.

## CHAPTER 2

## *Mining Partners*

Wilbur perhaps saw the gleam in my eyes as he spoke of his claims and stories of rich gold strikes that had been made at Cripple Creek, which I had already heard about from old-timers. Anyway, he asked me if I would like to go in with him on his mining adventure. I was surprised and elated to receive such an offer, but I told him that I didn't have the money to buy into or finance the operation of a mine. He replied that his claims were not a mine and that he was just developing them, that he had mining tools and would furnish the dynamite. Wilbur was honest with me. He said that his claims were just a raw prospect and a gamble, but if they turned out like some claims near his we would both become very rich. This last remark sold me. I was ready to start mining.

That evening we got together and worked out a satisfactory deal. We were both inexperienced in business, especially in drawing up contracts and agreements. However, we drew up an agreement stating that after I had examined the claims, I would have an option of furnishing $150 as a grubstake for the two of us during the following winter. We estimated this would last until the first of April, at which time I was to receive a half interest in the two mining claims that Wilbur had recorded in his name. The names of the claims were Okie No. 1 and Okie No. 2, after his native state of Oklahoma—which is also my native state. Included in the agreement was the provision that I was to help Wilbur extend the tunnel during the winter.

As we were both anxious to get to Cripple Creek and settle on the claims before winter set in, we didn't try to find cheap transportation to Colorado. After collecting our pay from the Placer Mining Company, we took the train to Denver. Riding on

## Mining Partners

the cushions was something new to me. Already I felt like a millionaire.

From Denver to Colorado Spring we took a bus, which turned out to be both a passenger and a cargo carrier; it stopped at every store on the way to unload and pick up cargo. We arrived in Colorado Springs late at night and proceeded to sleep in the bus station to save money. Because Wilbur knew a trucking firm that hauled freight to Cripple Creek, about 25 miles west of Colorado Springs, we got a ride there on a freight truck for $2 each.

We arrived in Cripple Creek in the forenoon. The climate was far different from the California weather that we had just left. The first snow of the season had fallen the previous night and there was an inch of it on the ground. The little town of Cripple Creek looked like pictures that I had seen of mining towns framed with snow-covered mountains, but it also looked like a tough little mining town put up in a hurry.

Wilbur's claims were about three miles from the town in a place called Gopher Gulch. His cabin was up a little way from the gulch bed, and fortunately could be reached by an unimproved wagon road. We needed this to transport our bedrolls and a few other things, including some supplies such as groceries and cooking utensils. We decided to do our shopping, then get a delivery wagon to take our stuff out to the cabin on the claims. However, after we had done our shopping, we were unable to get a delivery wagon to make the trip, so we went to a party that had pack horses, teams, and wagons for hire and rented a team of mules and a small dray wagon, which was the real thing for the snow and kind of road we had to travel.

We arrived at the cabin without any trouble. I was surprised to find it unlocked and asked Wilbur if anything was missing. He replied that there had been only the stove, a table, and two chairs left in the cabin and they were still there. He added that no one in the Cripple Creek area locked their cabins. We soon unloaded the little dray wagon and Wilbur took the mules and dray wagon back to town. I cut some wood, got a fire going, and fixed some supper to give Wilbur an idea of what he would have to endure in the way of cooking if our deal went through.

It was late when Wilbur got back. He said that he had been visiting some miners that he had met and found out that there had been a lot of activity in the Cripple Creek area and at a little mining camp a few miles away by the name of Goldfield. He remarked that tomorrow we perhaps would be taking in some ore samples to the assay office, and we would do more visiting with the miners in town and find out more about mining activity during the past summer when he had been away.

During the evening we sat around a kerosene lamp and a combination heating and cook stove and talked over mining in general. He told me the story of the fabulous Horace Tabor, the first Colorado prospector, who was a millionaire, and also the story of the famous Matchless mine that someone sold Tabor as a swindle and turned out to be worth millions. I had heard the story before, but I enjoyed hearing it again from Wilbur, as he seemed to be a little closer to gold mining in Colorado.

We were up early the next morning, and as some of the snow had gone, we walked around in the area of the cabin. Fortunately there was a spring near the portal of the tunnel. Wilbur had built the cabin just below the spring and piped the water into the cabin. How much convenience would one want, with your work only a few steps away, and running water in your abode?

As there was still some snow on the ground, the tunnel was about the only place we could examine and get ore sample to be assayed. The tunnel was driven into a hillside about 20 feet along the ledge, which was exposed along the hanging wall. The foot wall of the ledge was exposed in places, as the ledge varied from 3 to 6 feet in width, and the tunnel was 5 feet wide. The ledge was a true fissure vein, between two different types of formation, with a steep dip or pitch to it, which—according to my limited knowledge of geology at that time—was very favorable for an intrusive ledge with depth.

## Mining Partners 11

We spent several hours taking samples from the floor, top, and both sides of the ledge, in addition to the samples through the center of the ledge. We really had the ledge sampled good. We had taken 24 samples which were marked on a sketch we made of the ledge. After comparing the sampling locations on this sketch, we found that we had some duplication, so we selected 16 samples to be assayed from the 24 we had taken. We both were anxious to get the samples to the assayer in Cripple Creek. We had our lunch and took off. After leaving the ore samples at the assay office, we visited a friend of Wilbur's, then returned to our cabin. We had not brought a lantern and didn't want to get caught in the dark.

Upon arising the following morning we found all the snow gone, so we decided to take a walk over the two claims. There was considerable float and ledge matter or ore that had broken away from the ledge. In fact, there seemed to be several ledges on the two claims, but whether they carried any value and to what extent could only be determined by assay. As it would be another day before we could get the results from the ore samples taken in the previous day, we decided to visit some of the small mine owners in the area and perhaps some of the nearby mines that were in operation. During the past summer there had been several rich strikes made, that is, rich pockets of gold found in the ledge (which means that pure or native gold, referred to as free gold, is found in rock that can be recovered by crushing the rock and washing away the residue leaving the pure gold).

Gold appears in several different ways—in quartz or hardrock mining. There is the free gold referred to above, which is usually found in the oxide zone in shallow earth. Then there is gold in the sulphides that cannot be detected with a magnifying glass; this is treated with a cyanide process and by a smelter.

Wilbur and I learned by visiting several mine owners that there had been two large deposits of free gold found during the past summer and a few smaller ones. The largest one of $530,000 was found on upper Cripple Creek about 7 miles from the city. The other one of $108,500 was found less than 2 miles from the city. The $530,000 pocket was in a small deposit 15 feet long by 10 feet wide and 5 feet deep and was worked out in a few days. It yielded chunks of pure gold as large as a man's hand.

The $108,500 deposit was in a vein of talc on the foot wall and only 4 by 6 inches and 8 feet long. We visited this latter mine that produced the rich pocket. It was owned by two brothers, John and Frank McCoy, who were very courteous. They seemed to be pleased to show us where they had taken the rich deposit from the ledge—or rather, vein, as it was only 10 inches wide. I examined the vein closely and it seemed to have the same kind of material as ours, and in the same type of formation.

I asked one of the men who owned the mine if he would object to telling me what his assays were in the ledge outside the rich pocket. He replied that he would be glad to, and said that their assays ran from $3 to $13 per ton in gold and $5 in silver. He further remarked that, of course, this was not profitable ore to work and that they just relied on rich pockets—and they did find small rich ones quite often. The rich one they had discovered this past summer was the most valuable they had ever found. The two brothers agreed that they had taken out almost a million dollars worth of gold since they inherited the mine from their father 11 years previously. The boys said that they had no secrets, that they sold all their gold as soon as they mined it.

On leaving them, we visited several other small operations. All except one (that produced silver and lead concretes) were gold operations. However, no one was as friendly or free with information as the two McCoy brothers. Almost all, though, were of the opinion that ledges and veins in the Cripple Creek mining district did not carry values in a continued or solid form; that values, especially gold, were to be found in pockets mostly on the foot wall of the vein, and that there were several different types of ore that produced the gold value, such as: talc, quartz, liminite, and hematite.

## Mining Partners

We managed to gather a great deal of information by visiting the various mines in the district and were grateful. This together with our assays would enable us to evaluate our claims better. After we got back to the cabin, we went over all that we had learned during the day and tried to figure out what we had.

I knew when we took the samples from the ledge in the tunnel that Wilbur didn't have much faith in them, as he remarked that we might and we might not get a good assay test. He mentioned that the Cripple Creek district is known for its gold value to be in pockets instead of being distributed uniformly and continually along the ledge, which occurs in many mining camps. Gold pockets that were found in other mining districts were usually a hundred or a thousand dollars in value. Cripple Creek had produced gold deposits of almost a million dollars in one pocket. I volunteered that we were looking for just one of those million-dollar pockets.

The following day was beautiful. The snow had melted the previous day and the ground had dried out. After breakfast we decided to look the claims over again, as we had been advised that the assays we had taken a couple of days before would not be ready till noon. Again we found a lot of float or ledge matter lying in the gulch that cut through the claims.

I asked Wilbur if he had ever had any of the float assayed. He said that he had had a few assays made, which ran pretty high in silver and lead but only a few dollars in gold. However, he'd had very little of the float tested compared to the amount we walked over in the 40 acres of the two claims. I told him that we should pick up more of the float before the winter snow and have it tested, and if we ran into anything rich, we could trace the ledge or vein down from the float. He agreed that this was a good idea and put it on our program for future exploring.

We left our cabin in time to get to the assay office at noon, and arrived exactly at noon. The results of the assays were ready for us, but were not too encouraging. The assays ran from $2.10 to $7.40 in gold, and averaged $6.80 for the 16 samples we had assayed. Counting the silver and lead in the assays, they averaged

$8.50, which was not profitable ore to mine. However, we were not too disappointed.

We went down to a little coffee shop and over a couple cups of coffee commented on the assays. I asked Wilbur what he thought of them, and he answered the question by asking me one: "They are not very good, are they?" I think I surprised him by replying that I was not disappointed, that I didn't expect to find profitable mining ore in the ledge that his tunnel was on; if it had been there, he would have been working it instead of working in the placer mines in California.

He seemed pleased at my remark and further pleased when I told him that I was going to take up my option to go in with him on his two claims, as I thought that he had a good gamble. With this we loaded up our packboard with groceries and other mining supplies and headed back to our cabin.

# CHAPTER 3

## *Two Boy Mining Co.*

That evening we felt as if we were partners in the mining business. I suggested that since we would be mining the claims soon, why not give our company a name, so we decided on "Two Boy Mining Company." We were very enthusiastic about our new venture. Wilbur said that since he located and recorded the claims three years ago and built the cabin a year later, he had not felt like he had been in the mining business until now. We spent the next day cleaning out the tunnel, especially the portal of loose dirt and rock that had slid off the hillside into the opening of the tunnel. Once this was cleaned away we could wheelbarrow material from inside the tunnel to the outside dump.

I spent the second day of our newly formed mining company picking up float and marking the location where I had found it, before the winter snow covered it up. This we would have assayed later. Wilbur passed the day putting in a set of drill holes in the face of the tunnel, which we packed with 3 to 5 sticks of dynamite and set off at the end of the day's shift so that the powder smoke would clear out during the night. We worked out a schedule whereby we would put in enough drill holes that the blast would produce sufficient rock and muck to keep one of us busy all day shoveling and wheeling it out to the dump, while the other would put in another set of drill holes.

The system we worked out of blasting every night at the end of the shift, so the powder smoke and foul air would have all night to clear out, worked very good. Wilbur wanted to know where I learned the blasting and mucking system. I told him I learned it from my six months' course with the old-timers at the Little Mint mine in Arizona. We made approximately 3 feet every day in the tunnel. Wilbur would put 4 to 6 drill holes 3 feet deep into the face of the ledge, which, of course, was a day's work. Meanwhile I would muck and haul out the preceding day's blast.

Everything had gone along fine at the Two Boy Mine the first week of operation. Wilbur and I would work 12 hours a day and go into the little city once a week on Saturday nights to have a few cheers at one of the saloons, just to relax. This was later called unwinding.

I persuaded Wilbur to attend Sunday services in one of the two little churches in Cripple Creek when the weather permitted. When the weather was too bad to go to town, we conducted our own services in our cabin. I said that there were three of us in this thing and the good Lord was entitled to one day a week of our time.

We continued to make about 3 feet a day in the tunnel, which required no timbering. We hit some reddish-looking ore in the ledge the second week and had it assayed. It ran over $50 a ton in silver, but only a few dollars in gold. The ore was in a ledge pocket 5 feet long by 3 feet wide. We thought that this perhaps could lead to something, so we had one of the two McCoy brothers, who had a mine two miles from us, come over and take a look at our ledge. He told us that it was what is known as an ore shut, also referred to as a mineralized pocket, and that when these pockets are mineralized with gold they are usually very rich. This brother (John, the older of the two brothers) was very well versed in geology and mining.

John said that it appeared we had a highly mineralized ledge with very good possibilities. We worked on, excited by what John had told us. It wasn't long until we had some more good news. A few days after John had been at our place, I started one morning to muck out the preceding day's blast when I found something that put me sky high. It was some blue quartz that I picked up. It was so full of gold that at first I thought it was iron pyrites, which is widely found in most mineralized zones. I took the quartz out to the mouth of the tunnel where there was more light, and I could see then that it was gold. I called Wilbur, who came running; he knew by the tone of my voice that I had found something unusual.

Wilbur took one look and said that was what we were looking for; that was the real stuff. He asked me where I found it. I showed him a place on the foot wall of the ledge where it had narrowed down to about 3 feet wide. We went out and crushed up some of the blue quartz in a mortar, and upon panning it out we got a long string of gold, perhaps several dollars' worth. We then followed the tunnel to where I had picked up the first piece, and every piece of blue quartz we found there had gold in it that you could see with the naked eye. Of course, we thought that we were rich. We had no idea how much of the blue quartz there was, or if the other material near the blue quartz carried gold.

We were sure that all the blue quartz carried gold, so we picked up all of it we could find, which filled four 50-pound ore sacks. We crushed up and panned other material in the ledge near where the blue quartz came from, but got only a few colors. Needless to say, we declared a holiday and took samples of the blue quartz and other rock and vein substance near where the blue quartz came from to the assay office. When the assayer saw the gold in the blue quartz he remarked, "You don't have to have this assayed; you can see the gold in it." We told him we knew this, and that we had about 200 pounds of the blue quartz and we wanted to know how much it was worth. We left the assay office and and visited a couple of saloons, buying the boys a few rounds and, of course, telling everyone of our good fortune. Then, after picking up a few things at the store, we returned to our cabin.

The next day we got back on our schedule of putting in the drill holes, which we loaded with dynamite and set off at the end of our work day, mucking it out the following day. However, we were going to have to change our schedule for a couple of reasons. One was the fact that we were getting back in the tunnel so far that we could not wheel a day's blast out in one day. The other reason was also relative to the length of the tunnel. The powder smoke would not clear out over night. We had installed a small gas motor with a fan to pull the powder smoke out of the tunnel, but that had its drawbacks. The wind and weather had to be just right for it to work well.

A couple of days had elapsed before we returned to the assay office to get the results from our new discovery. From looking at the gold in the blue quartz, we had built up high hopes and imagination of a vast fortune. When we arrived, the assayer told us that with our 200 pounds of blue quartz we had "a good grubstake." The blue quartz assayed $20,290 per ton, which should make any prospector or miner jump with joy, but somehow it didn't have that effect on us. We had built our hopes up too high. It seems hard to believe, but we were both disappointed, and it was easy to reason why at the time. Seeing the gold in the blue quartz impressed us that we had a vast fortune. The rock and material in the ledge near the blue quartz assayed only a few dollars in value, which was mostly in silver.

We had driven the tunnel into the hillside on the ledge 60 feet, making it 80 feet in from the portal, including the 20 feet that Wilbur had driven the tunnel. Every day we had looked for the big pocket of free gold, but so far we had only the $2,000 worth in the blue quartz in our cabin unmilled. The tunnel was so deep into the hillside now we either had to put in a shaft from the surface to the back end of the tunnel to take out the powder smoke and provide ventilation, or get some expensive equipment to do the job. We got the price on the equipment and found that to have it installed in the tunnel would cost over $5,000, so that was out. Sinking a shaft from the surface to the back end of the tunnel in the winter time was not a pleasant thought. While trying to decide what to do, something happened that changed the whole picture.

I will always remember the occasion and date. It was on the 4th of March, 1916, a warm day for this time of the year. It had snowed continually for the two previous days. Wilbur and I had both worked on the drills that day. The formation was of very hard rock. We put in 6 holes and loaded them heavily with dynamite. We lit the fuse and walked out of the tunnel. We had just reached the cabin when the blast went off. There didn't seem to be anything unusual about the blast. Then a few seconds later there was an awful roar and noise, such I have never heard before. We peered out the window of the cabin and it looked like we had blasted the whole hillside off. It was just getting dark, but we could see the big white snowslide coming down over the portal of the tunnel. It missed the cabin by just a few feet.

We were afraid that there would be another slide during the night which perhaps would take the cabin, so we gathered up a few personal belongings and spent the night in Cripple Creek. The people in town told us that they had heard the slide. That night was a sleepless one for Wilbur and me. Before, I had only thought that we had problems. Now I knew we had problems. The next morning, with a few miners from the camp, we returned to what was left of the Two Boy Mine.

It was a sad sight. Thousands of tons of snow, rock, and dirt had slid off the hillside down on the tunnel and over the opening or portal of the tunnel. It was a question of whether it would pay to clear out a way into the tunnel. Another question was whether the tunnel would hold up under the massive weight of rock and earth. Some of the old-time miners said that the tunnel might have to be timbered before it could be worked in again.

Wilbur and I now had to make the decision of what to do. Trying to remove the slide until the winter freeze was out of the question; we both agreed on that. Just before the slide occurred we had talked of getting employment during the summer to purchase equipment. The problem there was to secure employment. Wilbur then advanced an idea that he had mentioned once before and I had turned down—why not put in a hitch in the army? He somehow liked the army. He had one brother in the army and one that just got out.

Wilbur had a strong point regarding joining the army. He said that the army was going to get us anyway by way of the draft. There was a big war going on in Europe, and from all we could read about it in the papers the United States would be in it soon; the sinking of the *Lusitania* hadn't been forgotten. I suggested we give the army deal some more thought and in the meantime go to Kansas for the grain harvest that I had worked at before; it had paid more than any unskilled labor I knew. Wilbur agreed and we headed for Kansas.

On our way we passed through Denver, where I noticed that Buffalo Bill's "101" Wild West Show was playing. I remarked that I was once a cowboy in Arizona and also rode in Waldcott & Chapman, Arizona Wild West Show, and that I was going to try to get a job in Buffalo Bill's Show. At the show I met a tall, lanky cowboy who said he was in charge of the Rodeo. When I asked him for a job, he looked at me and remarked, "Kid, you might've rode some calves, but a horse would kill you." This really got under my skin. I asked him to let me take a try at one of his meanest buckers. He reluctantly agreed. They brought out a blaze-faced black horse called "Midnight" that looked like a quarter horse. And the way that horse could buck—the likes I had never seen before!

When I got atop of him and they turned him loose, I thought that I was on the moon. I stayed with him the full required ten seconds (later Wilbur said I made a beautiful ride). The lanky boss, whom we called Slim, came over to me after the ride and said, "Kid, you got a job." I asked him if he had a job for my partner, pointing toward Wilbur. Slim asked what he could do. I replied anything that pays money.

We stayed with the show until the wheat harvest time in June, and only left the show for more money that the harvest paid. We kept busy during the entire grain harvest in Kansas and accumulated quite a stake between us.

After the grain harvesting days I reluctantly agreed with Wilbur to further discuss the army enlistment, after which we had so many things planned and how we were going to do them

## Two Boy Mining Co. 21

that I cannot remember all of them. However, one plan was certain. We would go back to Cripple Creek and take a look at things, and if we decided not to work the Two Boy any more, we would go to Alaska, after probably a stint in the army. We often talked about Alaska and remarked many times that Alaska was our next stop, and that we were going to explore the Yukon and northwest territory of Canada. So back to Cripple Creek we went. There, we decided to dispose of our high-grade ore and straighten up other matters.

We contacted the two McCoy brothers who had a mine and stamp mill (a mill that crushed gold ore, and the gold can be recovered) two miles from our mine and asked them if they wanted to buy our rich quartz. They said that they would come and take a look at the gold quartz. One of the brothers, John, soon arrived. When he saw the quartz studded with gold, he remarked, "This is just like money with all that gold in it." He said that he was interested in buying the quartz, but he would want to take the entire 200 pounds to the assayer to get an average test. John had some pack horses on which we packed the quartz for the trip to the assay office. We got the assayer to put a rush job on the assay. He took only one average sample and had the results the following day, as all he'd tested for was free gold. The assayer gave John an accurate test of what he could recover from a stamp-mill job on the quartz, which was $1,820 for the 200 pounds of quartz.

We asked John what the quartz would be worth to him, and he replied that he didn't want to take advantage of us because we had to sell it. He said that there would be some expense and loss when running the quartz through the stamp mill. The brothers had been very good to us, and we wanted them to come out good on the quartz. We asked John if he could come out all right if he gave us $1,000 for the quartz. He said that he could and would like to take it and help us out by buying any equipment or groceries we had. We sold him everything we had at the cabin for $200. We had lost some valuable equipment in the tunnel. John asked us if we wanted a specimen of the gold quartz, which we appreciated. I kept my specimen for over 50 years, losing it only a few years ago.

# CHAPTER 4

## *Join the Army*

We closed our deal with the two brothers either the 10th or 11th of December. We split the money we got for the quartz and supplies fifty-fifty, which put my financial worth at a little over $800, the most money I had ever had in my life. I think Wilbur had a little more, perhaps $1,000. I didn't know whether to feel proud or sad over the recent turn of events. Looking back now, I know that I was just a mixed-up kid. The last thing we did before we left the cabin was for Wilbur to make me out a quitclaim deed for half the two Okie claims on a plain sheet of paper.

We left Cripple Creek the same way that we came, on a freight truck. And I was glad that the truck went slow, pulling out of Cripple Creek over the mountains, as I wanted to take a long look at the rough little city that I would never forget. At Colorado Springs we made connections with a bus to Denver, where we intended to enlist in some branch of the armed services—which one we had not yet decided.

We arrived in Denver in the late afternoon. The first thing on our schedule was to get something to eat. We were hungry after our long ride, in addition to being tired of our own cooking. Somehow this meal in Denver stands out in my memory more than any meal I can recall. As I recall, on the menu there was hamburger steak (my favorite dish), hash-brown potatoes, bread, and coffee for 15 cents. We both topped this off with two large pieces of cake, and the bill came to 40 cents for the two of us. Why I can so clearly remember this meal and the price of it, I can't understand. Of the thousands of meals I have eaten in restaurants during the last 50 years, I can hardly recall what I had to eat or what I paid for it. After the big dinner, we took in a show, with admission 10 cents. I remember the picture very well. It was a Western with William S. Hart as the star.

After the show we got a room in a hotel. As I recollect, the price was 20 cents for the room with a double bed. As usual, we arose early the next morning, but we might as well have stayed in bed as far as accomplishing anything. Wilbur wanted to enlist in the army right away, but I persuaded him to take in some more shows and see some more sights with me. I also tried to talk him into looking for another job, to no avail.

After a few idle days in Denver, we had another talk about the army. I was concerned for the length of time we would have to serve. My argument was that if we waited to be drafted, we would get out as soon as the war was over, if there was a war. Wilbur countered by saying there is a way to get out of the army when one wants to get out. This I bought, taking Wilbur's word for it. We agreed that whatever happened we would get together when we got out of the service, in case we were separated during that time. If necessary, we would get in touch with each other through our folks. Wilbur's folks lived on a small farm a few miles from Clinton, Oklahoma, about 30 miles east of Elk City, Oklahoma, which happened to be my birthplace. I gave Wilbur my mother's address, which was also on a little farm just outside of Duncan, Arizona. I had sent my mother some money from time to time so had kept in touch with her.

Now that we had agreed to go into the service, we had not decided what branch of the service we would enlist in. It didn't make much difference with Wilbur what branch he went into, but I wanted to get into a branch where I could learn a trade, in case I had to remain in the army for a long time. We decided to go to the recruiting office the next day and talk to them regarding the different branches of service.

We were waiting on the recruiting office steps when they opened up the next morning. They gave us the old story, "Join the Army and see the World." Regarding the different branches of the service, we were told that this was no problem, that once

## Join the Army 25

in the service we could transfer to any branch we wished. On this they sold us. We signed up and took the oath. This was another day that I will never forget. It was December 16, 1916. We enlisted in the 165th Field Artillery, and to this day I don't know why we chose this, or how we were talked into enlisting in this branch of the service. There were about 10 of us who enlisted at this time. As it was nearly noon when we left the recruiting office, we were taken to lunch in a restaurant, after which we were driven to Fort Logan, about 10 miles outside of Denver, fitted for a uniform and given some supplies, then assigned to a barracks. We were in the army now at the exhilarating salary of $15 per month.

The next morning we started on a six-weeks' training and drilling course, after which we were shipped northwest to Fort Worden, Washington, on Puget Sound, where we went through further drilling and training in the 165th Field Atillery, which I disliked more and more as time went on. We were moved around a lot to different barracks, but Wilbur and I stayed together in "F" Company. Then the first of March rolled around there was still no war. I tried to transfer to the Army Air Corps, as it was called then, but was informed that there was no more recruiting in that branch of the service.

I soon came down with the mumps and was sent to the hospital. Things seemed so much different here that it didn't seem like the army. The officers were not so strict; there was no drilling. As soon as I recoevered enough to move around, I visited the infirmary and operating rooms and thought—this is for me. It was the only part of the army I had seen that I liked. I had become acquainted with some of the hospital staff, and the more I talked to them the more I wanted to transfer to the medical department.

On Wilbur's next visit to the hospital, which was the following evening, I told him that I had been thinking of transferring to the hopsital, that here I would have an opportunity to learn something besides drilling and training which I could never use outside the army. He agreed with me and said that he, too, was getting tired of training with the heavy field artillery. He didn't think now that he would get to do any fighting and four months in the army was enough for him. He was going to try and get out in the summer. I told him if he got out I would, too, and we would go to Alaska, but in the meantime, I was going ahead with my transfer to the medical department and that I had an appointment with the hospital sergeant the next morning to fill out the formal papers for the transfer.

As my hospital stay extended, I made more acquaintances and friends. I met and talked with some of the doctors, and they said that there was no reason why my transfer to the medical department should not go through. Upon my discharge from the hospital, I returned to "F" Company and disliked it more than ever. I was about ready to go "over the hill" when I got a call telling me that my transfer to the hospital had gone through.

I was a very happy soldier when I packed my foot locker and other belongings and moved from "F" Company to the hospital. I became so engrossed in the work at the hospital that the days and nights literally flew by. I enrolled in a class of medicine and one of Latin. I had been assigned to the infirmary, which I found very interesting. I spent some of my off-duty hours in the operating room where I met Dr. Oliver Lemon, of middle age, a very social kind of a man. He had studied geology earlier in life and at one time had contemplated being a mining engineer. Naturally, we had something in common and became good friends. Dr. Lemon was of great help and comfort to me in my new vocation. His rank was captain in the army.

After transferring to the hospital, I did not see Wilbur very often. A week went by when I did not see him at all. Then one evening, the first part of April, he rushed into my room and said that something was about to happen, that "F" Company was moving out early the next morning but no one knew where, and that the officers were very tense. He said he would let his folks know where he was, and also me, if possible. He also said not to forget, when this thing was over, we were going to Alaska. I replied I'd double that in spades. After Wilbur left, I contacted

## Join the Army

others in the hospital to find out if anyone had any late news, which they didn't. I walked down to the PX and got a newspaper, which had the same old headline, "United States Closer to War." The date was April 2, 1917. I remember it because it was payday. The nation was then only a few days away from a disastrous war, but Fort Worden on Puget Sound in the far-away Northwest slept peacefully from its lack of knowledge.

The departure of "F" Company left a vacancy in my heart. I would walk down through the empty barracks and feel as if I had lost some friends. I not only missed my pal Wilbur, but others whom I had been with since our Denver-recruit days.

Fort Worden was partly empty on April 6, 1917, but there was a lot of excitement and moving around. There was a rumor in the air that we were at war. Of course, we had no radio or TV in those days and the local paper had not been delivered—which was not uncommon. The conversation was pro and con whether we were at war or not. I can recall some of the soldiers saying that the flag would not be lowered that night at retreat if we were at war. We all watched as the soldiers lined up for retreat, and the bugler stepped up and blew retreat, and the flag came down. A couple of soldiers shouted out, "We are not at war!"

When I arose the following morning, though, there was plenty of evidence that we were at war. Some of the soldiers had gone to Port Townsend only two miles away and brought back newspapers with large red headlines stating, "United States At War." The area on Puget Sound where Fort Worden was located was very thinly settled, with only the small fishing town of Port Townsend. And if no one told you we were at war, or you had not read about it in the papers, you would never know it. There was very little change at the hospital. Some new doctors came in and a few of the old ones were moved out.

Dr. Lemon was transferred to the General Hospital at Presidio near San Francisco, California. I talked to Dr. Lemon before he left, and he told me that he didn't think that he would be sent overseas because of his age. The vacant barracks where

"F" Company had been now filled with recruits. The hospital, though it now had more soldiers in it, was a lonely place for me. However, I was making progress in my pharmaceutic studies. I had taken the examination for sergeant, which I passed, and was given charge of the hospital pharmacy. Everything seemed to be working fine, but somehow I was not contented and happy. I now had only new recruits around me who came from almost all walks of life, and they didn't seem like the soldiers I had been around.

I had put in twice for duty overseas without any results, and I had written Wilbur's folks asking his whereabouts. The last they had heard of him he was in London. The latter part of August I was called into the office of the major, who was in charge of the hospital. He asked me if I knew Dr. Oliver Lemon. I replied that I had worked here in the hospital with him. He then informed me that Dr. Lemon had requested that 6 medics, including myself, be sent to Vancouver Barracks at Vancouver, Washington. I asked if we were going overseas. He replied that we were not. He told me that Dr. Lemon with other doctors was going to examine and muster in recruits for the Spruce Divison and that he had requested me along with the other men. If it had not been the major telling me this, I would have thought that it was some kind of joke. I had never heard of the Spruce Division.

I told the major that I would be glad to go to Vancouver Barracks and serve with Dr. Lemon. The next day after the request was received, we six men were on our way to Vancouver Barracks—which I had heard and read about but had never seen. From the Vancouver Barracks we were sent to some new buildings about a mile away called Barnes Barracks. There I met Dr. Lemon. He told me what this was all about. The Spruce Division had been made up mostly of loggers and truck drivers from the Northwest and Midwest to log and produce spruce lumber to build airplanes. This, of course, was before aluminum and metal planes had come into the picture.

## Join the Army

We were to give these men physical examinations and get other data in the process of recruiting and mustering them into the service. We really did a fast job putting these men through the procedure. Four doctors and 6 medics examined and mustered in over 2,000 men for the Spruce Division in a week. After the examination was over, and I wondered what next, Dr. Lemon asked me if I wanted to go with him to Waldport, Oregon, the headquarters of the Spruce Division, to operate the medical infirmary for him. When I told him that I had put in for overseas duty, he said in a low voice, "If you don't have to go, don't go." Then he told me about the basket cases that came into the General Hospital at Presidio. Having been a doctor all his adult life and being now past middle age, he must have seen some gruesome cases. When he described some of them that were coming back from overseas, it almost brought tears to his eyes. He said that it was not really known by the American people what was going on over there, adding, "I am giving this to you in confidence." I told him that I appreciated his telling me the things that he had, and I certainly would treat them confidentially. Then I said it would be a privilege to serve with him at Waldport.

After talking to Dr. Lemon, I offered a little prayer for Wilbur. I recalled the sentiment that both of us shared before we enlisted—that if we wouldn't come back all in one piece, we didn't want to come back at all. Of all the wars that our nation has been in, the First World War has proved to be the most cruel and terrible of them all.

The Spruce Division worked fast in the few days it took us to go to Waldport and set up our infirmary tent. They had started a sawmill, laid a lot of track for the logging train, and were logging. The area took in Newport, Waldport, and Yachats along the beach and as far as 15 miles inland in places. This was about 500 square miles, which had the finest stand of spruce timber in the nation. The government built railroads right into the forest to get the spruce out. Our medical unit consisted of Dr. Lemon, two privates, and myself, a sergeant. We set the infirmary up in

Above left: Floyd Marsh in his first uniform in the 165th Field Artillery, Denver, Colorado, in January 1917.

Above right: Floyd Marsh in the Army Hospital Corps, Vancouver, Washington.

Left: Wilbur Foster (at right), 165th Field Artillery, killed in action in France in 1918.

## Join the Army

a large tent in Waldport and served small camps in the vicinity. Dr. Lemon liked fishing and visiting, so I carried on and was known to all the fellows as Doc. I had two privates to assist me.

I had been keeping in touch with Wilbur's folks at Clinton, Oklahoma. The last they had heard from him was a letter, postmarked London, which said he was in France some place. Just before the holidays, Dr. Lemon was called back to the base hospital at Vancouver, Washington, as some overseas cases had begun to come in there. He asked me if I wanted to go back with him. I told him that I did. It had been nice at Waldport during the summer, but I had heard that the winters were a different story, and too, I wanted to get some direct information on what was going on "over there." After being relieved by a new doctor and two privates, Dr. Lemon, one of the privates, and myself returned to the base hospital at Vancouver Barracks.

At the Vancouver hospital I was assigned duty in the pharmacy which was near the surgical ward, where I spent a lot of time visiting. After talking to some of the boys who had come back for further surgery and treatment, I offered another prayer, and this one consisted of thanks to the good Lord that I was not sent overseas. Of all the men I talked to who had come back, no one knew, or would say, that they knew anything about the 165th Field Artillery. During the winter I talked with many of the boys who had gone through hell "over there," and I felt a little guilty sitting it out "over here."

In the spring—I think that it was the latter part of March or the first of April—Dr. Lemon and I returned to Waldport. I was glad to get back to the big, open spruce country and wasted no time getting around to visit some of the camps and renew my acquaintance with the good people I had met in Waldport.

One day while hiking along the beach a few miles south of Waldport, I saw someting that amazed me very much. Back on the beach about a hundred yards from the water line, there was a man working in the sand. As I approached him I could see that he was panning something. I walked up to him and asked, "Are you panning gold, or am I seeing things?"

"Yes, he replied, "I am panning gold." He was a friendly little man, about 60 years old, and I learned later that his name was Tim. He was using a rocker kind of device with which he worked the bulk of the sand off, leaving the concentrates, which consisted mostly of black sand. However, there were chromium, tungsten, and many other mineral concentrates in very small amounts, and from this Tim was recovering the gold by panning. After he found out that I had done some mining, I was in solid. We began to talk each other's langauge.

Tim showed me the gold that he had recovered from the black sand; he had it in a small jar. What he showed me he said was a week's work. It looked like a lot of gold to me. He said that he had been prospecting and mining for over 40 years, and had been panning the Oregon beaches for 10 years with his partner he called Shaky, who was away the first day I met and talked with Tim.

When I told Dr. Lemon about the gold-recovering operation I had run onto, he was very much interested and wanted me to take him to see it, which I did in a few days. We also visited another man recovering gold from the beach sand just south of Yachats. This fellow had a round type of bowl, about the size of a tub, that was spun around with a small gas motor and looked like a more modern set-up than Tim's. But this fellow had a secret operation. He wouldn't give us the time of day. He was very unfriendly. He would not show or tell us anything. As a parting sentiment, I told him that I hoped that we could keep the Germans off his back until he could make his fortune.

During the summer I visited Tim and Shaky's operation often. Tim lived in Yachats, where I visited him to see the many unique objects that he had picked up on the beach and panned out of the sands, in addition to gold. He told me that he had worked the Oregon beaches from Gold Beach to Newport and that there was no way of knowing where to look for gold, that sometimes it was way back from the water line where the tide reaches only in very severe storms. Sometimes he would make a good find along the water line, but the gold there came and

## Join the Army    33

went. He would have it rich one day, and the next day the gold would all be gone. Some fine type of gold would come and go with the tide. Occasionally storms would bring in a rich deposit of gold and leave it way back on the beach where it could be found several months or years later.

Tim reported that the riches place he had found on the beach was near the little town of Gold Beach at the mouth of the Rogue River, and that several years ago he had hit a spot there that was making him rich. He had taken out several thousand dollars' worth of gold in one week when a severe storm blew in and ruined a sand bar at the mouth of the Rogue River. However, Tim never told me how much gold he had taken from the beach in the last 10 years. He said only that it was all he'd done and that he and Shaky had made a good living and helped some of his relations. He knew he could never have found work that would pay him as much as he could make panning the beach. The type of gold that Tim was getting was different from any I had ever seen; it was called flour gold. It was hard to control in a gold pan.

I spent so much time with Tim that I almost forgot I was in the army, and I think that Dr. Lemon had other interests that occupied most of his time, too. The two privates who were supposed to take care of the infirmary were just about as attentive as I was. One morning I came into the infirmary about 10 o'clock and found a bottle of aspirin and a bottle of iodine on a table with a note on one saying, "This is Aspirin" and a note on the other, "This is Iodine." The boys had turned the infirmary into a "self-service" project.

Not only did we medics slow down and lose interest, but the entire camp seemed to lose interest in what they were doing. One could walk through the camp any time of the day and the only activity would be poker or a crap game. They were even taking up some of the rail track. It began to look as if they had found something better to make planes with—or the war was winding down.

An order came through the latter part of September for the medical unit to move to Toledo, Oregon, where the Spruce Division had a large mill. This was typical of other orders to move; we had only three days to get to Toledo. I made a rush trip to Yachats to see Tim. He was getting ready to move to Bandon, down the coast about 100 miles, where his partner Shaky had found a rich spot of gold on the beach. It was back from the water line and would give them a good place to work during the winter. I would miss Tim. He was a fine fellow. I liked him from the time I first spoke to him. He would give you the shirt off his back but would starve before he would ask you for anything.

He wanted me to come back when I got out of the army. He said that we could make a fortune panning gold on the Oregon beaches. He said that Shaky couldn't take it any more, that he was past 70 and was going to San Diego to live with a son. Tim said that he didn't want to be alone, and he didn't want to quit the beach. I told him that I would try and make it back when I got out.

I had told him about Wilbur and he said to bring Wilbur along, that there was enough gold on the Oregon beaches for us all. With the promise that I would try to get back, I told Tim goodbye and wished him all the luck in the world. The last thing he said to me was, "God bless you, boy. I hope that your partner makes it back." I often think of the old gold beach miner and his unqiue way of recovering gold. Today with the technology of gold recovery and the high price of gold, Tim's gold beach mining could be a bonanza.

# CHAPTER 5

## *Armistice Signed*

On arrival in Toledo at our new assignment, which was only 20 miles from Waldport and in the area that the Spruce Division was working, we set up our infirmary tent. From the many men there, it looked as if a number of camps had moved to Toledo— where there was a large lumber mill surrounded by a forest of spruce timber. However, the men didn't seem to be doing much. The camp was a little tent city, and like the last days at Waldport, it was full of men playing cards, rolling dice, and just plain loafing. There was no beach to stroll on or any other amusement, and no one was getting sick or injured—which made me feel useless and unneeded.

I spoke to Dr. Lemon about a transfer back to the base hospital at Vancouver. He replied that he had already put in a request to be transferred there, and that if his request was granted he was sure he could take me with him. We were waiting to hear from the transfer request when all "hell" broke loose one day in camp. It was either late in the afternoon or evening of November 10, 1918. It seemed like everyone was out in the streets of the tent city beating pans, cans, or anything they could get their hands on and yelling, "The war is over. The Armistice has been signed." I got out and mingled with the crowd, but could get no further details. Needless to say, no one slept in camp that night, contrary to a report that came in shortly after midnight that the Armistice had not been signed— which did not dampen the enthusiasm that was displayed during the night.

The next morning Dr. Lemon was down to the infirmary early. I asked him if the report was true about the Armistice being signed. He said he hoped that it was true, that he could not endure another night like the one we just had. Sometime during the day of November 11, 1918, it was confirmed that the Armistice had been signed. The medical unit was the first out of Toledo, headed for Vancouver and Barnes Hospital Barracks, as it was called at the time. There they would undo what had been done a year and a half previous; they would convert the Spruce soldiers back to civilian life. They had to have a physical "going out" as well as "coming in." We set a record recruiting them into the army and broke it mustering them out.

Within a few weeks after the Armistice was signed, things began to get back to normal. All the Sprucers and many thousands of soldiers were on their way home. I was transferred to the base hospital. I wanted to get out of the service the worst way, but was told that I had to wait until the draftees were out, and then apply for a transfer to the regular army reserve. This transfer to the regular army reserve I requested immediately. I had written Wilbur's folks in Oklahoma regarding his whereabouts but had received no answer. At this time there was no airmail, and the turmoil and movement of troops made correspondence a slow way of communication.

Dr. Lemon had been transferred to Fort Wright, near Spokane, Washington. For some reason I thought that I would like to be over there, so I called Dr. Lemon at Fort Wright, and asked him if he could get me transferred there. He said he thought he could and would make the request soon after the holidays. It was few days before Christmas now. Again I called Wilbur's folks in Oklahoma. They replied that Wilbur had been listed as "missing in action," that he was in the "lost battalion" that disappeared in the Argonne Forest in France. I told them that I was going to Fort Wright, Washington, and would write them from there and let them know my correct address. The few weeks that followed the signing of the Armistice seemed like years to me.

Soon after the middle of January my transfer to Fort Wright came through. I was glad to get out of the busy "mad house"— the base hospital at Vancouver. Arriving at Spokane, I needed

## Armistice Signed

my "longjohns," as there were about two feet of snow and it was very cold—but I liked it. From Spokane I took a trolley out to Fort Wright about 10 miles away. Upon arrival I reported to Dr. Lemon. He told me that my transfer to the regular army reserve should be coming through soon, and that I could take it easy without any assignment. In answer to my questions, he replied that from what he could ascertain, transferring to the regular army reserve was the only way for me to get out of the service unless I remained in another 10 months to complete my regular 3 years of service I enlisted for.

I had written Wilbur's folks giving them my new address and letting them know that I would not be here very long. I received a letter from them by return mail, and it was not good news. Wilbur was now listed as "killed in action." His dog tag and other personal belongings had been sent to his folks. This left me despondent. I had a sense of guilt. I thought that if we had stayed together, Wilbur might have been alive now. I walked through Fort Wright barracks one evening when a light February snow was falling and wished that snow was falling on me in Alaska, and that Wilbur was with me. Somehow I thought that I just had to go to Alaska now, and would like to think that Wilbur would meet me up there.

About this time, though, I did get some good news. Dr. Lemon called me into his office and told me that my transfer from regular duty to the army reserve had gone through. He then asked me what I was going to do. He knew I had planned to go to Alaska and also that I had not seen my mother and brothers in Arizona in a long time. Before I could answer his question he remarked,

"You should go home and see your folks and then decide on what you want to do." I told him that was the best advice I had received in a long time, and that I was going to take it.

The next day I did one of the hardest things I'd ever done in my life, and that was to bid Dr. Lemon goodbye. I told him I hoped the good Lord would reward him for all the fine things he'd done for me while serving with him, which made my service in the army much more pleasant.

On February 10, I took a trolley from Fort Wright to Spokane, where I caught a train for Duncan, Arizona. On the way I stopped in Los Angeles and went to Hollywood and Burbank, as I always had wanted to see a movie in the making. The studios were very nice. I spent over a day watching them make pictures. I saw Roy Stewart, Tim Holt, Hoot Gibson, and many others in action. Though I enjoyed seeing how motion pictures were made, it took the edge off my enjoyment of seeing the pictures on the screen, as I always liked to think they were "for real." After this enjoyable visit among the movie studios, I resumed my trip to Duncan.

It was a happy reunion with my mother and brothers. The boys had grown up and changed. Mother looked a little older. The farm looked the same and just as unattractive—after my being in the Northwest for several years with the cool summers and green forests. I asked my older brother, who had done a good job rearing a fatherless family, if he wanted me to help him on the farm. He replied that he had all the help that he needed and that he knew my heart was in the North. My brothers drove me around the country visiting friends of early days. It was a wonderful visit, and I was saddened when I left. As the train pulled out of Mormon Valley headed north, I looked back over the valley and the little town of Duncan, and knew I would never live there again. But the memories will be with me always.

Two days later I arrived in Seattle, Washington. I immediately went to the Northern Commercial Company, that was well versed on Alaska, to get some information. They told me where I might contact some people from Alaska, and also people going there. On contacting these people, I was told that if I were going into the interior as far north as Fairbanks, I would have to make the trip before the breakup of the rivers and streams in order to cross them on the ice; and also, at a later date, there would be problems getting over the trail after the snow started to thaw and get soft. I was advised that the snow trail would not be recommended for travel after March 15.

## CHAPTER 6

## *Arrival in Alaska*

I took a boat out of Seattle for Alaska the latter part of February. After stopping at Ketchikan, Juneau, and Cordova, we landed at Seward, the south end of the government railroad. This place I didn't like at all. I immediately took the train north to Anchorage, over a hundred miles of the crookedest railroad I'd ever ridden. In Anchorage I felt like I was in Alaska. It was odd to see it dark at 3 p.m. and dark until 9 a.m. And the shortest day of the year had passed two months previously. Dog sleds were everywhere, and sourdoughs tramping over the snow. I looked around trying to find a place where the sourdoughs, prospectors, and miners stayed. I was directed to such a place, and when I found it I thought that it fitted into that category.

I found out that there was no mining and very little prospecting around Anchorage, that the action was farther north, and that miners and prospectors were now going in over the trail or had gone into the interior for the summer mining, as the placer mines freeze up during the winter. Some of the miners spend the winter in what they call the "outside," in the states and what is now called the "lower 48 states." I became acquainted with some of the old-timers who were going to make the hike into the interior and arranged to go along with them and to meet with them on a certain date to start the long trek into the interior of Alaska.

The days in Alaska had begun to get longer and warmer in midday; however, the night was still cold enough to remind you that you were in the Far North. It was one of those days in the first part of March, 1919, at Anchorage, Alaska, that a party of seven was organized to hike over the Broad Pass between Anchorage and Fairbanks. The party consisted of 6 seasoned

## Arrival in Alaska 41

sourdoughs and one young fellow they called the Kid—that Kid was Floyd Marsh. The name "Kid" stuck with me during my three years' stay in Alaska.

The hike was to be made between the south and north end of the new government railroad. The railroad extended north from Anchorage about 30 miles to a small station called Palmer and extended south from Fairbanks about 85 miles to a terminal called Healey, a boom town in the North caused by concentration of many small contractors working on the railroad, also many prospectors and miners. There was also a small coal mine at Healey, along with some oil prospecting.

The hike consisted of approximately 100 miles between Palmer and Healey. I felt very proud being just a kid and being allowed to join this party of woolly sourdoughs hiking into the interior of Alaska. However, I was soon to learn that I did not realize what I was in for.

There was still about 16 inches of snow on the level around Anchorage and much more over the pass. It was an ideal time of the year to make such a hike; while the snow was soft during the daytime, at night it would crust over holding up a man's weight, making it unnecessary to use snowshoes. However, there was one problem to this: it was necessary that we do all our traveling at night after the trail crusted over or froze, and do our sleeping during the day.

We left Anchorage about noon on a very beautiful day; the sun was out bright, glittering on the snow. It didn't take very long for the two-car train on the new government railroad to reach Palmer, our jumping-off place for the big hike. At Palmer there was one small store where prospectors and trappers came for their supplies. When we got off the train at Palmer some of the old sourdoughs looked at me and asked,

"Kid, are you sure you want to make this trip?" I answered, "I sure am," as though it was just a trip around a city block. It was a challenge and adventure for me and I was very excited. As our arrival in Palmer was in the early afternoon and the snow was soft, we had to wait until the freeze at night before starting on our long journey.

Some of the old-timers had taken a nap in the afternoon and all of them got a good rest, but the Kid was all fired up like a fire-engine horse. I could not calm myself for a nap or rest. About 9 p.m. that evening, the trail froze enough to hold a man's weight, so we headed up the Broad Pass toward the interior of Alaska. The stars were out bright and it seemed as though there were more of them and they were brighter than I had ever seen before and the northern lights were flashing across the sky. It seemed that you could hear them crack as they flashed.

Roadhouses on the Anchorage-Fairbanks trail over the Broad Pass were 20 to 30 miles apart depending on the roughness of the trail. As I recall, the first roadhouse was about 25 miles from Palmer, but to me it seemed like a hundred. Everything went along uneventfully the first night, with the exception that the trail got a little soft the last couple of hours. We arrived at the first roadhouse about six in the morning very tired and hungry. I was about as tired and all-in as I have been in all my life, but I would not let any of the bunch know it. After a big meal (I guess you would call it breakfast) of moose steak and beans, we hit the hay. I slept like a log the entire day and had to be awakened when the freeze came at night, the time to hit the trail for the next roadhouse.

One of the sourdoughs in the party said that he knew an old-timer by the name of "Two-step Louie," who was prospecting on Crooked Creek a few miles beyond the summit of the pass and that his cabin was very close to the trail. Other old-timers in our party also said that they recalled "Two-step Louie" from the early days at Dawson. So we decided to pay Louie a visit and take the chance on how he would receive guests at 2 o'clock in the morning—but as we were cold, tired, and hungry we decided to take a chance.

We came upon Louie's cabin without any difficulty. It was a small one-room log cabin with a moss roof, located on the

## Arrival in Alaska 43

frozen bank of a small creek and beneath a large cliff of rock which served as a windbreak. To our pleasant surprise, Two-step Louie greeted us like long-lost relatives. It seems he was as hungry for company as we were for some hot coffee and a warm stove.

Louie soon got his wood stove roaring and some hot coffee brewing. Then he insisted that he cook us something to eat, and for this he didn't have to twist our arms. He apologized for not having any moose meat but said that he had some very good bear meat, and of course we told Louie that would be just fine. I had never eaten bear meat but I was hungry enough to take on some skunk. So Louie went out to his cache (a prospector's cold storage) and sawed off a bear steak for each of us. To my surprise, the bear steak was wonderful. I know that I have never eaten a steak before or since that tasted better than that bear steak. Louis said that it was a young, fat bear that he got just before hibernation the fall before.

Prospectors and roadhouse operators in Alaska get their winter's supply of meat just before the freeze-up in the fall. They put their meat in a little storehouse usually about 8 x 8 feet square, built on poles or posts about 10 or 15 feet high, with tin around the posts to keep such animals as bear and wolverines away from their meat supply. The storehouse, or cache, is reached by a ladder which is removed when not in use. When a steak is desired, it is cut frozen with a saw, usually a carpenter's saw, and is put into a hot skillet in a frozen state—and then what I mean is you have steak fit for a king. Many times in the last 55 years I have longed for a frozen moose, bear, or wild mountain-sheep steak.

So, after many cups of hot coffee and full of bear meat, we headed down the trail to our next roadhouse. After leaving Louie's cabin I asked why they called him "Two-step Louie," and they told me the story which went like this:

In the early days in Dawson, Louie came into town one day with $30,000 worth of gold dust. Some of his friends wanted Louie to deposit his gold dust in a safe deposit box with one of the saloons, but Louie would have no part of such a precautionary measure. He said that he could take care of his gold. So, to the dance hall Louie went that night. He was on the dance floor for every dance and buying drinks for the girls with his gold dust like it was going out of style. Sure enough, the next morning Louie woke up without a pinch of gold dust. His friends asked him what he had done with his gold and Louie replied that he two-stepped it all away. He would not entertain the thought that anyone had taken any of it away from him wrongfully, but insisted to this day that he two-stepped it all away. So, the name "Two-step Louie" stuck with him like his fingerprints and will be with him for the rest of his life.

Soon after we left Louie's cabin, we came to the summit of Broad Pass where we ran into a severe storm. For some time it looked as if we were not going to make it. We thought that we had lost the trail and were about ready to turn back to Louie's cabin when we came to some timber where the trail was protected and we could follow it. This, together with the fact that we were over the summit, made we decide to push on.

As we were now in the interior of Alaska, the nights were a little colder and the trail remained frozen into the early morning. We reached the next roadhouse in fine shape long before daybreak. We were all in high spirits, as we had only 30 miles left between us and the south end of the railroad, and with a reported good trail ahead of us and the summit behind, we felt like we had it made. But at this next roadhouse we received news that chilled us more than the cold blizzard we had encountered over the pass. The news was to the effect that there was a flu epidemic at Healey and that men were dying off like flies. We were all so tired that we agreed to get a day's rest before deciding what to do. After a good breakfast of wild sheep steak we hit the sack, but I might as well have stayed up, as I slept only about two hours. I got up and dressed. The roadhouse proprietor asked me where I was going and I told him to Healey. He said,

## Arrival in Alaska

"Kid, you are walking right into death. They are really dying off in Healey, and big strong men at that."

As there was a phone between the roadhouse and Healey, I called the only doctor there and told him that I had recently been discharged from the U.S. Army as a hospital sergeant and asked him if I could be of any help to him. He replied, "You bet you can," and asked me to come on to Healey as soon as I could get there.

All the sourdoughs were asleep and I hated to leave them without saying goodbye and knowing what they were going to do. However, I decided to go on to Healey and asked the roadhouse proprietor to have them get in touch with me at Healey. I arrived in Healey about dark. To my surprise I found a booming little city here in the frozen North. There were many small construction companies, miners, trappers, and prospectors for both gold and oil. I immediately looked up the doctor, a Dr. Lake, a fine, tall, slim, young-looking man, himself recently discharged from the army. He said,

"You can't imagine how glad I am to see you; we have only one female nurse and no other help with hospital experience." He wanted me to take over the night shift, which I told him I would. Then he took me through the two sick barracks where there were several hundred men lying deathly ill. I had seen some pitiful cases of sick and dying men in the base hospital at Vancouver and Fort Wright, Washington, casualties of the First World War, but I had never seen such a pitiful sight as these two sick barracks contained.

# CHAPTER 7

## *Moved on North*

The population at Healey consisted of Russians, Swedes, and Norwegians, and of course this made up the nationality of the patients. The Swedes and Norwegians were not so bad, but if you have ever taken care of a sick Russian you will know what we were up against. The Russians would develop a high fever and imagine you were trying to kill them. They would get right out of bed and take off through the snow. I have actually held men in bed while they died. To make things worse, we had a very limited medical supply—a little quinine, some aspirin, and a lot of whiskey. I do not recall just how many died during my stay there, but many nights as many as four or five died in the two barracks I attended.

When I had helped Dr. Lake for a little over two weeks, the flu epidemic slackened off somewhat and I decided to move on farther north. After all, I had come to Alaska for excitement and adventure, not work. But before I left Healey, I returned to the roadhouse where I left my hiking companions. I found that three of them had secured work with a contractor on the railroad, one was out in the hills prospecting, and the other two had moved on north without stopping in Healey.

I took the train from Healey to Nenana, 30 miles to the north. Nenana was a thriving little town of about 500 inhabitants, located on the south banks of the Tanana River, 60 miles southwest of Fairbanks. The government railroad was completed between Nenana and Fairbanks with the exception of a bridge across the Tanana River; however, this did not stop the train from crossing the river in the winter time. As soon as the freeze-up comes, a railroad track is laid on the ice across the Tanana River, which is about a half mile wide, and the train runs over the ice. This will give you some idea how thick the ice is on the large rivers in Alaska. Just before the spring break-up, the train is located on the north side of the Tanana River, the railroad track is taken up, and a ferry is readied for operation across the river between the train and Nenana for transportation during the summer months.

At Nenana I met a couple of middle-aged men who operated a small hotel called the "Hang-out." These two men had been in Alaska for several years and gave me a lot of help in the way of information about what was going on in that part of the country, also when and how to travel. But wanting to be a sourdough, I soon got tired of the "Hang-out" and moved into a small one-room log cabin and set up housekeeping. While still at a tender age, I had batched before in the states and could do a little cooking, that is, of its kind, and I like living alone. I had heard about a relatively late diggings (mine camp) by the name of Kantishna, discovered in 1906 by a man by the name of Dalton.

To get to the Kantishna diggings, I would have to take a boat for about 75 miles and a hike of about 30 miles. Of course there would be no boats running until after the break-up, which would be sometime in May or the latter part of April. This meant several weeks in Nenana, so I secured a few steel traps and set out to trap muskrats and mink, which were plentiful on the outskirts of Nenana. My trapping venture not only furnished excitement and the passing of time, it also helped build up my financial status for a grubstake. Being recently discharged from the army, I was not too flush. Besides, getting a lot of muskrats and mink, I found a land of a million ducks and I like duck. So it seemed like I had found the land of my dreams. Many a time coming in off the trapline very hungry, I would devour a whole duck; pot-roasted Mallard duck can't be beat. I cooked them many ways and almost lived on wild duck during my stay at Nenana.

Like everyone else in Nenana (and all Alaska) I was waiting for the big event and that was the break-up of the ice on the river. There was a large power plant at Nenana that had a loud whistle. A rope was tied to this whistle and to a stake in the ice of the river, so the second the break-up occurred, the whistle would sound off. There were large money pools made up as to the exact time the break-up would occur. The guess closest to the time of the break-up would win the pool, and surprisingly someone would always guess within seconds of the time of the break-up. I have been in on many pools but never was lucky. This first break-up that I experienced was certainly a thrill to me. As I recall, it happened the latter part of April in the early evening. I was devouring a fat Mallard duck that I had pot-roasted when the whistle went off, and needless to say the duck had to wait. I grabbed my coat and cap and off to the river I went, which was about 300 yards from my cabin. When I arrived at the river bank it seemed like every person in Nenana was already down there.

The sight of the big ice break-up in the Tenana River is hard to describe. It is a sight once seen you will never forget. There were chunks of ice as large as an ordinary house rising out of the water and into the air, and tumbling over each other with a roar like an Oklahoma (my home state) cyclone. I don't recall who won the big ice pool other than I know it was not I.

Now that the break-up in the Tanana River had occurred, it would not be long until I could make the trip to the Kantishna "diggin's" and get my hands on some of that stuff that the world was mad about—GOLD.

However, I was informed that the boat would not sail for several weeks. This gave me some additional time to run my trapline and continue building up a grubstake, which I badly needed. While waiting for sailing of the boat, I became acquainted with several prospectors who were making the trip. I ascertained from them what I would need for the summer stay in the Kantishna—which meant everything I would require for the entire summer, all carried in on a pack-board on my back. There would not be another boat into the Kantishna until late fall. The only way out was by hiking out over the Alaska range of mountains near the foothills of Mt. McKinley. This is an unmarked route which very few have ever made.

The date for sailing of the boat finally arrived the latter part of May. The vessel was a small sternwheel wood steamer. Aboard were five prospectors (counting myself) and several other people, one of them an attorney from Fairbanks, by the name of Cecil H. Clegg. I became very well acquainted with Clegg, who later played an important part in my life while I was in Alaska.

We were three days getting to the Kantishna landing. The boat, being a wood-burning steamer, had to stop along the way and load cordwood from the banks of the river, which the Indians had cut the winter before. We traveled only during the daytime; at night the boat would tie up to the bank of the river.

Our arrival at Kantishna landing was not very exciting. There were only two trappers to greet us, the diggings being 30 miles away. We soon got the boat unloaded and headed immediately for the diggin's.

Of the four other prospectors on the boat, I became well acquainted and very good friends with two of them, an old-timer and seasoned prospector by the name of Jack Ritter, and his partner, a young fellow only a few years older than I, by the name of Perry Blue. Upon arrival at the diggin's on Moose Creek we found a much livelier atmosphere than at the landing. There was a large building that housed the U.S. Commissioner's office. The commissioner was a fine young fellow by the name of Herbert Wilson. In addition to the commissioner's office, there were about 10 or 15 log cabins occupied by miners and prospectors; there was also a very small store. Knowing the difficulty of getting supplies into the diggin's one would readily understand the need for the store.

Prospectors who came up on the boat knew what they were up against in this primitive country (that is, everyone but myself), and all brought in ample supplies which they had packed in from the landing by pack-horses; as for myself, I had my complete summer supplies on the pack-board on my back. Jack

Ritter and Perry Blue wanted to take me in, but I told them that I wanted to go it alone.

There was a lot of placer mining in the immediate vicinity and I thought it advisable to get out and see just how recovering gold was done. I visited placer mines on Eureka, Eldorodo, and Moose creeks, where they were all operating sluice boxes. These were trough-like boxes 12 inches wide by 12 inches high with riffles to catch the gold from the gold-bearing gravel shoveled into them. This looked like a very simple method. Now, the problem was to find the gold-bearing gravel. One day while in the commissioner's office, Commissioner Wilson said to me,

"Kid, I know a good place for you and that is over on Yellow Creek about eight miles from here." He said that the creek had been worked out years ago, but there was a good cabin on it and a good area to prospect in, so I loaded my pack-board and off to Yellow Creek I went.

On Yellow Creek I found a small log cabin in good condition; however, it looked as though it had not been occupied for many years. After getting settled in my new home, I started to look around for some gold. To my great surprise I was not long in finding it. Yellow Creek had been a very rich creek; the gold lay in a very narrow streak in the old channel, which made many turns and bends, and the old-timers missed some of these turns and bends.

That is where I found the gold. I panned out what I though was about $100 worth and took off for the commissioner's office. I though that I had struck it rich and wanted to file on a claim. The commissioner was somewhat surprised, but not as excited as I was. He told me that it was some gold that the old-timers missed and that it was not a new strike. He said it would not be necessary to file on a claim, that I could work the ground without anyone bothering me—which the old-timers called "snipping." I returned to Yellow Creek less excited but determined to get some more gold. There were a number of old sluice boxes left; I patched them up and set up operation. Some days I really did well but other days not so well. Jack Ritter and Perry

Gold worth $650,000 leaving Anchorage on sled. This picture was taken two years before I arrived in Anchorage. This gold would be worth $6,150,000 on the current market.

Left: Some fish the author caught in Wonder Lake at the base of Mt. McKinley.

Right: My cabin on Yellow Creek where once I saw an Angel.

Blue heard of my good luck and paid me a visit. They seemed more enthusiastic about my finding the gold than if they had found it.

After about three weeks I ran out of hot spots and began to look around for new territory to prospect in. Ritter and Blue told me that they were camped on Rainy Creek about five miles away, so, after some time, I decided that I would pay them a visit. Upon arriving at their camp on Rainy Creek I found only Jack Ritter. Jack told me that Perry Blue had become very sick and was taken in to Kantishna where a miner's wife was caring for him.

It was getting toward midsummer and caribou had moved up into higher ground. Jack asked me if I would like to take a trip with him up into the Alaska Range in the Mt. McKinley foothills to get some caribou or wild sheep meat and also do some prospecting. This sounded good to me, so the next morning with our pack-boards loaded we took off for the Alaska Range. Jack said that he knew there was a glacier about 25 miles up into the range that we could make the first night and get away from the mosquitoes, which seemed to be having a convention at Rainy Creek.

On arriving at the glacier, I saw for the first time the midnight sun. It was beautiful.

We soon turned in for the night, or what was left of it, but the mosquitoes saw to it that we didn't get much sleep; they seemed to have followed us from Rainy Creek. We had mosquito nets and built a smudge fire, but they seemed to get through our defense. The next morning we moved on higher up into the range. All day long we saw herds of caribou and wild sheep. In the late afternoon we made camp on a small creek we named Green Creek after the many large green boulders along the creek bottom. After making camp we started out to get some fresh meat as were tired of beans and hardtack. Since the wild sheep were high and hard to get, we decided on a caribou. About a half mile from camp we spotted a herd and picked out a small one to take, perhaps a yearling. As shooting wild game

## Moved on North 53

was nothing new to Jack, he told me to shoot the caribou. I brought him down with a 306. It was getting late and we were both tired, so Jack suggested that we take the liver and come back the next morning to skin and quarter it up for jerky. As the trees were very small in this area, we had a hard time finding a tree tall enough to clear the caribou's head from the ground, but we eventually did.

We returned the next morning for our caribou, and much to our surprise, no caribou! A bear had taken it during the night. It was not losing the meat that we were so concerned about, but the thought that a bear large enough to carry off a caribou was only a half mile from our camp and us sleeping in only a mosquito-proof tent.

Green Creek proved to be a very promising place in which to prospect. We found a black shoot-like substance in the river-bed gravel that we were informed later was tin. We also found a large deposit of coal croppings from the creek bank and a seepage of oil. We would have liked to stay all summer there, but our supplies were getting low. This, together with cold, rainy weather that had set in and the thoughts of the bear, persuaded us to head back to the diggin's. So, early one morning after getting another caribou and cooling the meat out on the glacier, we set out for our home camp. We had it all downhill on our trip back, and we needed it, as we were loaded down with caribou meat. We made the trip back without an overnight stop, getting into Kantishna about 5 or 6 o'clock the following morning.

I returned to my cabin on Yellow Creek but the pickings there were slim. I became very short of grub, living on beans and groundhogs, or mountain beaver as they call them. There were some groceries at the little store at Kantishna, but flour and sugar were 50 cents a pound, and even at a dime a pound, I could have purchased only a very few pounds. Of course, I had my gold from Yellow Creek, but I was not about to part with that.

Suddenly I became very sick. One morning I didn't feel like getting up, and after that I could not get out of bed. However, I had the foresight to go down to the creek and get a pail of water before I got too sick to do so. I lived entirely on hardtack and water. I lost track of the days and nights as they went by; at times I would lapse into unconsciousness. The chipmunks would come near my bed and eat my hardtack. They kept getting nearer to me all the time and would get on my bed. I had horrible thoughts that when I became unable to raise my hands, the chipmunks would begin to eat on me while I was still conscious. Then one day (I don't recall whether it was in the morning or afternoon, but the sun was shining through the window) the door opened.

Now I don't know exactly what an angel looks like, but Jack Ritter standing there in the door looked to me like an angel. He asked "What's the matter, Kid?" I replied, "I'm sick." He suggested that he get some help to take me into the diggin's, but I asked him not to do that. I would be all right if I had something to eat. I knew that I was starving. Jack opened up his pack and made me a cup of tea—Jack always carried tea. I had never drunk tea and didn't like it, but the tea that day tasted better to me than anything I had ever drunk. Jack, together with the good people of Kantishna, soon restored me to full health with wholesome food, which to this day I am very thankful for.

The time was getting late in the summer, and the caribou had begun to migrate back to the low country. I soon recovered my former strength with good, fresh meat, and I tried to furnish everyone in Kantishna with fresh meat for their kindness to me. As Perry Blue had also recovered from his illness, I spent a lot of time with him and Jack. Perry Blue had studied Mining Engineering and knew a lot about geological formation. He asked me one day why I didn't try to find the ledge from which the placer gold came on Yellow Creek. He told me how to look for float, particles broken away from the ledge and drifted down to the river bed and often downstream. This became my next big project.

Fanny Quigley, a miner's wife, coming from the Alaska Range with pack dogs loaded with caribou meat, Kantishna, Alaska, 1921.

Alaska pack-dog team in the Kantishna District, Alaska.

A picture of caribou that Jack Ritter and I took in the Alaska Range near the foothills of Mt. McKinley.

I tried to find the gold vein from which the placer gold came on Yellow Creek, that the old-timers had worked out. I picked up several pieces of quartz in the river bed with gold in them and finally traced the pieces up the river bed to where it went up the river bank toward the rim of the mountain. Tracing the quartz float up the mountain side about 300 feet from the river bed, I found where the quartz float went into the ground. I knew then that the vein was in there somewhere covered with overburden.

After about ten days of hard work I had opened up a cut into the mountainside to the solid formation, and there was the vein. It was a beautiful sight, an 18-inch quartz vein with gold sticking out of the quartz that one could see with the naked eye. It really looked like a bonanza. Crushing the quartz up and panning it out, I would get a string of gold in the gold pan two or three inches long. This strike really excited the commissioner, and everyone else in the diggin's. The news spread throughout the Kantishna district that the Kid had hit it rich, and if there was ever a celebrity in the Kantishna country the Kid was one now. It was almost embarrassing to have old sourdoughs look up to me with such respect when they had spent a lifetime looking for something it had taken me only a few months to find.

Needless to say, I was not long staking out a claim on my new discovery and I named it "The Oklahoma" after my native state. Now my big problem was to get supplies and equipment in to work my newly found gold mine.

I was sure of one thing and that was I had to go back to Nenana and get a job to earn enough money for supplies and equipment to work my property. As the small sternwheel boat had made the last trip into Kantishna, I had only one choice to get back to Nenana and that was to hike out over the Alaska range of mountains to the new government railroad—about 80 miles of an uncharted route.

After making the rounds of the diggin's saying goodbye to everyone, I put three days of food in my pack-sack and with my 306 I took off across the unknown toward the railroad, with

## Moved on North 57

nothing to go by but dead reckoning. On my side, I had guts and youth and the encouragement and faith of everyone in the diggin's that the Kid would make it. I was advised by one old-timer that he had a hunting cabin on the head of McKinley River about 25 miles up into the range, which I could make for the first night stop. I had no trouble finding the cabin, but it was of little comfort to me as the field mice kept chewing my fingers and toes most of the night.

Early the next morning, while cooking a batch of sourdough hotcakes, I looked out the cabin door. On one side of the cabin I could see a herd of caribou feeding, and on the other side a herd of wild sheep. I thought what a wonderful country to live in and said to myself that I would never leave Alaska. Starting out from the hunter's cabin this second day of my journey, I had taken a good look at Mt. McKinley, which was on my right and a bearing on the direction that I should travel—almost due east with about 10 degrees north. I picked out low passes in the range to travel through. If I had to go either to the right or left in order to hit a pass, I always readjusted my directions after going through the pass.

Late on the second day out from the diggin's, I was surprised to see a couple of prospectors with a pack-horse coming down a small stream that I was crossing. I had expected to see no one in that part of the world, and I guess that they were just as surprised to see me. They asked me where I was camped. I told them that I was not camped any place, that I was going out to the railroad. They looked surprised and told me that I would never make it with the supplies that I had. They said that they had been eight days coming from the railroad and had been traveling all the time. I didn't want to give the old-timers advice, but I told them that I thought they had been lost and pointed out to them that, in this particular part of the range, they should have been crossing the streams instead of traveling downstream as they were doing, since downstream was south and they should be traveling west. I gave them the direction to take to hit the headwaters of the McKinley River and said to follow it down to the cabin that I had stayed in the night before. I never heard of them again; I hope that they made it.

Soon after leaving the two prospectors with the pack-horse, I ran into a glacier which really got me to thinking. I had not been advised that I would cross a glacier in this part of the range. However, I thought that my directions were right and I would take a chance on crossing the glacier—which I realized was dangerous this time of the year as glacier bears would lie in the ice and pop out on one without any warning. So, getting the 306 in position, I started out across the glaicer with only the good Lord and the Northern Lights as my guide. It was beginning to get dark now but the moon was out and it was almost as light as day. After traveling a few miles across the glacier, to my very pleasant surprise I could already see the other side as it happened to be a very small glacier.

Soon after crossing I came to a small river, the largest stream that I had encountered on my trip. I learned later that this was the Toklat River. It looked like a dangerous stream to cross. While it was not very wide, it was swift and I could hear rocks rolling downstream. I debated with myself for a while whether to cross before I made camp for the night. But, knowing that I could not sleep thinking of having the stream to cross the next morning, I decided to make a try for it then. Taking off all my clothes, which I hoped to keep dry, I stepped into the stream, which was ice-cold water as it came out from beneath the glacier. It was about waist deep but was so swift I could hardly stand up in it. I finally got across after losing a couple of toenails.

I quickly built a fire to warm up and cook something to eat. After devouring a big caribou steak and some hardtack, I spread out my sleeping bag and crawled into it for a good night's sleep. When I awoke the next morning, I thought that my watch had gone haywire as it showed almost 10 o'clock. I hurriedly threw some sourdough hotcakes together and got on my way. The traveling was really rough this third day out. It seemed that the mountains got steeper and there were more of them. I wondered at times if I was traveling in the right direction. Mt. McKinley, though, seemed to be in the right place and I appeared to be traveling in the right direction.

I saw a couple of bears this third day out and many herds of caribou and wild sheep. When dark came on this third day, I was somewhat saddened as I had expected to be at the railroad. Instead, I did not know exactly where I was, and had no sight of the railroad. I did not plan on camping out the third night; however, just before midnight as I crossed over a low pass I noticed that the streams ran in another direction. That seemed right as the railroad ran through a valley at the place I expected to hit it. I figured that any of these streams would lead me to the railroad, so I picked out one and headed down it. About 4 a.m. on the fourth day I came upon a beautiful sight—the government railroad—but at this point I did not know which way the nearest station would be. I only knew that Nenana would be to my left, so that is the direction in which I headed.

I had gone only a few miles when I came to Station No. 42, which meant that I was 42 miles from Nenana. I soon got a work train to Nenana. Much to my surprise, it seemed that everyone in Nenana knew the Kid and had heard the news that the Kid had hit it rich in the Kantishna. After visiting a few friends, I took the train to Fairbanks. I had several reasons for going to Fairbanks. The first was to have the ore of my claim assayed, which to my amazement, assayed over $500 a ton in free gold, as well as other values. I also had some gold to cash in, which was the nuggets from my placer mining; this came to over $2,000.

While in Fairbanks I paid a visit to my good friend, Cecil H. Clegg. During this visit was the first time I had met Mrs. Clegg, who was a schoolteacher in Fairbanks. They had, of course, heard of my good luck and insisted that I stay with them a few days and tell them all about it, which I was glad to do as some good home cooking was what this boy was looking for. After a couple of days' visit with the Cleggs I went back to Nenana, where I had been promised a job in the government warehouse.

Arriving back in Nenana, I located a small log cabin where I set up housekeeping and in a few days took up my job in the government warehouse as shipping clerk, sending out supplies to contractors on the new railroad.

The work was not hard, so I decided to get my trapline back in operation. Winter had just set in and it would be a means to supplement my wages and build up capital for supplies and equipment to open up my gold mine. It was a little early for muskrats but mink and marten were plentiful, and in those days I got a good price for marten. With the good wages I was getting, together with the fur I was shipping, I was making so much money I wondered why one would want a gold mine.

## CHAPTER 8

## *An Alaska Sweetheart*

I had more money and was making more money than I ever had made in my life, but it soon dawned upon me that there was something more in life than just money. After all, I was a young man of only 21 years. As you know, a man of that age wants other things in life besides money. Needless to say, the nights up there were long and lonesome for me. There was very little social activity going on in Nenana. After getting acquainted with some of the people who worked in the office of the government warehouse, I met a little Russian girl by the name of Mary Kirkenoff.

Mary was a wonderful girl, very pretty and a world of personality. Mary and I hit it off together like twin jets. She was two years younger than I, the sweetest girl I had ever known, and the only Russian I had ever met in my life that I liked. Mary also had wonderful parents. The Kirkenoff family had been in Alaska before the famous Seward Purchase of Alaska from Russia and lived in one of the largest houses in Nenana, with a large porch facing north (how well I can remember it!). Mary and I would sit on the porch night after night watching the northern lights and I would tell her about a world that she had only read and dreamed about—the States.

Mary had never seen a streetcar or ridden in an automobile, had never seen a circus or a stage show. This gave me a lot to talk about, in addition to telling her how sweet she was. With the friendship of Mary, the long winter nights soon rolled by and the spring break-up was approaching all too soon. I had begun to get my supplies and equipment together in order to take the first boat into Kantishna to open up my gold mine. Mary wanted very much to go back to the Kantishna with me, and hinted that we make it legal, but I was not about to get hitched. The only thing I wanted to make legal was a million-dollar bank account from the "Oklahoma."

Getting supplies and equipment together to open up a gold mine was a bigger job than I thought. So one day I made a decision that proved to be a wise one and that was to pass up the boat trip into Kantishna and go over the snow the following fall with a dog team. This change of plans really pleased Mary for it looked as though I was going to have to choose between gold and love. The break-up of the ice on the rivers and the melting of the long winter snow is the sign of spring in Alaska, and Alaska is blessed with a beautiful spring and summer. I had picked up my traps from the trapline and got the shotgun out. I brought in ducks and geese to the Kirkenoff residence until I know that they were sick of the sight of them, but I never got tired of eating them, especially the way Mrs. Kirkenoff cooked them.

The spring months soon passed by (thanks to Mary). About the first part of June, I received a letter from Cecil Clegg at Fairbanks that a big event was going to occur in Fairbanks about the 20th of June. Some airplanes were coming in from the states and he asked me to come up for the occasion, which I did. On the 22nd day of June, 1921, the "Black Wolf" squadron of about ten planes landed in Fairbanks; they were biplanes with a picture of a black wolf painted on their sides. These were the first airplanes to land in Alaska. What a sight this was, as well as one of the biggest celebrations ever held in Fairbanks up to this time. I was favored by being the guest of the Cleggs during the celebration, which I enjoyed every minute. After the celebrations the miners and prospectors returned to the hills and I to Nenana.

As I began to get my supplies together, Mary suggested that we pick some wild blueberries to include in my grocery supply, since blueberries are a favorite food in this cold climate due to the non-freezing quality of the berries when packed in sugar. So, about every day that we had off from our jobs (which was only Sundays in those days) Mary and I would go into the woods and pick blueberries—did I say berries? Well, we always came back with blueberries.

In the late summer the supplies and equipment were pretty well put together for the trip back to the diggin's. I had selected a good dog team of five dogs, four Alaska Huskies and a large gray Malamute that I named "Jake"—an outstanding dog. He seemed to be smarter than the other dogs, but was a fighter, especially with dogs ahead of him. So I conceived the idea of making a lead dog out of Jake, and what a lead dog he made! Jake would follow a frozen, wind-blown trail, or trail over a frozen lake of clear ice, and would immediately turn right or left at the command of "Gee" and "Haw."

As I recall, the first big snow came in the latter part of October, but I wanted to wait until some trappers had gone in over the trail and packed it some before traveling it with my heavy load. I had given up my job at the government warehouse and was spending my days with my dog team on short trails around Nenana, and my evenings, of course, with Mary. I would often get to thinking of the long winter nights that I was going to have to spend alone in the Kantishna and sometimes think about Mary's idea of making it a team was not such a bad one, but good judgment prevailed and I decided to go it alone.

About the middle of November I loaded my supplies and equipment in my 10-foot sledge and with Jake in the lead I headed out over the trail for the Kantishna. The first cabin on the trail was 30 miles, which I did not make the first day because of the heavy trail. About 20 miles from Nenana I made camp for the night. After bedding the dogs down in the snow, I stretched my sleeping bag out on some tree boughs and turned in for the night. The next morning I was surprised to find about two feet of snow over me. With the new snow I had a very heavy trail this second day out and only made about 10 miles to the first cabin. Here I had some good luck as that evening two trappers came into the cabin. They were traveling light so they broke trail for me the next day and I made the 30 miles to the

Knight's roadhouse on the Taklat River. This was the river I had crossed on my way out about 60 miles upstream in the Alaska range.

Late the next day I came to a wide tundra about 10 miles across, on which the trail had been wiped out entirely by the wind. Jake put his nose to the ground and started out across the tundra. Every once in a while he would put his nose down to the wind-swept snow and make a turn to the right or left, and I prayed that he was making the right turns. After about three hours I came to some scrub timber where the trail was protected from the wind and there was the trail. Jake had brought me across the 10 miles of tundra and kept right on the trail. A few miles farther on I came to a large lake and Jake again followed the obliterated trail across the lake.

On this day out, my plan was to make an old ghost-mining camp by the name of Diamond City, which was 30 miles from Knight's roadhouse. Not knowing how far I had come this day, I did not know where I was and it was very dark. I could only keep going and put my trust in old Jake, in whom by now I had a lot of faith. Soon I came onto some old cabins, most of them with the roof fallen in. I selected one that looked pretty good and made camp.

I had just got a fire going in my sheet-iron camp stove when there was a knock on the door. I opened the door and there stood an unkempt man with a heavy beard. He looked lean and hungry but as though he would fight a buzz saw barehanded. He stuck out his hand and said,

"I'm Harry Owens," and before I could tell him my name he said, "You must be the Kid." I asked him how he knew and he said that I looked like a fellow that would do the things that he heard about.

After I had fed my dogs and we had a bite to eat, Harry and I had a wonderful visit long into the night. He told me that I was lucky to hit it rich in such a short time and advised me to clean up and get back to the states. He told me that he had gone to Dawson as a young man of about my age and had been in al-

## An Alaska Sweetheart 65

most every new mining camp in the north. Now he had wound up as a trapper in Diamond City, where the gaiety and laughter had long since gone. He told me that he was the only person in Diamond City and that it was lonely. I judged Harry Owens to be a man in his middle forties, but from his stories of the early days in Dawson and other mining camps, I would say that he had experienced a hundred years of excitement.

The next morning after bidding Harry goodbye, I took off on the last leg of my trip of about 25 miles to the Kantishna diggin's. It was cold but a beautiful day. I had some mountains to go through and a few ridges to cross, but I had a packed trail and everything went well for me the entire day. Just after dusk as I came over the rim of Moose Creek, I could see the candlelight through windows of log cabins on Moose Creek at the diggin's, and the large building of the commissioner's office. It was a beautiful sight to me. I felt like going up to my lead dog, shaking his paw, and saying, "Jake, we made it." I know that old Jake would have understood.

Arriving back in the Kantishna was a happy occasion for me and a surprise to my friends there, as they did not expect me until later in the winter, or just before the break-up in the spring.

After a good night's rest I visited many of the old-timers who had been so kind to me on my trip into the Kantishna the previous year. I heard the sad news that Perry Blue, partner to Jack Ritter, had passed away three weeks before my arrival. I visited Jack Ritter on Rainy Creek and found him sitting alone in his cabin. He looked lonely and he looked old. He had aged a lot within the last year. He said, "Kid, I am glad to see you," and told me that he hoped that I would make my stake and get out of the country while I was young and had a lot of life ahead of me to enjoy. I asked Jack what he was going to do and he replied that there was only one thing that he could do and that was stay in the country, that he had most of his life behind him, and that he was going to stay in the north that had claimed the better years of his life.

Jack surprised me when he asked if I wished to see Perry. I replied that Perry was dead. He said, "Yes, he is dead, but we have delayed the burial until we can get some word to his folks in the states." There was no wireless station in the Kantishna and shortwave radio sets were unknown at this time, and there was mail in and out of Kantishna only once a month. Jack said that perhaps it would be several months before they buried Perry. He told me that the body was in a tent down at the diggin's and would stay frozen all winter.

After a day's rest at the diggin's I headed for my cabin and claim on Yellow Creek. The trail to Yellow Creek was unbroken; it took me two days to break a trail and get my supplies into the cabin. I found everything at the cabin as I had left it over a year ago, but now I had more responsibility. Instead of having one mouth to feed, I now had six—my own mouth and five hungry dogs. After getting settled in the cabin I snowshoed to the McKinley meadows, about six miles away, and got a big bull moose for my winter meat supply, which I divided with my dog team. I could not see myself eating moose steaks and my dogs eating dried salmon. After getting the moose hauled into camp, cut up, and put away in my meat cache, I proceeded to start work on my claim, "The Oklahoma." It was getting on toward the latter part of November now and I wanted to get some gold ore out and over to a stamp mill on Moose Creek before the break-up.

Since I was driving a tunnel into the side of a mountain, it didn't take me long to get under cover and a nice place to work. The ore looked wonderful. I could see pieces of gold sticking out of the quartz ore. I took out a few tons and returned to the diggin's to show miners there the rich ore I was taking out. It was not long until "The Oklahoma" was the showplace of the country. I had worked on my tunnel about three weeks and had about 25 tons of high-grade gold ore. Then one day I noticed that there was no gold showing in the ore, but instead some iron pyrite where the gold should be. I also ran into a different formation of talc and iron clay. I could hardly believe my eyes.

I worked long into the night trying to find more gold ore but with no results. Needless to say, I did not sleep much that night. The next day I went to Rainy Creek and brought Jack Ritter back with me to try and find out what happened. After looking around a bit, Jack said,

"Kid, you have hit the bottom of the pay streak." The gold ore was in the upper oxidized zone and when I hit the lower sulphide zone and the iron ore I had the gold worked out; I would find no more free-milling gold ore. He told me that this was typical of this particular area. I believed Jack, but I had a couple of other miners look at the ledge and they told me the same thing. It was hard to believe, but I sadly realized that the bottom had fallen out of my dream of a gold mine.

The time was about a week before Christmas. One night while sitting in my cabin looking out the window at the Northern Lights I made a decision, one of the few I have made in my life that changed my entire future. I asked myself if I wanted to stay in the north and live the life of Jack Ritter or Harry Owens, and I also thought of Perry Blue, who came up here a young man in the prime of life and now lay frozen in a tent at the diggin's. I also thought of the poem written by Robert W. Service, which went like this: "Twenty years on the Yukon moiling and toiling for the muck called gold, twenty years on the Yukon, twenty years, and I am old."

After all, I had not done bad for the short time I had been in the North, I had my gold ore to sell, a claim, and supplies. This together with the money I had in the bank at Fairbanks would yield me a small fortune. I would get Mary and go back to the States. This was a pleasant thought, but another thought came to me that made me very depressed and that was the fact that I could not take, my dog team to the states with me. I had become very fond of my dogs, especially old Jake, to whom I felt as close as a step-brother.

I went over to Rainy Creek and told Jack Ritter my story. He said, "Kid, I am not going to try to talk you out of going outside (the States) but now that Perry is gone I was going to ask you to team up with me." He said that he would have put the proposition to me sooner but he was afraid that I would think that he was after a chunk of "The Oklahoma." He said,

"Kid, if you want to stay, we will team up and next summer go back to Green Creek in the range where we found the tin pebbles, coal, and oil seepage and hit it rich. Don't let the disappointment of 'The Oklahoma' get you down." He said he had had many such disappointments in the past 20 years, but he also advised me to use my own judgment.

With this in mind I went back to my cabin to do some more thinking, and I believe that it was on Christmas eve that I decided to return to the States. Several miners came over to Yellow Creek to bid on my gold ore. Johnnie Lake, who had a small stamp mill on Moose Creek, had the advantage of the other miners and offered me $8,000 for the high-grade gold ore and claim. So, "The Oklahoma" was sold. I had no problem selling my supplies for more than twice what I paid for them in Nenana.

The last thing to sell and the hardest to part with was my dog team, as I would have a difficult time selling the dogs in Nenana. I decided to sell the dogs in the Kantishna where I could get a good price for them. Harry Owens, the trapper from Diamond City, bought my team and sleds for $1,000. After selling everything I realized over $10,000. This was all paid to me in gold. If you ever had $10,000 in gold in a money belt around your waist, you know how loaded down I was to mush out on a snow trail over a 100 miles to Nenana.

I picked a day the mail sledge would leave the diggin's for Nenana to start my trip out, as I knew that I would have a broken trail part of the way. I recall the time of my departure from Kantishna was a cloudy, dreary day between Christmas and New Year's, 1921. The mail sledge left the diggin's early, long before daylight, but I was right there behind them, with the thoughts of my return to the States, with Mary (I hoped).

The man with the mail said he was going to make Knight's roadhouse the first night, which was about 60 miles. I told him that I perhaps would stay in Diamond City with Harry Owens, which was only about half the distance. The trip to Diamond City was very good as I had a fresh-broken trail ahead of me. I got to Diamond City in the late afternoon, but I decided against staying with Harry Owens overnight, as I could not stand to tell old Jake goodbye the second time, so I hiked on down the trail toward Knight's roadhouse 30 miles away.

As I left Diamond City (a city of only one resident, Harry Owens), I could not help thinking of the trusty dog team I was leaving behind. I paused a moment in the trail and looked up into the northern sky and offered a little prayer that went like this: "O Lord, if there is a Heaven for dogs, please find Jake a place up there."

After leaving Diamond City I wondered if I had made a mistake by trying to make Knight's Roadhouse from the diggin's in one day, as it was getting very dark and the trail was not very good. About midnight I heard a dog team coming up behind me. It was a trapper going into Nenana with furs. He asked me where I was going and when I told him he asked me if I thought that I could make it, and I told him I thought I could. He asked me if I had a light. I told him I had a lantern but my hands were so cold that I could not hold a match to light it. He lit my lantern for me and told me that he was sorry that he had such a heavy load that he could not take me with him. He wished me good luck and advised me to be sure and stay on the trail. Soon after the trapper went by, the trail got much worse; a strong wind had come up and drifted the trail full of snow making it hard to follow.

I had fallen in the snow and put out my lantern; now I was in the dark again, my hands too cold to light the lantern. I was hoping that I could stay on the trail until daylight; then I would be all right. I came to some timber which offered some shelter from the wind, but it was still bitter cold. I decided to try and get some wood together and pour the oil from the lantern on it to start a fire. Then I heard another dog team coming down the trail toward me. I was a little way off the trail and they almost missed me.

I hollered and attracted the dogs' attention. It was the mailman and the trapper; they had come back on the trail to get me. Those two men were the most wonderful sight I had ever seen. I told them that if they would take me into the roadhouse I would give them a $1,000. They replied that they would take me into the roadhouse but that I was not going to give them one penny. To my surprise I was over 10 miles from the roadhouse and I never would have made it. We got into Knight's about 4 o'clock in the morning. Needless to say, I was several hours thawing out. I don't think anyone at the roadhouse slept any that night; the next day we all took a holiday and slept in.

The next leg of my trip would be the last mushing over the trail as 25 miles from Knight's roadhouse was a station on the government railroad where I could catch a work train into Nenana. The day I left Knight's roadhouse was a good day for hiking, cold and clear. I made the station in the early afternoon and was advised by the stationmaster that there would be no regular train through until late the next day, but he told me that a special train was coming through from Anchorage in a couple of hours bringing a new judge on his way to Fairbanks. He also told me that the new judge was Cecil H. Clegg. I asked him if I could get on the train. He told me that I could not, that the train would not stop unless he flagged it down and he would have to have a good reason to do that. I convinced him that I was a good friend of Clegg's and got him to flag down the special train, but he warned me perhaps the conductor would kick me off.

As the train (only one car) came to a stop at the station I immediately boarded it. Judge Clegg was sitting in the end of the car as I entered, and before the conductor got to me, Judge Clegg had got out of his seat and shaken my hand. Then I had it made. Judge Clegg asked me what was the trouble that I was leaving Kantishna, and I told him the whole story. He listened

## An Alaska Sweetheart 71

like a father, then asked me to come up to Fairbanks. I told him that I would, that I had to go to Fairbanks to get some money I had there in the bank. Then Judge Clegg said,

"Son (he always called me son instead of Kid), will you promise that you will come to Fairbanks and see me before you do anything?" He said it in such a way that it sounded important.

Arriving back in Nenana, of course I made a beeline to see Mary. She sensed something had happened. She looked pale and asked me what had gone wrong. I did not have the courage to tell her that the bottom had dropped out of my gold mine, but I told her the truth that I had sold the "Oklahoma." I also did not have the courage to tell her that I was going back to the States. But later that night while Mary and I were sitting on the Kirkenoff's large porch watching the Northern Lights I popped the big question. I said,

"Mary, I have something to tell you and also something to ask you." I told her that I was going back to the States and I asked her to marry me and go back with me. Mary didn't answer me but she buried her face in my arms and sobbed. Then I knew the answer. After a while she said, "This is the happiest moment of my life to be with you forever and live in the wonderful United States."

After leaving Mary that night, I wondered if I had acted in haste in asking Mary to marry me and go back to the States, since I had an appointment with Judge Clegg in Fairbanks and he might have different plans for me.

# CHAPTER 9

## *Appointed U.S. Commissioner*

After a couple of days in Nenana, I went on up to Fairbanks. Before taking the money out of the bank that I had there, I kept my appointment with Judge Clegg. He asked me if I had any particular reason for returning to the States. I told him that I did not, other than that I thought I could get a little more out of life in the United States than I could up here in the North. He said, "Son, Alaska is becoming a great country and we need people like you with youth and determination to develop it." Then he told me the story of how he became judge. He said that the Republican administration which had just elected President Harding was replacing some key positions held heretofore by Democrats, and he had several of these positions to fill; one was for U.S. Marshal in the Koyukok district, and another for United States Commissioner in the fourth district office located at McGrath. This hit me like a bolt of lightning. Before I realized what I was saying I replied that I would like the U.S. Commissioner position. Judge Clegg called in his clerk to make out the forms for the appointment.

The document of my appointment as U.S. Commissioner in Alaska has been treasured by me over the many years as one of my prize possessions and I would like to reprint it here for you:

"IT IS ORDERED that Floyd Marsh be and he is hereby appointed United States Commissioner in and for the Territory of Alaska, ex-officio Justice of the Peace, Probate Judge, Coroner and Recorder, in and for said Mt. McKinley Precinct, bounded and described by order heretofore duly entered in this court: his place of residence to be at and the same is hereby designated as the town of McGrath, in said precinct: and that he be and

## Appointed U.S. Commissioner 73

hereby is authorized and empowered to execute and fulfill the duties of said office according to the Constitution and Laws of the United States and that he have and hold the same office, with all the power, privileges and emoluments to the same of right appertaining, until the further order of this court of the Judge thereof.

"IT IS FURTHER ORDERED that the said Floyd Marsh be and he is hereby authorized and empowered to take into posession from W.F. Green, the present custodian, all papers, documents, books, moneys and property of every kind belonging to the United States upon giving proper receipts therefor.

"Signed this 10th day of January, 1922"
(Signed) Cecil H. Clegg, District Judge

I felt very proud of the above commission and walked out of Judge Clegg's office in a kind of daze. But as I walked toward the depot to take the train back to Nenana I thought to myself: boy, you sure got yourself in a mess in the last few days. Here I have obligations to take on a wife and responsibilities of a United States Commissioner. But the immediate problem at hand was how to break the news to Mary that I was not going back to the States and that there would be no wedding, at least for a while, as there would be a trail of 250 miles to hike over to get to McGrath, and living quarters to establish. So, I would have to leave Mary once again.

Arriving back in Nenana and building up some courage, I confronted Mary with the new development. She greeted the news with mixed emotion. She said that she did not know whether to be happy or sad. She asked if she could go to McGrath with me and when I told her of the difficulties of her going to McGrath at this time, tears came to her eyes. She looked like a little girl that had lost her ticket to Fairyland. I felt so sorry for her. I took her in my arms and said,

"Mary, as sure as there is a Heaven above, I will come back for you, or send for you." Then that night, long into the night,

Mary and I sat on the Kirkenoff's large porch under the northern lights and planned our future.

We decided that I would stay at McGrath only two terms of office as U.S. Commissioner. I told Mary by that time we would have a fortune made and would go to the States to live. With the money I already had, together with my income from the U.S. Commissioner's office, plus other opportunities I had heard about at McGrath, I was sure that I would be a very wealthy man in two years. I left Mary that night with a heavy heart, but with high spirits and hope for the opportunity that lay ahead for us.

It was hard to comprehend the responsibility that had been handed to me; I could sit as a judge, could jail and fine people for any crime less than a felony, which meant confinement in jail for not over one year and a fine of not over $1,000 or both fine and imprisonment. When I told Judge Clegg that I knew nothing about law, he told me that was all right; that Alaska being a territory the only laws that I would have to familiarize myself with were the compiled laws of the Territory of Alaska, which he gave me. He told me that I would only try minor crimes, that felony cases would be bound over to his court. Needless to say, the set of compiled laws of the Territory of Alaska was my bible for the next several months.

The long trail into McGrath started at a small station by the name of Nancy on the government railroad about 60 miles north of Anchorage. It was known as the Anchorage-Iditarod trail and had the reputation of having its share of casualties among the trails of Alaska. As the train (two cars) pulled out of Nenana I felt a heavy heart as this part of Alaska had been both cruel and kind to me. It was also in this part of Alaska that I had twice almost lost my life. It was also in this part of Alaska that I had found both gold and love, and I think that these two things, gold and love, have a greater impact on a man's life than any other thing as either one of them will inspire a man to accomplish much; they act as a fuel for energy.

Left: Floyd Marsh in Fairbanks, Alaska, January 1922, at the time he was appointed U.S. Commissioner, Fourth District, Territory of Alaska.

Right: Larry Cross the summer before his foot was frozen.

Dog freight team on the McGrath-Anchorage trail that traveled on my trip to McGrath.

The railroad ran through the Broad Pass route that I had traveled three years previously going into the interior. As I looked out of the coach window I thought of the many things that had happened in the last three years and offered a little silent prayer of thanks to the Lord for having his arms around me during this time, and I asked him to stay with me a little while longer as I had a tough job ahead.

The train arrived in Nancy late in the afternoon and I was advised that it would be two days before the mail sled would leave for McGrath, which made one trip every two weeks. The freight sled also made one trip every two weeks. They alternated, making a dog team in over the trail once a week. Wanting to go in over the trail behind a dog team I had to lay over in Nancy a couple of days. In Nancy there were a station-master, two trappers, and a miner working on a prospect tunnel nearby, so I had company and a nice visit with these old-timers during my wait for the mail sled. From them I got some very valuable information about the trail and roadhouses into McGrath.

I was told that the distance to McGrath was about 250 miles and the roadhouses from 20 to 35 miles apart, and that it was an 8-day hike. I was also told that this was the worst time of year to go in over the trail as at this time the trail was less traveled and the storms were worse, there were only a few hours of daylight. They also advised me that just before the break-up in another two and a half months there would be hundreds of miners going in over the trail to work in the placer mines in Iditarod, Flat, Ophir, and McGrath during the summer, and they all would come out just after the freeze-up in October and November. These two times of the year were the best to travel the trail. Of course, this did not solve my problem at hand. I would not only have to travel the trail alone, but I would have the elements of cold, storms, and darkness to buck.

After a couple of days of rest at Nancy and getting all the information I could about the trail and roadhouses, I hit out one morning about four hours before daylight behind the mail sled

## Appointed U.S. Commissioner 77

in a northwesterly direction toward McGrath 250 miles away. I was soon alone on the trail as the mail sled made two and three roadhouses a day and I was to make only one, and that one I had to make or there would be no more "Kid." As I mushed along the bleak white trail in the center of Alaska that led into seemingly nowhere, with only danger and death as my companion, I thought of a lot of things. I thought of my widowed mother and six brothers back in the states. I thought of Mary and her faith and confidence that I would make it—this gave me courage. It was not being alone that bothered me as I had been a loner since I was 14 years old when I left home and crawled into a boxcar. I also thought of a phrase I had read many years ago which went like this: "You can write it on paper or carve it on stone, he who travels the fastest, travels alone."

This first day out was a very bad one, in spite of a freshly broken trail. The going out was very tough; I saw no sun at all this first day. There was a "white-out" the entire day, something like a fog we have in the states, only everything is white and you can see only a few feet ahead. I arrived at the first roadhouse, which was about 30 miles from Nancy, quite late in the evening. The elderly couple who operated it were expecting me and really rolled out the red carpet for the new commissioner. They were very much interested in what they had heard about the "Kid" and seemed to have my record pretty well up-to-date. This elderly lady was the last woman I saw until I got into McGrath. The other roadhouses were operated by old-timers who prospected during the summer months and trapped in the winter, in addition to operating their roadhouse.

The next two days were good days on the trail. What short time the sun was out it was nice and bright and the trail was easy to travel. I arrived at roadhouses two and three in the late afternoon of both days. The first three days had gone quite well for me with the exception of the first day, which was a little rough. At the third roadhouse I was advised that the next day I would cross the Great Divide of the Alaska range, and this would be the most hazardous part of my trip. I had been told about the trail over the summit and about the lives that had been lost there. The distance to the next roadhouse over the summit was only 20 miles but mostly upgrade. I was also told that, just before I reached the peak of the summit, there was a small cabin alongside the trail with a stove in it and a phone connected with the next roadhouse six miles away operated by an old-timer known as "Old Joe." I was to call Joe when I arrived at the cabin and let him know when I was to leave the cabin for his roadhouse.

I arrived at the little cabin about dark. True to what I had heard about the pass over the summit, I could sense a storm up in the pass as the wind was blowing and the snow drifting at the little cabin. After resting a few minutes and warming up some, I called the roadhouse and told Joe that I was coming over the pass. He advised me to wait a while; that he would go out a way on the trail to see what the conditions were and would call me back, which he did in about 30 minutes. He reported back that the trail was pretty bad and asked if I was the "Kid." When I told him I was, he said that he had been going to advise me to stay at the cabin all night, but from what he had heard about the Kid he thought that I could make it. I told him that I appreciated his confidence very much, that I did not want to stay at the cabin all night. When I told him that I was going to give it a try, he said that he would start out from the roadhouse to meet me with a lantern and a dog on a leash, because his dog team was laid up with fish poisoning.

I traveled about two miles from the cabin and reached the summit of the pass when I encountered one of the worst storms I had ever been in. The trail was drifted smooth. I could not even be sure I was on it any longer, so I had to make a decision either to try to get back to the cabin or wait where I was for Joe. I decided to wait for Joe, for a while at least, so I tramped out a circle in the snow and kept walking in it. I knew better than to stop.

## Appointed U.S. Commissioner

In about 30 minutes or so I saw a light coming toward me. It was Joe and his dog. I was only about 100 feet off the trail, but if I had kept going I would not be writing this story today. Old Joe was everything I had heard about him, kind and understanding; even his dog was friendly for a Malamute. Joe said, "Kid, you played it smart, just like an old-timer, to stay put when you realized that you were lost." He said I would never have made it back to the cabin as my trail had been drifted smooth with snow. Going on to the roadhouse I really appreciated how a smart dog works an obliterated trail. I have worked coon dogs in the south on coon trails, but to see a Malamute dog work a frozen, obliterated trail—especially when your life depends on it—is a wonderful thing. I am sure that Joe and I never would have made it to the roadhouse without the dog.

After a big supper of moose meat, Joe and I had a fine visit. Joe was on the order of Harry Owens but much older. He said he was 60 years old and had gone to the Klondike in the Yukon Territory through Skagway in 1898. When I told Joe about Mary and our future plans, tears came to his eyes and he said in a mellow voice, "That part of life has passed me by." He said that when he left the States in '98 that he had a sweetheart of school days. He went to the Klondike to make a stake and then planned to go back and marry her. Because of the poor mail service up north—and many months with no mail at all—he had lost contact with her, but never gave up hope. In 1905 he had made his stake and gone back to Seattle for his Nell, but she had married several years previously. Joe said that everything seemed so much different after so many years away that he could not content himself with life in the States.

The Lewis & Clark Exposition at Portland, Oregon, was going on at that time, so he decided to visit Portland and find something that would interest him, but to no avail. After a couple of weeks in Portland he went back north again. He said, "Ten years ago I purchased this roadhouse and it is here that I am going to live and die."

Joe asked me to stay over with him a couple of days to visit and rest up. I told him that I would but the roadhouses along the trail would expect me on a certain day as the mail sled ahead of me had advised them the days to expect me. Joe agreed, then the phone rang. I was wondering if some other poor fellow was in trouble, as the phone line only went to the small cabin on the other side of the pass. It was a call from the cabin. After Joe hung up, he said that there was a dog team coming through. When I asked him if he was going out to meet the team, Joe replied, "Not that fellow. He will make it when no one else can. That is the fellow they call the 'night rider.' Because he travels at night, and mostly day and night, he makes emergency runs over this part of Alaska."

Very shortly, "night rider" pulled in at the roadhouse with the finest dog team I had ever seen, consisting of seven fine, big Alaska Huskies. They looked more like Shetland ponies than dogs. Joe asked him if he was going to stay overnight and he replied that he was not, that he was taking some medicine to Iditarod for a severely sick child (I learned later than he got $2,500 for this trip). "Night rider" would open up the trail and also notify the roadhouses ahead that I would be a day late, so I could stay over with Joe for another day. After a short visit, a big moose steak, and many cups of coffee, he took off down the trail for Iditarod, over 200 miles away, while Joe and I hit the sack. This was sometime after midnight, and needless to say, I did not need anyone to rock me to sleep that night.

Joe and I slept late the next morning. After a big breakfast of sourdough hotcakes (Joe could really put out the sourdough hotcakes) we attended one string of his trapline. The string of traps we attended that day ran up a large canyon into a high range of mountains; the snow was deep most of the way, which necessitated snowshoes. We arrived back at the roadhouse late in the afternoon with a catch of a marten and two mink. Joe said that we had traveled about ten miles; it seemed like a hundred to me. But I enjoyed the scenery very much, the awesome, massive beauty of this great white wonderland, the day bright and clear with the towering snow-covered mountains all about us. I realized what Robert W. Service meant when he mentioned in his poem: "The icy mountains hem you in with a silence you could almost hear."

While Joe was putting his catch on drying boards, I proceeded to take a little nap, but not for long. I soon heard a yelping dog team coming into the roadhouse, but it was going the wrong way to break a fresh trail for me as it was coming from McGrath. However, I got the latest news from McGrath and the other mining camps in the vicinity. The driver of the dog team was a fur trader in McGrath going out to Anchorage with a load of furs. He told me that the trail to McGrath was good at the time he came over it and that the people of McGrath were expecting me and looking forward to the arrival of the new U.S. Commissioner. He also told me that the first roadhouse out of McGrath, by the name of "Big River Roadhouse," was to notify the N.C. Store (Northern Commercial) when I arrived there and a party from McGrath was coming out on the trail to meet me.

We all retired early that night. The fur trader was to hit the trail at 4 a.m. the next morning, and Joe and I were tired from attending his trapline.

When I awoke the next morning the fur trader had already hit the trail for Anchorage. I took on a big breakfast as it was the last meal I was going to get until I reached the next roadhouse 30 miles away, and 8 to 10 hours later. I told Joe that perhaps I would see him sometime in March as I intended to get me a dog team soon after arriving in McGrath; I wanted one to see the country and also to cover my territory. Also I planned to go back for Mary when the trail became packed and the traveling was easy in the spring. Joe said to be sure and let him know when I was coming through with Mary, and with a chuckle he said, "I will have the Bridal Suite fixed up." I hated to tell Joe goodbye. I had never met a man with whom I had become so well acquainted in such a short time; I liked him very much. If old Joe is living today (which is very unlikely) he is 113 years

McGrath mail dog team that broke the long trail into McGrath for me.

old. But wherever he is, God bless him; I hope that he is doing well.

Long before daylight I was on the trail for the next roadhouse. It was a fine day and the sun came out for a couple of hours, which was all the sun we had at that time of year. There had been no new snow since the fur trader went over the trail, so I had a good trail to the next roadhouse, where I arrived in the late afternoon. Two trappers ran this roadhouse; that is, they trapped in the winter and mined during the summer months after the break-up and the creeks furnished water for their placer claims. Placer mining is the kind of mining that the old-timers like. It is instant money, washing gold from the gravel in the creek beds. They told me that they had mining claims recorded in the commissioner's office at McGrath, which I would see when I took office. These two fellows (I don't recall their names) were about middle-aged and interesting men to talk to.

The next day on my way I met a dog team with a sick man. The driver of the team was a trapper taking the owner of the next roadhouse into Anchorage. The owner said that there would be no one at his roadhouse that night but that it was unlocked (as all buildings are in Alaska, or were at that time). He told me to make myself at home, to cook my supper and breakfast, and where there was a bed. He also told me that I could leave my lodging fee in a tomato can on the table with my name. There was a standard price all over Alaska of $5 for two meals and a night's lodging. When I arrived at the roadhouse, it was dark, of course. I went in, lit up some candles and built a fire. I was hoping someone would come along for company, but no luck, so after while I went to the meat cache and sawed myself off a steak. The owner had told me that there was moose, wild sheep, and bear meat in the cache and, naturally, it was not labeled, so I just got myself some meat. After a big supper and with no company in sight, I hit the hay.

After cooking myself some breakfast the next morning and with a couple of sourdough hotcakes in my pocket for lunch, I hit out for the last roadhouse between me and Big River roadhouse. This place was called East Fork roadhouse. I found the owner a very friendly old-timer who had for many years lived in McGrath, and he gave me the lowdown on McGrath and surrounding vicinity. He said that the opportunities in the country were many and told me that I was a lucky fellow being appointed U.S. Commissioner of this district. The next day's hike to Big River roadhouse was a bad one. It had snowed during the night and I had a heavy trail. I arrived at Big River roadhouse late at night. Two young fellows operated it, and I wondered why such fine, young-looking fellows were up in this part of Alaska. I presume that they wondered the same about me. Larry Cross was the name of one of these fellows, with whom I became very well acquainted, and he later played an important part in my Alaska life. These boys told me that they were to call the N.C. Store (Northern Commercial) when I arrived, but at this time of night the store was closed, so they got in touch with the wireless station and notified the fellow there, who in turn advised them that a party would come out on the trail to meet me the next day.

After a long visit with Larry Cross and his partner I hit the sack, very tired but with high spirits and the comforting thought that the big hike was behind me and tomorrow there was a ride into McGrath, part of the way at least. The next morning I "hit the bear rug" (in front of my bed) early, and was soon on my way to McGrath 22 miles away, the last leg of my journey. I had traveled down the trail toward McGrath about 5 miles when I met two dog teams of nine big Alaska Huskies each. With the dog teams were Pete McMullen, U.S. Marshal of the district of which I was U.S. Commissioner; a Mr. Loomis, manager of the N.C. Store, and Captain William Greene, who operated the sternwheeler *Quick Step* during the summer months, on the Kuskokwim River.

After a warm greeting I was put on one of the dog sleds and we were in McGrath very shortly. What a royal welcome I received. It was fit for a king. I wondered where all the people

## Appointed U.S. Commissioner 85

came from. We came in at the N.C. Store on the banks of the Takotna River. The banks were lined with people. Mr. Loomis gave a welcome address. My acceptance was short, friendly, and appreciative. I said that I had come to McGrath to be one of the community and hoped that the people of McGrath and my district would treat me as such.

# CHAPTER 10

## *Take Office As U.S. Commissioner*

The big blow-off came that night in a great log building (I think they called it the community hall). A large crowd gathered, including all the people of McGrath, miners in the vicinity and I think all the Indians and trappers. Though Alaska had prohibition the same as the States, liquor flowed freely. I hardly knew what to do, but Pete McMullen, the marshal, put me at ease. He told me that he was to enforce the law and that I was only to administer justice. What bothered me was the Indians taking on too much firewater. At that time they were a ward of the government and were prohibited liquor. Of course, Pete and I did not see any Indians drink liquor, but we knew that those who were in a huddle in the back of the building were not playing football. Pete told me to take my hair down and have a good time. I did feel like unwinding after what I had gone through.

One thing that puzzled me very much was the extremely attractive young ladies at the party. They seemed out of place up there. I asked Pete who they were; he had a good laugh and said they were ladies of easy virtue from the tenderloin district of McGrath and Takotna. He said that everyone mixed with everyone up here. With this in mind, I did not get too friendly with any of these ladies, as it might become embarrassing when Pete brought them up before me to pay their taxes, which he did every once in a while.

I retired that night in a haze of bewilderment to think it was possible that this could happen to a poor Oklahoma farm boy who got his education and learning in a cotton field.

My first day in office as U.S. Commissioner was a busy one, taking over the books and legal documents from former U.S.

## Take Office As U.S. Commissioner 87

Commissioner, W.F. Green. I had set my office up in the United States Wireless Station, operated by a young fellow in the signal corps by the name of Leo Bundy. Leo was about my age, a very likable and congenial chap and good company.

We worked one full day and part of a night getting the books transferred, as Green wanted to take a trip outside (the States) as soon as possible. He mentioned something that made me realize I had taken on a bigger job than I had expected. He informed me that I was also the doctor of the precinct. I had heard people call him Doc, but I never realized that he was a doctor. He told me that his wife was staying in McGrath and that I was welcome to use his office in case of any emergencies. I asked him if he was the only doctor in the 10,000-square-mile district and he said that he was, but in the 20 years that he had been in the district he said that he had had very few medical cases, and they were minor ones. He had also had a few teeth to pull.

Dr. Green told me that he was going outside to see his mother, whom he had not seen in over 20 years, and expected to come back in over the trail before the spring break-up. He said that Judge Clegg had informed him that I had been a hospital sergeant in the army and that he thought I could take care of any emergency cases. I replied that I had spent almost three years in the hospital corps in the army but that I had never pulled a tooth or delivered a baby.

After all the U.S. Commissioner data was transferred from Green's office to my office in the Wireless Station, I proceeded to get acquainted with the people of McGrath and to find out what made this booming little town tick. I found some very interesting people. Right at this time, history was being made in McGrath by a fellow by the name of L.B. Loomis, manager of the Northern Commercial Store. Loomis told me that he had an idea and was getting a patent on it—an armored car to pick up receipts from business places and also to transfer money and valuables from place to place. He was leaving for the States before the break-up to have this car build (the first armored car of its kind). I thought to myself, Mr. Loomis you have been up north too long. To my big surprise, when I returned to the States several years later, as I was walking down a street in Portland, Oregon, an armored car passed me and on the side of the car were the words "Loomis Armored Car." I could hardly believe it, but before my eyes was an enterprise for which the idea was hatched out in the frozen North. I met Loomis (who is now deceased) many times after that and we would hash over old times in Alaska.

I spent about a week visiting among the residents of McGrath and vicinity when Pete McMullen, U.S. Marshal, suggested that I see some of the communities in my district such as Takotna, Ophir, Flat, Iditarod, Holy Cross, and a few others within a radius of one hundred miles of McGrath. Bethel, at the mouth of the Kuskokwim River 400 miles away, was in my territory and I intended to visit it by boat after the spring break-up.

Pete advised me what I would need for the trip through the district, which was about 200 miles to Holy Cross and back; we would visit the other communities on the way. Pete had a fine dog team of seven Alaska Huskies. We picked a good day to start our trip, about the middle of February. Pete sent word to Takotna 12 miles away that we would be there for breakfast on a certain day and we arrived at this little mining town per schedule. Takotna had about 30 people (winter population) consisting of miners and trappers. We had a fine breakfast and a friendly meeting with the top brass of the town at "Lillian's Place." After thanking our hostess and town officials for the wonderful breakfast and congenial meeting we headed down the trail for Moore Creek. At our next stop, about 30 miles away there was one store and a few log cabins. From Moore Creek we went on to Flat, which was another one-store town, but some type of hang-out for toughs. I think it was a pool hall and that you could buy a drink there if you knew the right people. From here we went on to Iditarod for the night. At this point we were about 60 miles from McGrath—not much distance for a good dog team, but we had done a lot of visiting on the way.

Iditarod had been a very rich mining town. There was still a lot of mining going on in the summer months when there was water available for placer mining, but at this time there were a lot of cabins vacant that would be filled up when the miners came back in the spring. Winter population of Iditarod and vicinity was about 40 people.

That night Pete and I got together with some of the business people of Iditarod for a meeting and exchange of information. Though I had been away from the States for over two years and away from Fairbanks and Nenana for some time, I felt like a walking bureau of information judging from the questions asked me and, of course, I had some questions I wished to ask these folks. I was interested in what kind of life they lived, how they passed the long winters, what they did for recreation. I think that one can find out more about human nature at a place like this than on 42nd and Broadway, New York. Never have I encountered people anywhere who were so relaxed and with such contentment as these people. They seemed to be at peace with the world. It was quite a contrast to the mad rush and hustle and scramble over the dollar I had seen back in the States. I was surprised to learn that some of the old-timers had been in Iditarod since it was discovered and had never been out as far as Anchorage; some of them were old men and some not so old, but all shared the never-dying hope that tomorrow they would strike it rich. That night, when Pete and I were alone, I remarked to him what a power the lust for gold has over man, and said that I hope that Alaska never gets that tight a hold on me, and Pete replied me neither.

The next morning Pete and I went over to what they called the Big Hump between Kuskokwim River watershed and the Yukon River watershed. It was 40 miles from Iditarod to Holy Cross Mission on the Yukon River, with no roadhouses or other stops on the way. However, Pete's fine team of Alaska Huskies took us over the 40 miles in good time. I really enjoyed the ride. There is no traveling so smooth and comfortable as riding on a dog sled. When it became dark and there was no scenery I slept most of the way.

We reached Holy Cross in the late afternoon, which at that time of the year was dark, but on our arrival at the Mission we could sense a festival air. The little town was packed with people and as we pulled up in front of the large roadhouse there, they swarmed around our sled. Someone told us what had happened, that the wireless station at McGrath had notified Holy Cross that Pete and I would be there on this particular day. In addition to receiving a royal welcome, the people of the Mission had a wonderful dinner planned for us, of which we gladly partook. But this was not all, they had a meeting planned that evening in one of the halls, and unprepared as I was, I had to give a talk to those people. Needless to say, it had to be right off the cuff—this was difficult enough; but, I would be talking to a strange people in a strange land. However, it was the kind of crowd I liked to talk to. They sat and listened with awed silence. I wondered if some of them knew what I was talking about. As for Pete, he got all the play from the kids with his big star and the "45" on his hip.

I was told that I was the first U.S. Commissioner whom most of these people had ever seen. Dr. Green had never visited Holy Cross and for me to make a trip down there upon taking office put me in as solid as a Democrat in the South.

We decided to stay over a couple of days at Holy Cross to let the dogs rest up. Also, we were undecided whether we would go on down the Yukon about 50 miles to Russian Mission. The two days at Holy Cross passed very rapidly; we were treated like celebrities. While we were at Holy Cross, several middle-aged natives came up to me and said that they wanted me to marry them. I asked them if they had a marriage license, but they didn't understand what I was talking about, so they brought one of the officials of the Mission to me, to whom I explained that I would have to issue a marriage license to these people before I could marry them. He understood, and it was decided

## Take Office As U.S. Commissioner 91

that they would come to McGrath when I got back and secure a marriage license and get married in McGrath.

After the exchange of wireless messages with McGrath and Fairbanks, Pete and I decided to return to McGrath instead of going on to Russian Mission, as this time of the year there was heavy shipment of furs going through McGrath, and all these furs had to be examined by the commissioner and a territorial tax collected for each respective type of skin.

I thought that the natives of Holy Cross had seen all of the U.S. Commissioner that they wanted to see, but the morning we left it seemed like all the people of the entire town and vicinity were down at the roadhouse to see us off. I felt a duty of service to these people and wondered what I could do for them. I thought to myself that I could at least explain to them the function of the Commissioner's office, so just before we left I stood in the doorway of the roadhouse and told the people of Holy Cross how Pete and myself appreciated the warm welcome that we had received. I told them that the U.S. Marshal and U.S. Commissioner's office was their local government for their guidance and that we stood ready at any time to give them help and information.

And with the words "Goodbye, good luck, and God bless you," we took off back over the big hump toward McGrath.

As Pete and I were anxious to return to McGrath we did not intend to do any visiting on our way back, not even an overnight stop in Iditarod, as we did on our way to Holy Cross. The trail was good as it was getting toward the latter part of February. With no fresh snow, the trails are always good at this time. The weather was beautiful, but cold, and there were only about three hours of daylight. The moon and stars were out so bright that it was almost as light as day.

I was doing a lot of sleeping on the way back. The dogs were fresh after a week's rest in Holy Cross. We were making good time and remarked what a fast and good trip back we were having. We had stopped at Moore Creek for dinner and after a short visit took off for McGrath about 40 miles away. We had traveled 10 or 15 miles from Moore Creek and were on the headwaters of Takonta River. I had fallen asleep when Pete reached down into the sledge, took hold of my arm and said,

"Wake up, we are in trouble." Before I could ask him what the trouble was, he said there was a pack of timber wolves following us and he could hardly manage the dogs. I could hear the pack's blood-curdling howl and yelping. What made it so weird was that the timber wolves would follow us for a time in silence, coming up on each side of the sledge, then drop back in a pack, yelping. The dogs were almost unmanageable. Pete said,

"We have to do something fast. If we don't come across a moose or a caribou soon to shoot for them, we'll have to shoot one of our dogs to leave for them." He then suggested that if I could hold the dogs he would shoot one or two of the wolves and they might leave us. We had two 306's and two revolvers with us, but the dogs were too unruly for one person to hold. I fired several shots at the wolves as they came up alongside of the sledge, but the wolves were darting among the large boulders and brush so fast that I was really shooting in the dark. As the moon had gone down now it was quite dark and the wolves were getting a little closer. Pete could see that I was getting very concerned. He said,

"Don't worry about the wolves getting you and me; when they get close enough I will kill a few of them and they will go away." Perhaps we would lose our dog team, but this did not make my blood pressure go down a bit. We were then approaching a large clearing. The wolves did not follow us out into the clearing but stayed on the edge in the timber, though still following us. In this clearing there was an old, abandoned roadhouse. Pete ran the dogs inside the roadhouse. We shut the doors behind us and took on the wolves, wagon-train and Indian-style. The wolves began to circle the old roadhouse, and as they came out into the opening we picked them off with our 306's. Pete remarked that a moving picture of this would be worth a million dollars. I was not shooting from a moving sledge now so I soon got myself a few wolves. With Pete also shooting, we soon discouraged the wolves. They had no more appetite for human flesh or dog flesh, whichever

## Take Office As U.S. Commissioner 93

one they were after. We picked up four large timber wolves that we had killed. We know that there were many more shot up so badly they would not make it very far.

After the episode Pete said, "This was very unusual." In fact, he knows of only one other instance of a wolf pack attacking a dog team and that was an attack on himself in the Koyukuk country north of the Yukon, many years ago. Pete was glad that there was a witness to this attack, as some people thought that he was stretching his imagination when he told them about the timber wolves attacking him and his dog team in the Koyukuk.

Pete not only had a witness to this attack but he had some evidence in the form of our large timber wolves we brought back to skin. This being in the middle of winter, the wolves had a valuable hide.

When we got on the trail again, it was getting late, so we decided to stay the balance of the night in Takotna—and to our surprise we were only a short ways from Takonta. We were also surprised to learn that the residents of Takotna and the miners in the vicinity knew that the wolf pack was in the country. The wolfgang had killed a packhorse near Takotna a few days previously. Women and children were staying inside their houses after dark and men were all carrying guns when they traveled. The supposition was that the wolf pack had come down from north of the Yukon, where there was no food, and were on their way to the lower Kuskokwin where there are animals that they could kill for food.

With only twelve miles to McGrath, we finished this off in short time the next day. Arriving back in McGrath I really ran into a mess. There were trappers all over town waiting to have their furs checked out so they could ship them to the fur houses in the States, and there were a great many mining claim locations to be recorded. Leo Bundy, with whom I shared living quarters, had done some of the recording, but that didn't take the trappers off my back. They wanted to get clearance to ship their fur and I was the only one who could give them this. Bundy remarked that he would help me with the recording, but he would not help me with some of the other things that were coming up. I asked, "Which other things?" and he replied, "Mrs. Carter (wife of the clerk in the store) has an abscessed tooth which has to come out right away." This hit me pretty hard, but the next remark from Bundy really laid me out. He said,

"Atwater's wife is going to have a baby and you know who the only doctor within 400 miles is—yes, the commissioner." If airplanes came into McGrath then as they do today, I would have taken the next one out, but under the circumstances I was stuck and had to make the best of it. Then I looked over on the back of my desk and there was a letter from Mary that had arrived while I was away. After reading Mary's letter I felt a lot better. It is surprising how a letter from one so dear to you will put the stuff in you to do a job which otherwise seems impossible.

That evening while I was busy checking furs, Mrs. Carter came into the office. She looked like she had the mumps unilateral (on one side), but no luck. She didn't have the mumps. After an examination I found that she did have a bad abscessed molar. I didn't feel like pulling any teeth at the time after what I had been through the last 24 hours, so to stall her until morning I told her I could not give her any novocain (I didn't have any anyway). Because of the infection in her jaw a shot would spread the infection. I also told her that it would be better for the swelling to go down some before pulling the tooth. I advised her to go home and put hot packs on her jaw, that this would reduce the swelling and also relieve her of some of the pain. Of course, this sounded like professional advice and it was also smart thinking on my part to stall for time, which I needed.

The night before I had slept very little, with the timber wolves chasing me, and now, tonight, the wolves would have company in the form of an abscessed tooth and an unborn baby. In addition to a stack of mining-claim locations to record, I would have several thousand furs to check, everything from muskrats to timber wolves (how I hate to mention that last one). Surprisingly enough, the next morning the world looked a lot brighter. For some reason I had much more confidence in myself, physically. I felt like a million dollars. Being a young man as I was in those days, I could recoup overnight.

Bundy and I had just finished our sourdough hotcakes when I looked out the window and there across the ice of the Takotna River came Mr. and Mrs. Carter. With a chuckle, Bundy said, "This I want to see." I told him if he would sit this one out, I would give him a ringside seat for the baby episode (this sounded like horse play but it was a good thing to break the tension). I had a horrible feeling that perhaps by Mrs. Carter coming over early that the tooth had become worse, but to the contrary, she was a lot better. The swelling in her jaw had gone down considerably and she had had very little pain during the night. (I said to myself, "So far, so good, Dr. Marsh.) Hopeful that I would get a negative answer I asked Mrs. Carter if she still wished the tooth pulled. She replied, "I certainly do. I don't want to go through the pain I have suffered the last few days any more." Mrs. Green (Dr. Green's wife) was very cooperative. She got the dental instruments out and sterilized them, and said that she would assist me.

I have been in many tight spots in my life, but I have never had a situation that had me cornered like this one. Then all at once I got hold of myself. I thought, old boy, you have assisted in many major operations in the three years spent with army hospitals in the First World War, amputating arms and legs from men. Now a little tooth is not going to get you down. Then I began to act like a professional. I asked the little lady to get up in the dental chair (she was little, about 100, and cute). As Mrs. Green handed me the dental instruments, I worked like a real dentist. I removed the gum line from around the infected tooth and deadened the gums with warm salt water. The tooth came out very easy. Mr. and Mrs. Carter were grateful and I was much relieved. However, the next morning I was a little concerned when I saw Mr. Carter coming toward the commissioner's office taking long steps. I remarked to Bundy that perhaps Mrs. Carter had developed complications and that Carter was coming after me, but Carter walked through the doorway with a big smile and said,

"My wife is feeling fine this morning and had the best night's sleep she has had in a week." He asked me how much he owed me. I replied, nothing, but he laid a $20 goldpiece on my desk. Carter didn't know it but the big smile that he displayed when he came through the door was my pay.

When Carter left I said to Bundy (to build up my ego a little), "What do you think of Dr. Marsh now?" Bundy replied, "I will reserve my comments until after you deliver the Atwater baby." Bundy was a fine boy. His and my own philosophy of life were quite the same. We needled each other just enough to keep the long winter nights from getting boresome.

I went out on the large front porch of the wireless station, which was my office, and looked out across the big valley where the Takotna River ran into the Kuskokwin River. Beyond stood the tall, rugged snow-covered mountains at the head of Nixon Fork River. That was a beautiful picture of a wilderness and wonderland where men dared to tread. What a country, what a world to live in!

After a week back in the office at McGrath I had just about dug out from under the pile of recording mining claims and assessment work, also with checking and collecting the territorial tax on fur being shipped to fur houses in the States. I had found time to do some hunting; there was plenty of moose in the low country at this time of the year. I had brought in two since returning from Holy Cross, a little over the bag limit, but there was an unwritten law in Alaska at that time that a resident could take all the game necessary for his own use.

I had been using Pete McMullen's (United States Marshal) dog team for hunting and other trips over the country and had become very fond of them. Pete had told me that he was resigning and leaving for the States just before the break-up. He said that he had been in Alaska since '98 and that he was going out and live the rest of his life in a warmer climate. I told him that I wanted his dog team and he promised me first chance at them, but said that he had to get all he could for them as he did not intend to work any more once he returned outside.

## Take Office As U.S. Commissioner 97

While in McGrath, between trips over the country, a grizzly looking man walked into my office one morning. He had a heavy beard, looked dirty and mean, and this was a picture of what I would imagine Dangerous Dan McGrew looked like. He said, "My name is Sam Hart. I want to sign a criminal complaint against Lew Maddox and I want a warrant for his arrest." I was very much surprised as Lew Maddox was a prominent sled freight hauler between McGrath and Anchorage. I asked Hart why he wanted to file a complaint against Maddox, and he replied that Maddox had shot one of his lead dogs that was worth a thousand dollars. Here my thought was to keep the commissioner's office out of the mess. I told Hart to collect damages for the loss of his dog he would have to bring suit in a civil action in the district court in Fairbanks, but I didn't know Sam Hart. He looked up at me with steel gray eyes staring out of a heavy, dirty, gray-bearded face and said,

"You don't know me; I am an attorney. While I have not been in a courthouse for over 20 years, I know law." He said that he wanted a conviction in criminal court against Maddox for maliciously killing his dog. He would bring suit for damages in a civil suit. I remarked,

"You are going to make a torte case out of it." (A torte case is a civil action for damages growing out of a criminal case.) He looked up at me kind of funny and said,

"Commissioner, you do know something about law. I had almost forgotten about this type of case since it has been so long since I have had a law book in my hands."

I told Hart that I thought that Maddox was on his way to Anchorage and if he wanted to sign a complaint for a warrant he could do so. I would issue the warrant and leave word for Maddox to come in and accept service on it when he arrived back in McGrath and there would be no use for the marshal serving the warrant.

Before Maddox got back from Anchorage there was another legal matter I didn't know quite how to handle. I received a wireless message from Nenana that a man waiting trial for claim jumping and theft of gold in the McGrath district before I took office had been apprehended in Nenana after jumping bail at McGrath. This gave me a bright idea whereby I could save the government some money and also see my Mary at Nenana. I immediately wired Judge Clegg for permission to go to Nenana and hold court there, thus saving the government the expense of sending the U.S. Marshal after the prisoner. I received a wire back from Judge Clegg stating that he had sent me instructions by mail regarding the defendant Fred Ballieu and I should receive said instructions any day. Within a few days I did receive the instructions, but they were not to my desire. As much as I disliked them, I still have them to this day. They have turned yellow and are a bit torn, but I treasure this legal document as testimony of where I have been. Judge Clegg's orders read like this:

"IN THE UNITED STATES COMMISSIONER'S COURT, MT. McKINLEY PRECINCT, FOURTH DIVISION, TERRITORY OF ALASKA, UNITED STATES OF AMERICA, Plaintiff, Vs. FRED BALLIEU, Defendant. No. 30 Criminal. To the HONORABLE FLOYD R. MARSH, Justice of the above entitled court; comes G.B. ERWIN, United States Attorney for the Fourth Division, Territory of Alaska, and moves for an order dismissing the above entitled prosecution on the grounds and for the reason: That the defendant Fred Ballieu states he would enter a plea of guilty of the violation complaint at McGrath in Nenana Commissioner's court and stand trial. That it will entail gross expense upon the Government to return the defendant to McGrath and the end of Justice can be best attained by dismissal of above entitled prosecution."

Needless to say, this punctured my bubble of hope for seeing Mary. It had been several months now since I left Nenana and I was getting lonesome to see her. The United States Marshal had more definite plans for his departure from McGrath, which now was set for the middle of March, a little over a month away, and I had a lot to do. It was planned that I was to buy Pete's dog team, take him out to Nancy on the government railroad, which was about 60 miles north of Anchorage, and was to pick up the new

## Take Office As U.S. Commissioner

United States Marshal, Donald Olin, and bring him back to McGrath. However, I had a few personal plans I hoped to work in with the above mentioned ones as Mary and I had not been idle in our preparation for our new home in McGrath. We had planned that—after I took Pete McMullen out to the railroad, and before I picked up Marshal Olin—I was going to take the train from Nancy to Nenana, about 150 miles north, and pick up Mary. We were to get married in Nenana and I would bring her back to McGrath as my new bride.

I had located a nice little log cabin not far from the wireless station and this is where Mary would help me while away the long, Alaska winter nights. How I dreamed of the time when Mary would share this little log cabin with me. I was as busy as an old hen with a flock of young chickens, fixing up the cabin. I was really on cloud nine. To break up my thoughts a knock came at the door. I opened the door and asked Lew Maddox to come in. He replied, I hear you have a warrant for me. I replied that I did. I said, "Lew, I am sorry but it is my obligation and duty to serve this warrant on you." Lew was pretty big about it. He said. "Commissioner, I hold no ill feelings toward you. I know that you have a job to do. As for myself I can take care of my end."

As Lew Maddox walked out through the door into the howling wind and drifting snow of 40 below and disappeared down the trail, I wondered if there would be another shooting of Dangerous Dan McGrew tonight. However, there were no reports of a murder the next day, so it was my duty to set a date for the trial and try to get a panel from which to select a jury. I selected twenty registered voters in the district for a panel, selecting those that lived either in McGrath or nearby so that I would not cause anyone any inconvenience. The trial date was set ten days from the date the warrant was served. I was informed later by Judge Clegg that this was really fast justice; in fact, a little too fast to be legal, but I was "King on the Throne" out here in this wilderness; no one questioned my authority or criticized my action.

On the day of the trial the jury panel all showed up, and about twenty other people came to take in the trial. The task of selecting a jury was the first order of business, each man acting as his own counsel. Maddox, who was well liked in the district, did not excuse one juror. Sam Hart, who was a loner, had very few friends and didn't seem to care about making friends; he picked the jurors over to some extent and excused about half that came up. I was afraid that he was going to run out of jurors; however, I had authority to put a limit to his selection, but I did not want to exercise that authority. A jury of 12 was finally selected, 11 men and a woman, a schoolteacher by the name of Lilly Boyd.

Since both men were acting as their own counsel, Sam Hart had the advantage over Maddox as he was an attorney; however, I think that Maddox's reputation and good will in the district had the advantage over Hart's knowledge of law. Once the jury was selected, Hart presented his case. He claimed his dog broke loose, went over to Maddox's place (about five miles from his place) where Maddox shot it. Hart had a point in claiming that his dog broke loose, as it was unlawful at that time for a man to permit his dog to run at large. Maddox testified that Hart's dog came to his place about 2 a.m. on the morning of February 26 and jumped on one of his dogs that was tied up and would have killed his dog if he had not shot the Hart dog. Hart, being an attorney, put on a good case. It was very interesting the way he presented various aspects of the law and his courtroom technique. He pressed hard for a case of malicious killing of his dog by Maddox. There was no question about who shot Hart's dog, he stated, but the only reason he shot the dog was to protect his own property, the life of his dog.

# CHAPTER 11

## *The Jury Verdict*

The case dragged on through most of the day, after both sides had presented their cases. I explained to the jury the law in the Statutes of the Territory of Alaska and instructed the jury of the possible verdicts they could bring in. I told them that they could bring in one of the three following verdicts: No. 1, Destroying another man's property with malice intent; No. 2, Willfully destroying another man's property where malice intent is not shown; No. 3, In protecting one's own property he may destroy or injure other property. I instructed the jury that Nos. 1 and 2 verdicts would be in favor of the plaintiff, Mr. Hart; and No. 3 verdict would be in favor of the defendant, Mr. Maddox. As the case came to a close, it was evident the jury favored Maddox and I think Hart sensed this.

After my instruction to the jury they retired to an upstairs room in the wireless station to decide their verdict. As the days were short this time of the year it was very dark by now, but everyone stayed around to hear the verdict and see the fireworks as some thought that there surely would be if the verdict went against Hart. Others said that Maddox could take care of himself. I was surprised the jury was staying out so long. I expected a speedy verdict for Maddox. A whispering story got out that the jury would be afraid to return a verdict against Hart. About 7 p.m. I went up into the jury room. I asked the jury if they wished to go home and continue the case the next day, or if they wished to go to dinner at a nearby roadhouse and continue the case. They said that they wished to do neither, that they would continue to meditate. The jury seemed worried and not too happy with the verdict they evidently were going to be obligated to return.

Pete McMullen, the U.S. Marshal, had been in court all day but had gone to his cabin when the jury retired to meditate. I sent for Pete and told him that I wanted him to be in court when the jury returned with the verdict. I returned to my makeshift courtroom where everyone was tense. Pete McMullen had come in. I asked him to come up in the front part of the courtroom and have a seat near me facing the crowd. In a short time a knock came on the door. I went to the door and there stood the foreman of the jury, a big, rough-looking Swede. He said to me in broken English,

"We got verdict."

A moment of silence followed the big Swede's announcement of "We got verdict." You could hear a pin drop on the floor.

I asked the jury to come in and take their seats. As the jury filed in they never looked to either side. As they took their seats their eyes were fixed on the front of the courtroom. I knew what their verdict was then, and I think that Hart did, too, as he had his eyes fixed on the floor. I asked the foreman of the jury if they had reached a verdict. He replied that they had. I asked him to stand up and read the verdict. The big Swede got up and started to read the verdict, but his limited English had him stuck. I saw he was messing up things pretty bad, so I asked Mrs. Boyd, the school teacher, to read the verdict which went like this: "We the jury find that Lew Maddox, the defendant, killed the dog of Sam Hart, the plaintiff, on February 26th at which time the dog in question was illegally running at large and was also in the act of destroying property of the defendant. We therefore find for the defendant Lew Maddox."

When Mrs. Boyd finished reading the verdict you could have heard a pin drop on the floor; no one moved. Hart still had his eyes fixed on the floor. I glanced over at the U.S. Marshal and he had his eyes fixed on Hart. I broke the tense silence by asking Hart if he wished the jury polled. At the same time I looked at the jury; they all appeared nervous. I could sense their concern at having the jury polled, as it would be known how each juror voted. Hart put everyone at ease, especially the jury, when he

## The Jury Verdict

stated that he did not request the jury polled, and you can bet that this was a relief to the Commissioner also.

I thanked the jury and witnesses and with a rap of the gavel the court adjourned. Everyone began to leave with the exception of Sam Hart. He sat in his chair still looking at the floor until everyone left the courtroom, then came up to the commissioner's desk and politely asked what the court cost was. I remarked that it was late and suggested that he came back in the morning and I would figure out the cost, but Hart said, "No, I want to take care of it tonight." He said it in such a way that I did not want to argue with him. I figured out the court cost and he reached in his hip pocket and pulled out a leather poke and poured out a number of gold-pieces on the desk, picking out the right amount for court costs, then putting the balance back in his poke. He stalked out the door in the cold, dark night. This was the last time I ever saw Sam Hart. He left the area and no one from McGrath ever saw or heard of Sam Hart again.

The next day, Pete (the U.S. Marshal) and I got together to plan our trip out to the railroad. Pete was retiring and leaving for the states, and I was to bring back the new U.S. Marshal. Pete mentioned that it was now the first part of March and the trail might be getting so soft we would have to do our traveling at night. I told Pete that I was ready any time, but that there was one thing that had to happen before I left. Pete asked what that was. I told him that Mrs. Atwater would have to have her baby. Pete remarked that there were midwives in McGrath that would take care of her, but I told him that I was supposed to be the doctor in the district and I wanted to be there in case of an emergency. We decided to meet again the next day to decide what to do. I remarked to Pete that I would pray that Mrs. Atwater would have her baby that night. Between the recent court case and Mrs. Atwater's baby, I didn't sleep much that night.

In addition to taking Pete out to the railroad and bringing back the new U.S. Marshal, I would be returning with Mary. With all this in mind, I arose early the next morning. It was a beautiful day; the sun was out bright, dancing on the several feet of snow on the ground. I decided to take a walk out through the little village of McGrath and dropped by the N.C. Store. To my great surprise I saw Mrs. Atwater shopping there. It was evident that she had given birth to her baby. I asked one of the clerks when Mrs. Atwater had her baby, and he replied, "A couple of days ago." I asked him who attended her in the birth; he said, "No one." He said that these squaws (Mrs. Atwater was a half-blood) go off by themselves and have their babies like a cow does a calf. This was something else I learned about the country, and this I liked.

I immediately looked up Pete and told him that I was ready to hit the trail any time. It was decided that we would leave McGrath the next day, and we were to contact the railroad at a small station known as Nancy about 60 miles north of Anchorage. Pete was to take the train to Anchorage and meet the U.S. Marshal, Donald Olin, at the old Cook Hotel and inform him to remain there until I notified him to meet me at Nancy for the trip back to McGrath. I was to take the train to Nenana about 200 miles north of Nancy to meet Mary and bring her back to McGrath as my wife. As scheduled, the next day we loaded up for the trip. The entire village was out to give Pete a warm and heartfelt farewell. Pete had been at McGrath a long time and everyone loved him. Women and children were crying and old sourdoughs were blinking their eyes to hold back the tears, and as we slid down the glittering white trail away from McGrath, I could see a tear in Pete's eye too.

I had purchased Pete's dog team. I was very proud of this fine team. They were something on the order of the first dog team I owned in the Kantishna country. That is, all but old "Jake," and there was no dog that could ever take the place of old "Jake" in my admiration. As a lead dog I have never seen his equal. This first day on the trail was ideal for traveling. The weather was not cold and the sun came out bright and shining, which made fast travel. There were seven roadhouses between McGrath and the railroad. We figured if we were lucky enough

## The Jury Verdict

not to hit any storms, we could make it into the last roadhouse in three days and arrive at the railroad on the fourth day.

As we were late getting out of McGrath this first day, we arrived at the Big River roadhouse (the first) about noon. Larry Cross, one of the owners, a boy about my age, and a fine fellow that I had become well acquainted with, was at the roadhouse. I told Larry that I was going out to get Mary, and I could see tears come to his eyes. I knew, and Larry realized, that life was passing him by. Larry was of the age that he needed the love and companionship of a woman instead of a partnership with another man. After a short visit and a lunch of moose meat, we headed down the trail to the next roadhouse 30 miles away, where we intended to spend the night. As the sun was soon down and the icy Alaska mountains closed in on us, we had a slow trail the latter part of this first day. However, this was pleasant traveling compared to three months before when I had hiked over this trail into McGrath. This time I was riding. Pete and I would take turns riding the runners and guiding the sled while the other one rode in the sled.

We arrived late at our first night's stop. This roadhouse was known as the East Fork's roadhouse, run by an old-timer who knew Pete well. After he and Pete had a long farewell visit, we hit the hay. With the excitement of leaving McGrath and the first day on the trail we were tired. Pete suggested that we sleep in a little late the next day to rest up a bit and also to let the sun get up and slick up the trail to make a faster trail. After a late arising and a hearty breakfast of sourdough hotcakes we hit the trail. It was a beautiful day; the sun was out and we had a fast trail. As we intended to make only two roadhouses this day, I asked Pete if he thought it possible that we make the third roadhouse, as it was at this roadhouse that I met old Joe on my trip into McGrath. Pete said that it was all right with him. As the dogs wanted to travel, we let them go, and for a while we made good time. We stopped for lunch at the first roadhouse about midday. Here we were informed that old Joe had become very sick a week earlier and had been taken to a hospital in Anchorage.

Soon after we left this roadhouse we hit some steep grades. We were getting higher up into the mountains. It was cold and the trail was slow, so we abandoned the idea of making three roadhouses this day. It was a good thing that we did as we were very late getting to this second roadhouse, which was run by two old sourdough miners turned trappers. They knew the country and trail very well, so that night we planned the remainder of our trip. The trappers suggested that we try to make three roadhouses the next day, as we had a good, even trail to Joe's roadhouse. Then, six miles from Joe's roadhouse, we would hit the summit, then downgrade and a good trail to the next two roadhouses.

Now, at this third roadhouse, we would be only one roadhouse away from the railroad and be getting an early start this last day we could make it into the little station at Nancy in time for Pete to catch the 3 p.m. train to Anchorage. This schedule suited us fine. We would cut a day off the time we planned on Pete getting into Anchorage. The next morning we hit the trail real early. We were at old Joe's roadhouse a little after daylight. We had only a cup of coffee at Joe's and shot the breeze a few minutes with the old-timer who was looking after the place.

Leaving Joe's place, we were very fortunate that there was no storm over the pass (at the summit). This was very unusual and we appreciated the weatherman giving us this break. Once over the summit we really made time. At one place we were going so fast around a curve that I dumped Pete in the snow. The dogs got into a fight and we had quite a time. We got the dogs straightened out, had a good laugh, and were on our way. There was a good trail now and we arrived at the second roadhouse in the early afternoon, had a little lunch here, a short visit, and took off for our last roadhouse, or the first roadhouse 30 miles away from Nancy. An elderly couple ran this roadhouse, with whom I had had a nice visit on my way into Mc-

Grath three months previously. This couple was very glad to see me and wanted to know everything that had happened since I went through on my way to McGrath. I have often thought of this elderly couple and treasure them among the wonderful people I met and made friends with in Alaska.

The train which I would take to Nenana came through Nancy from Anchorage at 9 a.m. and the train that Pete was to take to Anchorage came through from Fairbanks at 3 p.m. We knew that we could not make it early enough into Nancy for me to make the 9 a.m. train to Nenana, so we decided to take it easy and get to Nancy in time for Pete to get the 3 p.m. to Anchorage. We had a late breakfast and a nice long visit with the old couple at the roadhouse the next morning, then headed down the trail for our last 30 miles. We arrived at Nancy shortly after midday. Instead of staying overnight at Nancy I decided to go into Anchorage with Pete so I could meet the new U.S. Marshal and visit a while longer with Pete. The 3 p.m. (combination) train from Fairbanks was on time, consisting of one passenger coach, three box cars, and two work cars. I had arranged to have my dogs taken care of until I got back from Nenana, so the next day I would stay on the train and go to Nenana. In about an hour and a half Pete and I were in Anchorage.

We went to the old Cook Hotel where we met Donald Olin, the new U.S. Marshal. Donald seemed to be a fine fellow, much younger than I expected to see. He told he something that made me very happy. He said he was just married and intended to send for his wife as soon as he got settled. How pleased this would make Mary. Besides, Donald seemed like a fellow whom I would like to work with. Pete was going to be in Anchorage for a few days. He and Olin were down at the train the next morning to see me off for Nenana. I told Olin that I would notify him when Mary and I left Nenana so he could meet us at Nancy for the trip to McGrath. I hated to tell Pete "goodbye." Postponing it for one more day didn't help a bit. I have never met a man I like better. About the only thing I could say to Pete when I left him was, "God bless you." Pete, no doubt, is not around any more. If he is, he would be over 100 years old.

We soon passed through the little station of Nancy on the way to Nenana. As we went through the passes and around the curves of the mountains of the Alaska range, I fell asleep with one thought on my mind and that was—Mary.

I woke up when the train stopped at a little station on the north slope of Broad Pass. This was a very busy little place, more so than any of the stations I had noticed along the government railroad. I was very much surprised when a bearded, rugged fellow came up behind me and slapped me on the back. I turned around and Harry Owens stuck his hand out and said, "Kid, I am glad to see you." Harry was the trapper I met several months previously in the little ghost town of Diamond City in the Kantishna district. Harry said to me, "Kid, you have really been making history over there at McGrath. We read all about your activity, about the U.S. Marshal Pete McMullen and you making the trip to Holy Cross on the lower Yukon where you got tangled up with the timber wolves." I, of course, was glad to see Harry and get the news from the Kantishna district.

I asked Harry what he was doing in these parts. He told me that he had pulled his trapline at Diamond City and was here in the Broad Pass district to do some prospecting after the break-up this summer. He said that the Oklahoma" I discovered and sold in the Kantishna was operating, that they had struck a new body of ore and it looked like a winner. After some inquiry I found out what made this place buzz with activity. This was the jumping-off place from the government railroad to the Kantishna and Mt. McKinley National Park. Soon a road would start in from here to these areas.

The conductor came into the mess hall and announced, "All aboard, north to Nenana and Fairbanks." Soon I was once again on the single coach special winding through the snow-covered mountains of Alaska. What a beautiful sight Alaska is in the spring of the year when the snow and ice covers the mountain peaks, rivers, and valleys, which resembled glittering

## The Jury Verdict

jewelry show-windows from the reflection of the sun or the northern lights. We soon passed through Healy, a place I will always remember. On my way north 2-1/2 years earlier, I helped out here in a very severe flu epidemic in which many old sourdoughs and native children died because of the limited medical supplies and help. I will always treasure the thought that I helped ease the pain and saved many lives during this terrible epidemic.

Nenana was only a short way from Healy. We arrived there in the mid-afternoon. Nenana looked about the same—no change in the few months since I had left, but those few months seemed like so many years, as I was away from Mary. Needless to say, as soon as the train arrived at the little depot in Nenana, I made a beeline for the Kirkenoff residence to see her. Mrs. Kirkenoff came to the door and before she spoke I knew that something had happened. My first words to her were, "What has happened?" She told me that Mary was in the hospital very sick with the flu. I went immediately to the hospital, a small hospital built and operated by the government after the flu epidemic several years previously.

At the hospital I was informed that Mary was very sick, with a temperature of over one hundred degrees, and I was also advised that only the immediate family was permitted to see her. When I told the head nurse who I was, she changed her attitude. She seemed to know almost as much about Mary and me as I did. The nurse then gave me permission to see Mary, but asked me to talk very little and limit my visit. I hardly knew Mary, she was so pale and very thin. I will never forget how she cried; in fact, we both had a little cry as we realized that our immediate plans had gone astray. I told Mary that I would stay in Nenana until she got better, then go back to McGrath and we would make further plans.

In a few days Mary made a wonderful recovery. I recall that her doctor told me that I had done more for Mary in the last few days than he had done in the last two weeks. Seeing that she was doing so well, I decided to go to Fairbanks to see Judge

Clegg, which turned out to be a very constructive visit, as I brought him up-to-date on what was going on in the Mt. McKinley precinct. In the few days I was in Fairbanks we went over a great deal of territory law, which would put me in a better position for my next court case. When I returned to Nenana, Mary had recovered so much that they had taken her home, but her doctor advised against her going to McGrath for some time. Mary and I both realized that the trip over the trail to McGrath for her at this time was impossible.

I contacted Donald Olin, the new U.S. Marshal, at the Cook Hotel in Anchorage and was advised that the trails on the south slope of the Alaska range were getting soft during the daytime, so we decided to hit the trail for McGrath as soon as possible. We decided to meet at Nancy the next day, and upon my arrival there, which would be about 3 p.m., we would take off over the trail the same night so that we would have night traveling all the way to McGrath. I left Mary that evening, not telling her that I would leave Nenana the next morning for the trip back to McGrath. I wanted her to have a good night's sleep that night, as I knew that I would not—and I did not.

I awakened early the next morning and had several hours before the train would be through Nenana from Fairbanks to Anchorage. I had an early breakfast at a small restaurant, then went to see Mary and broke the news to her that I was leaving for McGrath. I found her in a very cheerful mood. After visiting with her a while I said, "Mary, I am leaving for McGrath today," and before I got her reaction I went on to mention the plans that I had formalized. I told her that she could take the train to Anchorage in June, then a boat to Bethel that made a weekly trip from Anchorage to Kodiak and Bethel. I said that I would let her know when the sternwheeler *Tanana* from McGrath would be in Bethel and that I would meet her there and we would be married. The wedding would be unique in that I would have to issue our marriage license, since this was my district and no one else would have the authority. We could get a local minister or a ship captain to marry us. This seemed to

## The Jury Verdict

please Mary very much. Her eyes sparkled and that radiant smile came to her face that had been in my memory since the first day I met her. She seemed in high spirits when I left. I will always remember the last words she said to me, "Floyd, darling, if anything would happen to you, nothing in this world would be worth living for, so do be careful on the trail, please, just for me, and I will see you in June."

After saying goodbye to Mary and the Kirkenoff family, I headed for the little depot in Nenana to catch the train for Nancy. Once again I left Nenana with a heavy heart and more so on this occasion, since this was the trip I planned to have Mary with me. I slept most of the way to Nancy as I had slept very little the previous night. I did not get off the train at the lunch stop where I had met my good friend, Harry Owens, on my way north a week ago. The combination passenger freight and work train arrived at Nancy on time, about 3 p.m. The new U.S. Marshal, Donald Olin, was waiting for me. Donald told me that everyone coming in or going out over the trail was traveling at night, as the trail was too soft to travel over during the day. We kept testing the trail for traveling condition and it was after 10 p.m. before the trail froze enough to hold up the dogs and sled. The dogs had been tied up over two weeks and they were ready to travel. I put Donald in the sled and I took the runners on starting out. This was Donald's first dog-sled ride, and he got a big thrill out of it. When it came his turn to handle the dogs, he did a very good job of it. I thought to myself how fortunate I was to get a fine fellow like Donald to work with.

Since the first part of the trail was upgrade into the mountains, we didn't make very good time, reaching the first roadhouse in the early morning about 4 a.m. We didn't take time for breakfast, just loaded up with coffee and took off for the next roadhouse, which we hoped to make before the trail got soft. We arrived at the second roadhouse just as the trail was getting soft; the dogs and sled went through the snowcrust at times. Here we had a big breakfast, and after a little visit with the proprietor, we retired, asking him to call us about 6 p.m. so we could get on the trail early. This being high in the mountains, the trail should be frozen over earlier at night. I awoke early; I think about 4 p.m. It seemed cold so I got dressed, went out on the trail, and found it freezing over very fast, so I called Donald.

We had a big breakfast of wild sheep meat and got started on the trail for what we hoped would be at least three roadhouses. We did make the three roadhouses that night stopping only at the roadhouses on the way for coffee, sometimes a bite to eat, and to let the dogs rest. When we reached the third roadhouse, we had traveled almost a hundred miles that night, a long distance even for the fine dog team we had. We were fortunate in having a good, fast trail. At this point we were a little over half way to McGrath. We were now in the "interior." The trail would be frozen longest at night and we had a downgrade trail most of the way into McGrath.

At this third roadhouse we decided to sleep only a few hours and try to get on the trail by 6 or 7 p.m. so that we could make the Big River roadhouse only 22 miles from McGrath. We did make the Big River roadhouse that night, but got in late as the trail was getting soft. I was looking forward to a nice, long visit with my good friend, Larry Cross, one of the proprietors, but I was saddened very much when informed by Larry's partner that he was in McGrath with all the toes on his left foot frozen. I called McGrath and was told that Larry was in a lot of pain. Anchorage had been called, but doctors there advised against trying to get him out over the uncertain trail.

I learned from Larry's partner what had happened. Larry had been caught out on the trail with shoepacks and the weather turned very cold. (Moccasins are a must on a frozen trail.) Larry's partner told me that he had been in McGrath for three days and they feared gangrene had set in and that his toes would have to be amputated. They were in hopes that Dr. Green or myself would show up. Dr. Green had not come over the trail, so this left me on the hook.

## The Jury Verdict

I called McGrath and was informed that Dr. Green had left Anchorage three days previously and should not be very far behind us. I talked to Mrs. Boyd, the schoolteacher, who was taking care of Larry. She told me that Larry was running a high fever and that something had to be done very soon. I told her that I would be in McGrath as soon as the trail froze over enough to travel. I lay down that day to get a little sleep while waiting for the trail to freeze over, but slept very little, thinking of the decision I soon would have to make upon which perhaps would depend a man's life. Between naps during that day I would ask myself if I could amputate a man's foot. Before I ended my broken sleep that day I decided that I would try, if it meant life or death for Larry.

I was up and around long before the trail was frozen over enough to travel that evening. I again called Mrs. Boyd at McGrath and she told me that Larry was still in severe pain, that his entire foot had become very swollen and that she feared that it had become infected. I told Mrs. Boyd to keep hot packs on Larry's foot and that I should be in McGrath about midnight. Olin and I got on the trail about 7 p.m. and arrived in McGrath just before midnight. I went immediately to see Larry, who was in an old rooming house near the Northern Commercial Store. Mrs. Boyd met me at the rooming house and told me that Larry was asleep for the first time in two days. She said that the hot packs had worked wonderfully. I told Mrs. Boyd that I was going to my office in the wireless station, and that if Larry woke up in excess pain to have one of the Indian girls attending him call me. I asked Mrs. Boyd to come to the wireless station about 8 a.m. with all the information she had of Dr. Green's arrival and departure at Anchorage. This information, with what Mrs. Green had, might enable us to locate about where Dr. Green would be. But before Mrs. Boyd arrived at my office the next morning, one of the Indian girls attending Larry came to my office and told me that Larry wanted to see me.

I immediately went to see Larry. He seemed much worse than I had expected to find him. He looked at me pitifully and said,

"Floyd, you are going to help me, aren't you?" I said, "Larry, I will do anything in the world that I can for you." He then said very much to my surprise, "Will you take my toes off? They are killing me." I thought, what faith this man has in me, and this faith seemed to give me the courage that I needed. I said, "Larry, we are trying to locate Dr. Green, and if we cannot I will operate on your foot." This seemed to please Larry very much. He told me that the hot packs had relieved much of the pain and given him some rest and sleep. I decided to have him immerse his entire foot in warm water, which would further relieve the pain.

I then went back over to my office, and with Mrs. Boyd and Mrs. Green—together with the information they had—attempted to locate Dr. Green. We wired the Cook Hotel in Anchorage and received the information these women already had. Dr. Green had left the hotel three days previously for McGrath, one day later than Olin and I had left Nancy. We also wired the station agent at Nancy, who informed us that Dr. Green had left Nancy one day after Olin and I had left. We received some additional information from the agent at Nancy that Dr. Green was in the company of a trapper friend of his, and the dog team they had was not the type of dog team Olin and I had. It was the opinion of the agent that they would be more than a day behind us, in addition to accidents and other time-consuming things that could happen on the trail.

Later in the day I went to see Larry again and told him what we had heard from our trace on Dr. Green. It was not very encouraging. Larry wanted me to operate that day, but I told him that it would be better to have his entire foot soaked in warm water for 24 hours before operating. I found out later that this was a good idea, but at the time I was stalling, hoping that Dr. Green would show up. I told Larry that if Dr. Green did not get in that night I would operate the next morning.

## The Jury Verdict

I retired that night with a prayer and a hope on my mind that Dr. Green would get in before the next morning and also a prayer for myself.

Soon after retiring at the end of the first day back in McGrath —which had been one of extreme anxiety for me—I was awakened by one of the Indian nurses attending Larry. She told me Dr. Green had sent an Indian runner in from the second roadhouse from McGrath with a message that he had heard about Larry Cross and was coming in early the next morning. Needless to say, I had a good sleep that night, which was the first sleep I had in two nights.

The next morning I was up early and went to the combination roadhouse and rooming house where Larry was. He had heard the good news about Dr. Green; in fact, he had later news than I had. Dr. Green had called the McGrath roadhouse from the Big River roadhouse 22 miles away and said he expected to be in McGrath about 8 or 9 o'clock in the morning. Larry seemed to be quite relieved that he could be operated on soon. He also had less pain and his temperature was down because of the all-night soaking of his foot in warm water. About this time the new U.S. Marshal, Donald Olin, came over to the roadhouse to tell me that a miner by the name of Ronald Olson from Iditarod was at my office and was cut up pretty badly. He had been in a fight with an Indiam-Eskimo by the name of Roven Tunda a few days previously, and his wounds were in bad shape. I went to my office immediately and found this to be true. He had a deep cut the full left side of his face, extending from the hairline to the lower jaw, and his left hand and left forearm were cut quite badly. I dressed his wounds and advised him to stay in McGrath a few days to see if any further infection developed. I was sure he had some infection at this time.

Olson told me that Tunda lived on the lower Kuskokwin River near Bethel and was a wood cutter for some of the steamers on the river. I contacted Captain Wm. Green who operated the two stern-wheelers on the Kuskokwin, the *Tanana*, and the

*Quick Step.* Captain Green told me that Tunda had worked for him cutting wood every winter; that at this time he owed Tunda some money and he was sure he could have Tunda come in and accept service on a warrant that Olson had sworn out for him. I also sent word to Bethel and Iditarod asking Tunda to come to McGrath, which would save himself and also the government money. This pleased the new marshal as he didn't care about a 200-mile trip on the trail at this time of the year. Traveling could be done only at night and it was somewhat uncertain at that.

About 9 o'clock I returned to the roadhouse expecting to find Dr. Green there. But, instead, I found about everyone in McGrath and vicinity waiting for the big event. By this time the trail had begun to get a little soft and some concern was felt about the doctor. Soon one of the strongest teams of Alaskan Huskies in McGrath started down the trail to meet Dr. Green. They had gone about half way to the Big River roadhouse when they met the doctor and his traveling companion, a local trapper. Their dog team was just about played out and it was doubtful if they could have made it to McGrath. Dr. Green said that soon after leaving Nancy he had heard about Larry from a fur buyer on his way out to Anchorage, but he could not make any better time because of the heavy load and a soft trail most of the way.

When Dr. Green looked at Larry's foot he clinched his jaws. I could see he was very much concerned—which he tried to hide from Larry and the others. I had worked with doctors enough that I knew from the doctor's concern that we had a problem on our hands. Dr. Green said to me, "Let us get at this right away." We had started across the ice on the frozen Takotna River to his office to sterilize the surgical implements for the operation when the doctor stopped and said, "We will have to tell Mrs. Boyd to prepare Larry for a major operation." This meant his stomach would have to be completely empty and particular so as I asked the doctor if we could use ether for the anesthetic. I also asked him if only the toes would have to be re-

## The Jury Verdict

moved. He replied that this would have been the only thing necessary a few days ago, but now we would have to go back much farther.

We soon had the necessary implements sterilized and with Mrs. Green we returned to the roadhouse to operate. The doctor's wife was to assist him in clamping and tying blood vessels, while I was to give the anesthetic. When we returned to the roadhouse we really had an audience. Larry suggested that no one watch the operation. Dr. Green concurred with Larry on this and his request was carried out. We got started with the operation about midday, which gave us some natural light. This, with the best lights we could get in McGrath, was still poor lighting for a major operation. The operating table consisted of some boards placed on sawhorses. On the boards was placed a heavy quilt and a sterile bed sheet. While this seemed to be a crude set-up for a major operation, it was not too bad as boards have no spring, or give, to them and in some respects resembled a regular operating table.

Now that we had the operating table set up, there was no chair high enough to sit on while administering the anesthetic. While we were trying to locate a suitable chair, someone brought in a nail ket, which was just the thing. Everything seemed so crude I shuddered at the thought of a major operation under these conditions. Larry saw I was somewhat concerned and asked me if everything was all right. I assured him that it was. As I started the anesthetic with chloroform, Larry said to me, "I thought you were going to give me ether." I told him I was, but it would be easier to start out with cholorform. Dr. Green and I had planned to use ether for the main anesthetic as it is a heart stimulant while chloroform is a derivative. We chose ether because we both anticipated a lengthy operation. It finally got under way and I felt a relief from the last two days of anxiety. I used a homemade mask to administer the anesthetic, which permitted some air to filter through and so took some time to get Larry under its influence.

I switched over from chloroform to ether as soon as Larry was under, and informed Dr. Green that he could start operating. I was very much surprised and somewhat depressed when I saw the doctor start the amputation. I was thinking only the toes had to come off, but the doctor began in the center of the instep, and there was so much blood from the start I wondered if the doctor was going back too far on the foot. He seemed very slow and not too sure of himself. After the operation had been in progress for almost an hour, he had cut only about half way through the foot and I could see that Larry was losing a lot of blood.

By keeping a finger on the artery under the jaw I could feel that the blood pressure was going down, and by watching the operation I could see that clamps were not being put on blood vessels. The large ones were not being tied as both the doctor and his wife were elderly people. It was evident that they could not see properly, especially with the kind of light that we had. It was also obvious that I had to do something and do it fast, so I asked Mrs. Green to administer the anesthetic and I would assist the doctor. This worked out fine. I soon got clamps on the small blood vessels and tied the larger ones. Blood was soon cleared from the cut and the doctor could see to work. The doctor remarked, "Boy, you have worked at this before." The foot was soon removed at the instep, and as he had gone back far enough on the foot, there was plenty of skin to cover the amputated part of the foot. I was surprised at the neat job the doctor had done. He had been out of surgery for over twenty years, but he still had the skill of a fine surgeon.

There was no bleeding from the wound, which meant we had the large vessels well tied. Now I began to worry about infection setting in and mentioned this to Dr. Green. He replied, "Thank the Lord that the man is alive and has his infected foot off. We will just have to pray for the best." On this I agreed. Larry slept for perhaps a half hour after the operation, which is unusual for ether. Mrs. Green became concerned that he did not respond soon after the operation. I felt his pulse, which was strong, thanks to the ether, and told Mrs. Green that Larry was all right and that it was good for him to sleep as long as he could. The longer he slept the less pain he would have to endure.

There were several hundred miners, prospectors, trappers, and just about everyone else in McGrath waiting outside the roadhouse when the operation was over. Dr. Green asked me to talk to the crowd and tell them about the operation, which I did. I told them that Dr. Green had performed a wonderful operation, that it was too early to know all the results, but that I was sure it was going to be successful. There was one thing I was certain of, though, and that was that Dr. Green had saved Larry's life. After this little spell I went in to see Larry. He responded to my questions and said he felt very sick from the ether, which we expected, but he had no feeling of pain in his foot. This was the first relief he had had since his foot was frozen.

I returned that evening to my office in the wireless station, very tired, to meet two problems. One was the big Swede that had been cut up in the fight. I sent him over to Dr. Green, but the other problem I could not send over to Dr. Green. That was a big stack of recordings of mining claims and assessment work; also a large bunch of fur had to be checked for territorial tax, and given clearance. This was in addition to some official reports that were past due at the Territorial Capitol at Juneau. A lot of this stuff can accumulate in 30 days, even when the mail is brought in by dog sled. But, I was not going to dig into it that night. I hit the hay early and again that night I offered a little prayer, thanking the good Lord for the operation going as well as it did, and I also put in a good word to the Great Maker for Larry.

The bright sun beamed down on the rugged mountains and valleys that made Alaska a fairyland at this time of year. The days had begun to get warmer. A pool had been made up for the guessing on the date of the break-up on the river. This was one of the biggest events of the year. However, to me a big event had just occurred and that was the last mail sled had arrived in McGrath and what I was looking for was in it, a letter from Mary. She said that she was much better than when I left Nenana, but she was lonely and anxious to come to McGrath. She said she could get passage on a Coast line boat from Anchorage to Bethel, arriving in Bethel on June 5 or June 20, and wanted to know which date would be best to meet a river boat from Bethel to McGrath.

I immediately contacted Captain Greene, who operated the stern-wheeler *Tanana*, on the Kuskokwim and was told he expected to leave McGrath for Bethel about June 1. This should put him in Bethel about June 5 or a few days after, depending on the supply of wood (for making steam) the Eskimo-Indians had cut and piled up along the banks of the Kuskokwim for him. I immediately sent Mary a wire that the June 4 arrival in Bethel would be ideal for connection with the river boat to McGrath. I also told her that I would meet her in Bethel and we would be married by my good friends Captain Greene and spend our honeymoon on the sternwheel river boat, *Tanana*, back to McGrath.

What a wonderful feeling to think that soon I would have someone to share with me the lonely life in Alaska! I liked the people and the way they lived up here and admired their outlook on life. I was fast building up a security for the rest of my own life, but the loneliness was almost unbearable, especially for a young man of 23 years. This age was much in need of the love and companionship of a woman instead of the constant association with rugged miners and trappers. My heart would beat just a little faster when I thought that soon I would have the most adorable and lovable girl I ever had known. To dispense the loneliness, together we would build our security for the future and some day would return to the States to live and forever enjoy our happiness together.

I visited Larry Cross often. He was coming along very well. A couple of weeks after the operation he was hobbling around on crutches and had returned to his roadhouse on the Big River and very bravely accepted his life as one of the many clubfoots that

## The Jury Verdict 121

inhabited Alaska. Many had met the same misfortune he had. I soon had caught up with all my work at the office and all the current reports had been made to the Territorial Capital at Juneau. The fur trappers were coming in with their last catches, so fur checking for the season was about over for the winter. I spent a lot of time fixing up the little log cabin I had purchased for Mary and myself. It had become the show-place of McGrath. The women in this little town had brought me many useful and ideal things to set up housekeeping.

Only a very few nights were cold enough to freeze the trail, but when we did get one of these nights, the U.S. Marshal and I would take all-night trips with my dog team as they would soon be laid up until fall or early next winter. The Marshall and I often visited the Atkin gold dredge about ten miles from McGrath, where a crew was in preparation to start gold dredging as soon as the break-up came. We also visited all the diggings in our district near McGrath, as once the break-up came the only way to get to these places would be on foot. There were a lot of people in McGrath now. They all came in over the trail ahead of the break-up.

CHAPTER 12

## *The Mines Open*

This was my first spring in McGrath and I could hardly imagine why so many people were in McGrath. Where had they come from and where were they going? I soon found out—they came from out on the coast and some from the States, where they had spent the winter. They all came to McGrath for one purpose, "GOLD," and the many people had many ways of getting the gold. Some came to work on the gold dredges and placer mines, some to dig gold for themselves, and many others who came for gold did not intend to work or dig for it. Some had marked cards and loaded dice. Many beautiful women came to McGrath. Some came to dance for the gold; others intended to get their gold, but not to dance for it. They had an easier way down in the tenderloin district.

All this meant more work for the U.S. Marshal and me. However, we did not intend to stop something that had been going on since McGrath was discovered. The gamblers and girls were visited by the U.S. Marshal from time to time, and told to appear at the U.S. Commissioner's office. They were to pay a fine in lieu of a tax and license; and, of course, when anyone got out of line, a legitimate arrest would be made and the subject brought before the U.S. Commissioner for trial. This happened quite often during the restless period when a number of miners were waiting in McGrath for the break-up so they could get out to the mine fields. Every day was like a carnival, with one thought and wish in everyone's mind, and that was for the big event, the break-up, which we all were waiting for daily.

The first part of May finally arrived. The break-up had occurred, and what a sight! Blocks of ice as large as a house were coming down the Kuskokwim River and the Takotna River, and

## The Mines Open

as these rivers came together at McGrath it was a spectacular scene never to be forgotten. You saw large chunks of ice coming together and piling up 30 and 40 feet high with a roar that could be heard for ten miles. The blocks of ice piled up at the forks of these two rivers causing a flood that covered most of McGrath, especially the south part of the town which was the part where the U.S. Commissioner's office and U.S. Marshal's office were located. They were in the Wireless Station building, one of the few buildings on the south side located on high ground that did not flood.

The U.S. Marshal, Donald Olin, and I got out early the next morning after the ice jam to see that everyone got out of their cabins and to high ground. We had a rowboat and went from cabin to cabin picking up everyone who had not got out and helping them move what personal belongings we could. I recall a funny instance during this time of anxiety. We had noticed there was no activity or sign of life about the cabin of an old-timer whom everyone called "Lazy Luke." The water was about two feet deep around his cabin. We rowed up to one of his windows and could see Luke in bed. We asked him why he didn't get out and he answered he was going to get wet anyway so he decided to stay in bed a little longer. We left, but kept an eye on his cabin. The water continued to rise and in a short while we saw Luke coming out of his cabin in water waist deep. We rowed over to where he was, but we did not have to plead with him to leave his abode this time. We asked him why he finally decided to leave his cabin, and he said that he was about half asleep when he noticed something floating by his bed. After taking a good look at it, he found out that it was his coffee pot. It had floated off the stove and over to his bed. He said that he thought this was some kind of an omen that he should leave his cabin.

The Takotna River splits the town in two, with about two-thirds of the town on the north side and one-third on the south side. There was no crossing the river because of the large ice floes, so each part of the town had to shift for itself. On the south side of the Takotna River there were only a few cabins, in addition to the wireless station, that were on high ground and out of the reach of the flooding, so the few cabins and the wireless station building had to shelter about 40 people. There were 20 people, some women and, who stayed in the wireless station in which there were only four rooms. We not only slept very little, but we ate very little as the large N.C. Store and another large trading post were located across the Takotna River from where we were. The only store on our side of the river was a small one operated by an old fur trader, and most of his groceries were under water. The last few days we lived on ducks and geese we shot on the Kuskokwim.

Here occurred one of the times I almost lost my life. I was trying to retrieve some geese that I had shot and the ice floe broke in two with me on it. I went under both the water and the ice floe. When I came out from under the ice the old-timers on the river bank said that they had witnessed a miracle, that they never expected to see me again.

The ice jam lasted for three days. When it broke, it took the water another three or four days to recede so that we could retrieve some canned groceries to augment our diet of duck and geese. However, the food problem was not as bad as the sleeping problem. Twenty people sleeping in four rooms is not very comfortable. They slept on the floor, in corners, and any place that they could find a spot to lie or sit down. While it was a trying ordeal and a hardship at the time, I look back on it as one of the most challenging and interesting episodes I experienced while in Alaska. To think that 20 people were cooped up in a four rooms for over a week with no place to sleep, and very little to eat, and not one lost his composure and good nature. I often think what a wonderful world it would be to live in if everyone in it could go through what these 20 people did and come out with the same composure and feeling they had.

About four days after the ice jam broke, the water receded and the river cleared of ice chunks. People of McGrath crossed the Takotna River from one side to the other in rowboats and

## The Mines Open 125

launches. The mode of transporation was either by boat or on foot. The snow now was all melted and the large chunks of ice were on their way to the ocean. The placer mines and gold dredges had begun operation. Gold had begun to come into McGrath from some of the individual placer operators who had been working for a couple of weeks. McGrath had begun to take on new life. The boys with the cards and dice were operating on the gambling strip. The dance hall had opened up for the lonely miners who came to town to share their gold with the pretty girls—and they had plenty of takers. There were, on the average, about two cases a week that came before the Commissioner's court. However, this did not keep the Marshal and me too busy; consequently we had time to indulge in other activity.

The Marshal and I took long hikes into some of the mining camps and also did some prospecting and mining ourselves. I, being the recorder of the district, knew where all the new locations were being made. Soon after the break-up some new placer locations were filed for recording on a little creek high up on the Nixon Fork about 50 miles from McGrath. The locaters were very secretive about their new find, but it leaked out that they had found something very rich. Larry Cross had told me about this creek some time ago, but it was so hard to get into that I hadn't investigated it. Now, I got the bright idea to visit Larry, who was in the vicinity of the new find. I could then enjoy a social visit and at the same time talk over the prospecting possibilities of the area. Larry had done a lot of traveling in this country before he lost his foot. As there was a phone from McGrath to Larry's roadhouse on Big River, I called him and he was delighted when I told him that Marshal Donald Olin and I were going to pay him a visit.

Everything had settled down to normal since the flood caused by the ice jam, and all my work was caught up and very little coming in. The couple of weekly arrests and court cases that we usually had from the Tenderloin district could wait until we got back. I sent Mary a wire at Nenana telling her that I would be gone from McGrath for about a week, until about the 25th of

May. This would be a few days before we would take the boat for Bethel, and I asked her if she would be ready to take the boat from Anchorage to Bethel about the first of June.

The weather was very beautiful now. Donald and I got our prospecting packs ready for the trip to Larry's Big River roadhouse, a visit with Larry, and a prospecting venture. These trips I just loved and Donald was a very generous and a wonderful partner to travel with.

As I recall from my notes, it was on the 16th day of May that Donald Olin and I set out for the Big River roadhouse where we were to pick up Larry Cross and head for the wilderness of the Von Frank mountains and the new prospecting grounds. The weather was beautiful; the glitter of the sun reflected from the surrounding snow-covered mountains. The trail was clear of snow and the rivers clear of ice. It was really one of the most beautiful times of the year in Alaska. We arrived at Larry's roadhouse in the early afternoon, and after a visit with Larry and his partner we laid plans for our prospecting trip to the headwaters of the Nixon Forks River, which started in the high wilderness of the Von Frank mountains where no prospector had ever been. Only a few trappers had even been in this territory, and that when snow covered the ground. Larry said that it was a rough place to get into and that it would take us at least two days, as it was all upgrade.

Early the next morning, Larry Cross, Donald Olin, and myself hit the trail at 4 a.m. for the rugged Von Frank mountains. The first day we made good time, considering the heavy packs we carried (pack horses could not get into the country). We covered about 20 miles this first day of the 35 miles that we estimated it would be to where we wanted to go. This first night we stayed in an old trapper's cabin; that is, what was left of it from the many years of gnawing and chewing by rats and chipmunks. We had to run a couple of mountain boomers (known by some as a mountain beaver, a 6 or 8-pound animal) out before we took over. The next morning we got a thrill when we

## The Mines Open

went outside the cabin and saw signs where a wolf-pack had been around the cabin during the night.

It was rough going the next day, with no trail. We traveled only by dead reckoning and compass. We slowly moved over the rough mountain country to a large divide between the Nixon Forks and the Kuskokwim River, traveling along the divide for several miles until we came to a small creek that came out of a glacier. At this elevation snow covered the ground, and the little creek was frozen over for a mile after it emerged from the glacier. Larry said that he thought this was the creek he was looking for. We followed the creek to where it was free of ice. By this time it was dark so we holed up for the night. We found a large cliff of limestone that was clear of snow and rolled our sleeping bags out as close together as we could. We slept with our rifles by our sides as the grizzly bears were coming out of hibernation at this time of year and they would be hungry.

I think that we all three awoke about the same time the next morning with the same thought in mind—"Gold." After a breakfast of hardtack, bacon, and coffee cooked over an open fire, we set out with our shovels and gold pans in this prospector's paradise. Results came quickly. Larry picked up the first nugget about the size of a dime in a little hole behind some rocks, then we all began to pick up nuggets. This was very unusual as we did not expect to find gold until we dug down near bedrock. We knew now that we had a rich find and that the big pay would be on or near bedrock, which we estimated to be three or four feet in depth at this location of the creek. After picking up what we thought would be about $1,000 in nuggets along the ripples and pot holes, we conducted a survey to ascertain how much of the creek was gold-bearing so we could file claims on it. We worked down the little creek (that we named "Lucky Lue") for about two miles to where it ran into the Nixon Forks. Here we ran out of gold so we knew the gold was from this point to the glacier. We then worked upstream from where we camped and found large nuggets and coarse gold.

Floyd Marsh panning gold on the Takotna River near McGrath, Alaska in 1922.

Big River roadhouse near McGrath, Alaska, operated by Larry Cross and his partner. The small building on the left is a "meat cache" elevated for protection from wild animals.

## The Mines Open

The gold was heaviest right at the glacier mouth. We cut a hole in the ice at this point and found some nuggets almost as large as a quarter. After panning gold and picking up nugget for three days, we decided to stake the creek from the mouth of the Nixon Forks to its head, which was up into the glacier. We were two days staking claims on the creek. In all, we staked 25 claims. After this, with our gold and packs on our backs, we set out for the Big River roadhouse. We made it back in one day from our rich find. We were very tired but just about the three happiest guys in all Alaska.

Larry's partner was waiting for us with an urgent message for me. It was from Captain Greene of the sternwheeler *Tanana;* he was leaving the next day for Bethel. I immediately got Captain Greene on the phone and told him I would be in McGrath early the next morning. He told me that he would like to leave McGrath about noon. Little did I realize that we had been away from McGrath for 12 days. We had expected to be gone only a week.

I slept a couple of hours at the roadhouse. Shortly after midniht I awoke Donald Olin and told him that I was going on into McGrath and that he could have his sleep out and come in later, but he insisted that he accompany me. It was a beautiful night. One would hardly know that it was night, with the Northern Lights illuminating the snow-covered mountains like day. We arrived in McGrath about 9 a.m. I had previously wired Mary that I would be gone only a week and was anxious to wire her now and tell her that I was leaving for Bethel and to ask her to meet me there on June 5. When I arrived at my office in the U.S. Wireless Station I found Leo Bundy, the operator, in a sweat and turmoil.

The power at the station had gone off two days previously and he was unable to send or receive messages. The dredge master of the Akins dredge had just arrived and they were in hope of having the station in working order shortly. I just had time to record our newly located gold claims and get a few things packed for the trip to Bethel when I heard the 30-minute whistle of the *Tanana*, which meant that she would be leaving McGrath. Since repairs had not been made at the wireless station, I left the operator a message to send Mary at Nenana. I advised her I should arrive at Bethel on the 4th or 5th of June. I asked her to write me at Bethel in case she was unable to make the boat out of Anchorage, which arrived in Bethel on June 5, and advised her to take the next boat out of Anchorage, which arrived in Bethel on June 20.

It was the custom that the first boat leaving McGrath after the long winter and the break-up was a big event; a huge party had been held on the *Tanana* all the previous night, and now almost everyone in McGrath was at the boat slip when Captain Greene gave two short toots on the whistle to cut her loose. The swift current of the big Kuskokwim River bobbed the *Tanana* around like a cork. We were soon out of sight of McGrath around the many bends in the river. So many things had happened to me within the last few weeks I wondered if I was not just dreaming. Within the last week I had been a party to one of the richest gold discoveries in the McGrath area in many years. Now I was on my way to meet Mary and in a few days our dreams would come true. I had not had an opportunity to tell Mary of my latest good fortune—the rich gold find. I thought what a wonderful opportunity Mary and I would have. This new gold find would speed our plans of making a stake up here and returning to the States, and also visiting the many places in the world that we had often talked about. I was almost afraid to go to sleep this first night, afraid that I would awaken in the morning and find this all just a dream.

The trip down the Kuskokwim was very beautiful; however, unfortunately the Eskimos who were supposed to cut and pile wood along banks of the river, to make steam for the *Tanana*, had failed to do so and the crew had to cut wood from time to time to make steam for the boat boilers. This delayed our trip with the results that we arrived in Bethel two days late. There were several hundred people at the landing to meet us. I, of course, looked the crowd over for Mary, but without success. I

**MARY KIRKENOFF**
May 10, 1904—May 28, 1922

immediately contacted John Layton, Game Warden in my territory, whom I had asked to meet the boat from Anchorage and take care of Mary until I arrived. The Laytons were going to assist us in the wedding. John had a daughter about Mary's age who was going to be one of the bridesmaids. He told me that the boat from Anchorage had arrived two days earlier and had just left for Kodiak. Because the Post Office was closed, I would have to wait until the next morning to find out if Mary had sent me a letter on the boat that had just come in advising me that she would be on the next boat from Anchorage, which would be a little over a week now. In fact, I was so sure of Mary arriving on the next boat that the Stantons and I had begun to put things in order for the wedding on arrival of the next boat from Anchorage.

The next morning I was at the Post Office door when it opened. There was a letter waiting for me, but it was not from Mary. It was from Mary's mother, Mrs. Kirkenoff, and the letter was trimmed in black. Mary had passed away from virus pneumonia on the 28th of May, two days before she was to leave for Anchorage, which was the day we left McGrath. I stood there in that little sod Post Office like a statue. I could not believe that this could happen to me. The good Lord had been good to me since I came to Alaska, had given me prosperity and material things that I thought would bring happiness. Now I had lost everything that had been so dear and sweet to me. I felt a great emptiness that I had never felt before. It seemed that the whole world had dropped out from under me. I walked down that narrow dirt street of Bethel with no sense of direction where I was going. I soon found myself out on the tundra and wondered how I got there. I kept repeating to myself, "It can't be true; it can't be true." Out there on the great tundra of southwest Alaska I realized that I had reached a crossroad in my life, that I would have to make a decision that would have a drastic impact on my life.

After wandering around for some time, I returned to the *Tanana*. Captain Greene was aboard. He watched me walk up the gangplank and could sense that something was wrong. He asked me, "What happened, Commissioner?" Without answering him I handed him the letter trimmed in black.

The *Tanana* remained in Bethel for two days loading suplies for the many small trading posts along the Kuskokwim. During this time I stayed in my stateroom pondering over which road from here I should take. I had already accumulated a fortune and this would grow with the development of our gold dis-

## The Mines Open 133

covery on Lucky Lue Creek. I also considered the other phase of life, the social and enjoyable side. With the fortune I now had I could really live it up in the States. My memory wandered back to the occasions when I had seen old-timers being taken out of the wilderness on dog sledges with broken bodies from the clutches of grizzly bears, and sourdoughs I had helped take out of log cabins and buried in frozen graves. Once again one of Robert W. Service's poems came back to me that went like this: "I wanted the gold and I got it, I scrambled and mucked like a slave, with hunger and scurvy I fought it, I hurled my youth in a grave."

As we had all upstream going back to McGrath, the *Tanana* was eight days making it back. I had decided on this trip back what I was going to do, but I wanted to first talk it over with Donald Olin and Larry Cross before I told anyone. The *Tanana* arrived in McGrath just at dusk on a bright June day. Soon, about everyone in this little mining hamlet was at the landing to receive the many treats that the first boat in from Bethel after the long winter would bring—such as fresh fruits, vegetables, eggs, and many other things. Bundy, the wireless operator, had received a message for me from Nenana which contained the same news that Mrs. Kirkenoff's letter did. The U.S. Marshal, Donald Olin, met the boat to receive his prize package. His wife had come in from the States. Donald and his wife were very saddened to hear about Mary, as we had planned many things to do together. Of course, seeing Donald and his wife together increased the large emptiness in my heart for Mary.

I was informed by Donald that we had several offers for our new gold discovery. I suggested to Donald that he, Larry Cross, and myself have a meeting to discuss what we should do with our claims. So, the next day Donald Olin, Larry Cross, and myself met at my office to decide what to do with the Lucky Lue claims. We each stated our respective desires. Larry said that because of his clubfoot he did not think he could make it back to the property other than over the snow by dog sledge. Donald said that as he was U.S. Marshal in the district, the

Justice Department might not look upon his mining activities with favor, and as for myself, I had already decided that I wanted to return to the States. Now that they had expressed their desire to sell our claims, it was easy for me to make it unanimous.

Since we had made the discovery and staked our claims on Lucky Lue Creek, there had been several hundred claims staked in the vicinity. Representatives of several mining companies had inspected our ground with the results that we had several offers for our claims. We notified all who had signified their interest of a meeting whereby offers for the claims could be submitted. Jim Stricklin, a prosperous placer operator in the Iditarod district made us the best offer, $30,000 cash and 10 per cent royalty from gross production. We accepted Stricklin's offer, and typical of Alaska dealings in those days, Stricklin reached in his pocket and brought out $30,000. As he handed me $10,000 I asked him if he thought that my 10 per cent royalty would be worth another $10,000. At this point Donald and Larry Cross spoke up and asked if they could buy my royalties and, of course, I sold to them instead of Stricklin. I am very glad I did, as I learned later that it has proved to be a very good buy. During the next two years over a half million dollars in gold was taken out of the Lucky Lue Creek.

This $20,000 with the $30,000 I already had, made quite a fortune for a boy my age, and I definitely intended to go outside and enjoy it. As it was getting late in the summer now, I would have to make plans soon if I was to go out by boat and I did not want to wait until the freeze-up and go out over the trail. So I contacted Captain Greene of the *Tanana* and he informed me that he would be making his last trip to Bethel in a few days. I wired Judge Clegg my resignation. The former U.S. Commissioner, Dr. Green, was still in McGrath and accepted the appointment as U.S. Commissioner, so my resignation was accepted immediately.

To tell the people of McGrath goodbye was one of the hardest and most depressing experiences I have ever gone through, es-

## The Mines Open 135

pecially the people I had worked with and had been so close to. What made it so hard to say goodbye to these people was that I realized it was very unlikely that I would ever see any of them again, and this proved to be true with one exception. That has been Mr. Loomis, manager of the N.C. Store, who later built the Loomis Armored Cars. Later I visited with him many times in Portland, Oregon. Long afterwards I heard that Donald Olin and Larry Cross became very wealthy from royalties of the gold claims on Lucky Lue Creek and that Larry married a very pretty little half-breed I knew in McGrath, by the name of Nellie Campbell. I hope that wherever they are, that they are well and happy and that Larry still has some of his gold.

As the *Tanana* steamed down the swift Kuskokwim, I thought what a queer trick fate had played on me. Here I was going down the same river in the same boat I had a few weeks ago, but with a far different outlook on life. On the previous trip I was a very happy boy on my way to Bethel to meet Mary and was looking forward to happiness with her in Alaska. Now I was leaving Alaska with a heavy heart, having no idea where I was going or what the future held for me.

When we arrived at Bethel, there was a large ocean liner by the name of *M.S. Anvil* at the landing. I got the idea that I would take this boat back to the States instead of going by way of Anchorage, which would require taking a small coast-wise boat from Bethel. I had a problem and that was to get on this large boat—which had a large crew—without anyone suspecting that I was a walking gold mine. I had all my wealth around me in a money belt, and since I was unable to exchange all my gold coins for paper money, I was really loaded down.

The *M.S. Anvil* had accommodations for passengers, but there were none aboard. I would be the only paid passenger, and it put me in the position of a sitting duck. Captain Greene took me aboard the *Anvil* to meet the skipper, who appeared to be a fine fellow. While aboard the *Anvil* I met the wireless operator, a fellow by the name of Dick Stanton. Dick and I seemed to talk the same language. We even belonged to the same lodge. I asked him if I could come back that evening and talk to him. He said that he would enjoy it. I knew that I had to confide my predicament to someone, so that evening I visited Dick aboard the *Anvil* and told him my situation. He advised me against going back as a paid passenger. He said that they had a short crew and that he could get me on as one of the crew, telling the skipper that I was broke. Dick said that the skipper needed more men at the wheel and he would show me how to read the compass, which he did and got me signed on as one of the crew that evening.

The next morning I told Captain Greene and the crew of the *Tanana* goodbye, and with one old, battered suitcase I boarded the *M.S. Anvil* as one of the crew. A native Indian pilot took us out to the mouth of the Kuskokwim; then the ship's crew took over as we hit the rough, open sea headed for Dutch Harbor. The skipper called me to take the wheel, I walked up to the wheel like an old salt, very confident, and was doing all right as the skipper from the bridge would give orders of "southeast by a quarter east" or whatever the order might be. But soon we hit some very rough sea and I got so sick that I could hardly hold onto the wheel. I heard someone behind me and I turned around to face the skipper. He looked me straight in the eye and asked, "Where did you ever sail?" I replied, "This is my first trip and my last one." The skipper kind of grinned. Taking the wheel, he said, "Go below to your bunk." I did just that and stayed there for two days until we were coming into the port of Dutch Harbor. Dick Stanton had visited me several times and given me some tips on treating sea sickness. On one occasion he took me to the ship's kitchen to give me something to help sea sickness, and the cook they called Andy Gum ran us out.

After two days' stay at Dutch Harbor, the *Anvil* sailed through the Unimak Pass and headed out to open sea toward Seattle, Washington. I felt very good after the first attack of sea sickness. I again took the wheel and the skipper remarked that I was making a good sailor. I had made good friends with the entire ship's crew with the exception of the cook, Andy Gump, who was always giving me a bad time for mistaking the passengers' washroom for the crew's washroom. Dick told me that I didn't have to take the abuse from Andy and to slap him down, but I felt so good getting back to the States that I was not mad at anyone.

Early one morning we came in sight of land off the western coast of Washington and it looked awfully good after eleven days out of sight of land. The green waters of the Straits of Juan De Fuca had begun to replace the white salt water of the ocean. I felt wonderful that morning, and it looked as if I were going to make it back to the States with my little fortune. However, I again made the mistake of using the passengers' washroom. As I started out, Andy Gump showed up in the doorway. I started out past him but he caught me by the arm. I whirled around and let him have a hard right to the chin; Andy went down. When he got up he made a run for the kitchen, which was only a little forward of the washroom. I went up to the door of the kitchen just in time to see Andy reach up on the wall and get a meat cleaver. I ran forward to my bunk and got a 45 revolver (my First World War issue).

I looked back and saw Andy going up on the upper deck so I took a stairway near me to the upper deck. When I reached it, I saw Andy advancing toward me with cleaver in hand and I started to advance toward him. I had begun to wonder how close I should let him come before I let him have it with the "45." Then I heard the skipper call, "Andy!" We both stopped when the skipper called. He didn't direct any word to me, but told Andy to come up to the bridge. I returned below to my bunk. After some time Dick Stanton came to my room and told me that Andy wanted the skipper to put me in irons. The skipper told him that he would turn me over to the authorities when we arrived in Seattle. However, Dick said that he thought the skipper told Andy this just to cool him off as he had not received any such message. Still, I was not taking any chances.

When the *Anvil* came along the dock I jumped from the ship to the pier and started out across the dock. The skipper called out that he wanted to see me. Not wishing to be a fugitive from justice the rest of my life, I stopped. The skipper came up to me and said, "I want to talk to you." He told me that Andy was leaving the ship and that he wanted me to sign on as a crew member. At this, I was much surprised and relieved but I had no intention of ever sailing again on the *Anvil*. I wanted to get out of my predicament of the gun episode the best I could, so I told the skipper that I would see him later, but I have not seen him to this day.

As I walked down the streets in Seattle with an old battered suitcase and $50,000 in a money belt (most of it in gold coins) I suddenly stopped and looked around, realizing that I was back in a world that I had left three years before. I didn't know where to go or which way to turn.

# CHAPTER 13

## *Seattle Show Business*

As it was just about midnight and I was back in a place that was now strange to me, where people would rob and kill for money, I was a little nervous. There were two things on my mind: one was to find a hotel for the night, and the other one was to find a bank the next morning to relieve myself mentally and physically of the heavy load of gold that I carried.

As it was after midnight when I got a hotel room and retired, I had no problem getting to sleep even in the big, noisy city. But the next morning I was awakened early by the clamor of rushing traffic that I could hardly realize had increased so much during the three years I had been in the North. I lay in bed and just listened to it. It was difficult to imagine that so many automobiles and trucks had been built since I left the States. Later, when I visited some clothing stores and restaurants, I found out that a lot of other things had changed too—and that was prices on about everything.

When I poured out my $50,000, mostly gold, in front of a teller in a Seattle bank, he looked at me as though he thought I had robbed a bank. Then, on a second look, my clothes, and makeup, he was not so curious. Seattle being the first large city outside Alaska, odd characters such as myself were not unusual to the bank. After banking my wealth, I felt more at ease roaming around the city, but I could not make up my mind what to do. I was not ready to go back in the hills mining, especially with winter coming on. I kept watching the "Business Opportunities" in the classified section of the Seattle *Post-Intelligencer*, trying to find a business to get into. I had had no training or experience in any kind of business. I was really a "sitting duck" for anyone wanting to get rid of a white elephant. I wandered around, taking in shows and getting pretty bored, until about the first of December, when a fast-talking business broker got hold of me and told me what a fortune could be made in the moving-picture theater business.

The slicker sold me a theater, rather the lease on one, with about $500 worth of equipment, for $2,000. The theater was located on 55th and Meridian Avenue and was called "The Meridian Theater." Its equipment consisted of an old moving picture projector and an old, battered piano. There were three years left on a five-year lease; the rent was $50 a month, with two months' rent in arrears. This should have told me something, but it didn't.

I got in touch with the party who had played for the piano for the previous operator, a nice young lady by the name of Nellie Gibson. I engaged Nellie at once. She also advised me on the operation of the theater, which I needed. After cleaning and painting the inside and front of the theater—which set me back another $500—Nellie took me down to the Film Row and showed me how to select pictures to show. I recall some of the pictures I selected, such as "Mickie" with Norma Talmage, "The Sheik" with Rudolph Valentino, and a number of pictures with Douglas Fairbanks, Wallace Beery, William S. Hart, and some of the other old-timers who have long since gone.

The grant opening was just a few days before Christmas. The picture was "Blood and Sand" with John Gilbert. I put out 1,000 handbills for the opening, which I distributed myself throughout the neighborhood. I had high hopes for the grand opening, and wondered if the theater would hold everyone. I soon found out that it would; in fact, the restrooms would not have been crowded if all the people had been in them at the same time. After the show I counted the attendance; there were 27 counting both adults and children. With 25 cents for adults and 10 cents for children, the night was not exactly a bonanza. I was $1.30 short of breaking even on the labor cost. If I had not worked the box office myself, I would have thought that someone knocked down on me. However, I was not discouraged.

## Seattle Show Business 141

Nellie told me that we would have days like this, and remarked that people respond to different types of pictures.

After the holidays, business picked up some. I found out what type of pictures to show—westerns and rough-and-tumble pictures. I made a killing on "Dangerous Dan McGrew," "The Squaw Man," and "The Three Musketeers." I could pack the house on Saturday and Sunday matinees. Also, when I played highly advertised pictures, I got a good attendance, but I was only working for the film producers, as I paid much more for these pictures. I did just fair during the winter months. By April 1, I had almost all my money back that I had invested in the showhouse, but nothing for my labor and living expenses—except experience, which sometimes doesn't come cheap.

I decided that show business was not the life for me, that I wanted to get out and do some prospecting and mining during the coming summer. I went back to the broker who sold me the "Meridian" and asked him if he could sell the theater, rather the lease, for me. The broker gave me a "song and dance" about the summer not being good theater weather; therefore, it would not bring as much as when he sold it to me, but he said that he would give it a try and asked me to keep it open, as by doing so it would sell a lot better. Contrary to the broker's remark that the theater would not sell for what I paid for it, I listed it for what I had in it—which was $2,500—but I was going to take the best offer that I got, and the sooner the better.

About a week after I had the theater listed, the broker brought a middle-aged couple out to see it. It was on a Saturday night, and I was turning them away. As I recall, I was playing a Harold Lloyd comic. The attendance was mostly all kids (10 cents admission) but it looked good. After the couple was shown the theater, there was some talking between them and the broker; then the broker came over to where I was and said he could make a deal for $2,000. He next began to give me many reasons why I should sell—which was very unnecessary. I really wanted to yell "sell!" but I did not want to act anxious. I told the broker that if the buyer would pay the selling commission it would be a deal. After the broker spoke a few words to the buyer, he asked me to acknowledge an earnest money receipt, that we had made a deal.

It was certainly a relief to get out from under that theater. It was too confining—week days, holidays, every day for over three months. I asked myself, "Why get tied down in a deal like this when I have a small fortune in the savings up town?" Nellie promised to stay and help the new owners operate the theater. God bless her; she was a wonderful person. She helped me out very much. It cost me $500 and over three months of labor to find out that I was not the theatrical type.

## CHAPTER 14

## *Back to Gold Mining*

I remained in Seattle a few days. Selling the theater was so much faster than I thought it would be, I had not given much thought of where I would go. After shifting my finances around a little and taking a draft with me, I boarded the train to Spokane. I had considered going to Fort Wright when I first arrived in Spokane, then said to myself, "Why open up an old wound?" I purchased a T-model Ford in Spokane and headed for Idaho, which I had heard a lot about. I first went to the beautiful scenic Coeur d'Alene country with its large lakes, but I was a little early for its great fishing. I then went over into the Kellogg, Wallace, and Mullen area where there were a number of large mines, mostly silver, lead, and copper. I found out that this was a highly mineralized and rough country; but it is right in the Rocky Mountain range, a hard country to get around in to do any prospecting.

From here I went into the northern part of Idaho and on into Canada. This is also a highly mineralized country and a rough place to get into—all hard rock or quartz prospecting and mining. As I had no camping outfit to go out into the mountain for quartz prospecting, and there was no placer mining, I decided to head down into the centran part of Idaho.

I arrived in Lewiston at the time the placer mines were coming through there and into Lewiston for materials and supplies for placer mining, which starts in the spring and runs through the summer. At Lewiston I learned that there was quite a lot of placer mining near Orofino on the Clearwater River. I drove to Orofino about 70 miles to the east. At Orofino I found considerable activity. It looked like a prosperous little town; there were signs of mining everywhere. When I began to get acquainted and ask questions about the country, I found out that there was placer mining almost every direction from Orofino, and some recent discoveries had been made. After a few days I met a storekeeper who told me he knew of two young men who had several rich claims and were looking for some financing.

I made arrangements to meet the two young men, one a Norwegian by the name of Herb Olson, and the other one of German extraction by the name of Hans Waldberg. After talking with them for some time, I decided they were honest men and did indeed have some rich placer claims. They said that they had lost all their equipment and supplies in the April flood as the snow-water came down the Clearwater. They needed about $2,000 for supplies and a grubstake until they got set up to take out some gold. Their story sounded good. The next thing to do was to look at their claims. The two boys had an old Dodge sedan, which we drove up the Clearwater River to see the claims that were about 40 miles from Orofino. We arrived about two hours before dark. We looked the property over and panned out about $20 worth of gold in a very short time. The gold was quite fine but there was a lot of it.

This looked like a good deal to me. I wanted to buy an interest in the claims, but the boys only wanted to make a deal for the summer. They offered me one-third of the gold we would take out during the summer for my help and the loan of the $2,000 secured by the claims. There was no full-season record of production on the claims as the boys had located them late the previous summer. They had taken out over $5,000 worth of gold before the freeze came but had not worked any this year before the flood came. We spent the next day sampling the claims. I figured the three of us should take out between $30,000 and $40,000 during the summer just by shoveling gold-bearing gravel into the sluice boxes, as no heavy machinery could be moved in. Sensing that I could not get a piece of the claims, I told the boys that I would go in on the summer deal. So we went back to Orofino to draw up our contract and get supplies and equipment for operation. We hauled the general supplies

## Back to Gold Mining 145

and groceries in our cars, but had the lumber for sluice boxes trucked in within 5 miles of the claims and packed in with horses the rest of the way.

Since we were all young and husky, it didn't take us long to get into operation. We had sluice boxes built, set up, and ready to shovel in the gold-bearing gravel by the middle of June. We were up and shoveling in gravel as soon as we could see in the mornings and worked until dark. We never missed a day from the middle of June until the freeze, the latter part of October. In a few days over 4 months we had taken out a little over $34,000, and the last few days we had hit a spot on the bedrock where we got coarse gold.

Not a bad 4 months' work for me—a little over $10,000 and my $2,000 returned. However, the $2,000 was taken out of the gross $34,000 production before we split it up. Herb and Hans were fine fellows. I enjoyed their company and working with them. There was not a complaint or cross word among us during the time we worked together. The boys were down on banks for not lending them money for their placer operation. They appreciated my helping them out, though it was rewarding for me, too. They wanted me to stay in the area, and told me about a placer prospect about 60 miles from where we were on the south forks of the Clearwater, but I would have to wait until next spring to try and find it.

I drove the T-model to Lewiston and stayed there a few days, trying to figure out what to do. Then one day I remembered what Dr. Lemon had said to me when I left the service—Go home and visit your folks, then figure out what you want to do. And that is exactly what I decided to do. I sold the Tin Lizzie in Lewiston and took a bus to Portland, Oregon, where I stayed a week. I had often visited Portland when I was in the service at Vancouver, Washington, across the Columbia River. From Portland I took the train to Los Angeles where I visited a week with one of my brothers and some relatives living there before going on to Phoenix, Arizona, where my mother and some of my brothers now lived.

## CHAPTER 15

## *Trip to Phoenix*

My mother and three of my brothers were now in Phoenix, and we had a nice reunion. After we got over the joy of seeing each other again, there was a kind of sadness in our hearts as we had changed a lot. All the boys had grown up; some had married and moved to other states. It was like the little birds that left their nest. We would never all be back together as we once were. Phoenix struck me as being a fine city, a much better place to live in than Duncan, and also much different than Alaska. Here one could lie out in the sun in the middle of winter and eat oranges fresh off the tree. I thought that I should send a picture to the *Fairbanks News*.

I liked Phoenix so much that I thought I would invest some money here. It seemed like many people were coming into the area. Of all the places that I had visited since returning from Alaska, Phoenix seemed to be the main boomtown. One day I saw an ad in the local paper that a Land Sales Company was taking prospective buyers out in the country to look at land they had for sale. I told one of my brothers about it and asked him his opinion. He said he thought it was a good investment and that the land was only a short drive from his place just north of Glendale, which was on the northwest edge of Phoenix. We drove out to the land. It was just desert, but I liked it. The sunshine and the surrounding mountains, together with the unbelievable weather—I wanted a piece of it.

I told my brother that one would have to see other parts of the country to appreciate this. I don't recall what my brother said the land was selling for, but I thought that it was a good investment to hold, as the taxes were very low. The money I now had in the savings was bringing me 2%. When we got back to Phoenix, I wired Seattle for $10,000, and a few days later I took a promotional bus loaded with prospective land buyers to look at the desert land. The promoters gave us a long "song-and-dance" of what would be here some day, but they spread it on too thick. After a big turkey dinner in a large circus-type tent, they tried to get our names on the dotted line. When I came out to the place, I had fully intended to buy, but the salesmen oversold themselves and the land by making it look too rosy.

When I returned to my brother's place, he asked me if I had bought. I told him that I didn't though I got a turkey dinner out of them, and had a little laugh. But now I wonder who is laughing. If I had invested the $10,000 in the desert land, which I intended to do before I was oversold, I would not only have made one million, I would have made many millions. What then was desert land is now SUN CITY with almost a million population.

I had loafed over a month in the winter sun at Phoenix when one of my brothers suggested a trip to Duncan and the old farm. It was a nice trip about 140 miles up the Gila River. Duncan and Mormon Valley looked the same. After a few days visiting with old friends, we decided to drive over into New Mexico to Santa Rita, about 4 hours away, where another of our brothers worked in one of the largest copper mines in the nation. Leaving Duncan and going out over the Lordsburg Plains, we traveled in the same area that we had traveled with our father in 1908, with horses and wagon, and had seen buffaloes feeding on the grassy prairie.

At Santa Rita we saw one of the largest copper mines in the nation, and a mining wonder of the world. There was a large excavation in the earth about 8 by 10 miles across at the top and 2 miles deep, with trains traveling around the inside of the excavation on about a dozen different levels carrying ore to the smelter at Hurley, 10 miles away. To watch the trains crawl along 2 miles deep in the earth was a sight. There was every color of the rainbow on the huge walls of the excavation, caused by copper stains. It was truly the largest and most magnificent art gallery in the world.

Here I saw something pertaining to mining that I had never before seen or heard of, and that is making copper out of tin cans. We saw some men in a small creek below Copper Mountain on which the huge copper mine is located. There men were putting tin cans in ponds dug in the small creek and taking copper cans out of other ponds. We learned later their technique of making copper out of tin cans. The little creek came out of Copper Mountain through a fault. The stream contained such a strong solution of copper that it turned the tin cans into copper. These cans were like all other cans referred to as tin cans; in reality they were iron cans. Very few, if any, cans are of pure tin; they are only tin-coated.

I became quite well acquainted with the operator of the can-converting deal. He told me his name, which I never remembered other than Steve—it was a foreign name. He told me he had staked mineral locations along the little creek many years ago, and that he had done all right—which was the only information he would give me regarding his operation. Steve did tell me though, that others below him had tried his method, but the copper solution was too weak when it reached them. He said that his mineral locations joined the Copper Company property, so he had the little copper solution creek sewed up.

It looked as if Steve and his son, who was his only partner (though they hired other help), had a unique copper mine and processing plant. The only expense they had was finding tin cans. The little town of Santa Rita with its large copper mine was very interesting; the Spanish signs were everywhere. The Spaniards had built the little town before the foundations were laid for our largest cities. We visited many historical places, such as the old Spanish town of Silver City, which was headquarters for outlaws and cattle thieves.

Leaving New Mexico, we drove to Duncan and spent the night there, then went on to Phoenix the next day. On our way we drove through such beautiful little towns as Mesa, Tempe,

Widow Marsh and her seven sons. They are (from right): Claude, Floyd, Pete, Arthur, Joe, John and Ted. Picture taken in 1923 after my return from Alaska.

The large open-pit copper mine I mentioned at Santa Rita, New Mexico—2 miles deep and 8 miles across. The ore trains on several levels appear like toy trains.

and Scottsdale. I liked them all and told my brother that some day I was coming back here to live. Of course, I was in Phoenix in the wintertime, and as I found out later that was the best time of the year. It can get very uncomfortable in the summertime.

# CHAPTER 16

## *Back to the Northwest*

The latter part of February I reluctantly decided that I should be getting back up North. I tried to buy a car in Phoenix as I wanted to drive back through California, but was unable to get what I wanted. So I took a train to Los Angeles where again I was unsuccessful in getting a used car to my satisfaction. After a couple of days I took the bus to Sacramento, where I purchased a 1922 T-model Ford sedan. It was a better car than the one I bought in Spokane the year previously. I paid $335 for this last car, and I was proud of it. From Sacramento I headed toward Marysville, but stopped many places along the way where there was placer mining going on. Everyone was working low ground and creek bottoms before high water would hit them from snow melting in the mountains.

In Marysville I tried to find Mr. Schultz and the dredge I had worked on 7 years previously, but to no avail. However, at Yuba City 5 miles away I located what was left of the old dredge. It was being remodeled with a new screen and new sluice boxes and riffles modeled to recover more of the fine gold. I was very much interested in the latter, so I remained at Yuba City for several days. And for my appreciation of the knowledge I was gaining, I helped them on the dredge. It was after the first of March now and time I was getting back to Idaho to try and locate the placer that the boys I worked with the previous summer had told me about.

On my way back to Idaho I stopped in Portland one night and a day to pick up some supplies and a camping outfit. It took me three days to drive to Elk City, Idaho, as the roads were not so good in those days.

I arrived in Elk City about the middle of March, which is usually low-water time of the year and would be a good time to look for the placer ground the boys had told me about. This was a hard place to get any information. There were only two placer mines working. They were large outfits and were not giving out any information—if they had it. I found out from a small storekeeper that the boys had worked on some claims on the Clearwater a few miles downstream from the little town two years previously, but no one in the camp knew much about them. I had a good enough description of the place that if I got near the location I would recognize it, so I took off down the Clearwater to see if I could find anything like the description I had in my pocket. After driving downstream from the little town about 6 miles and walking aways, I found the place. It was in a sharp bend on the south forks of the Clearwater. It was a hard spot to find and a hard one to get into, about two miles from a poor wagon road where I left my car. As it was getting late I returned to the car and made camp for the night. It was wild, cold, and rough out there.

The following morning I arose early and had a breakfast over an open fire, after which I had to wait a little while for daylight. Then with my pack and a lunch, I took off for the place I had found the previous day. Arriving there, I again checked the sketch the boys gave me, to be sure I had the right location. Everything was in place except a sand bar in the bend of the river. This could have been taken out by a flood or ice flow. In shallow water along the banks and on a few sand bars, I found quite an amount of gold. It was very fine and would be hard to recover in an ordinary sluice box and riffles.

I stayed at my camp where I had the car parked for several days. I spent another day on the property that the boys told me about, as I didn't want to pass up anything, but finally gave it up as not being profitable to work. I spent several days looking over some higher ground and could find gold in small amounts in several places that I panned. I discovered some coarse gold high up on a bench of what I thought was an ancient channel,

## Back to the Northwest 153

about 100 feet above the present creek bed. On examining the place a little closer I could see that it was an old hydraulic placer mine, and what I found was missed by the old-timers, who had first mined this part of Idaho in the 1860's. I fixed up some old sluice boxes with riffles in the bed of the little creek, and selected some gravel from the old channel and slid it down to the sluice boxes, where I washed it out and recovered about two ounces of coarse gold—then worth $40; now worth over $350. How times have changed!

As this area was old workings and only gold in spots missed by early miners, I decided to move on. After breaking camp, I drove to Grangeville, the county seat of Idaho County, about 40 miles away. I thought there I might find out what was going on in the county, because all location and assessment work are recorded there. Grangeville was a nice town, the largest town in Idaho I had been in, other than Lewiston. In Grangeville I met and talked to a number of miners in both quartz and placer. There were many mining propositions in the area, but they were mostly sniping on old, worked-out claims. I had been in Grangeville about a week and was getting ready to leave when I met a small, middle-aged man by the name of Dan Taylor, who had mined the bars, banks, and islands of the Salmon River for many years. He seemed to be a man of means. He had property in Grangeville to prove that he had made a lot of money doing something.

Dan and I seemed to speak each other's language, and in a few days become well acquainted. We exchanged mining experiences and seemed to agree on the many methods of mining. He told me that he had a barge, two boats, and some mining equipment at White Bird on the Salmon River, which he had mined for the last 10 years, from Riggins to below White Bird, a distance of over 40 miles. He said that he was going to White Bird, 15 miles from Grangeville, to check some gear and asked me to go along; we would take a boat ride on the Salmon. I was glad to make the trip, as I had become interested in mining on the

Salmon River from my conversation with Dan. We drove to White Bird in Dan's new Chrysler, the first one I had seen.

At White Bird we got in Dan's shallow-draft motor boat to take a ride on the fabulous Salmon River. We first went to a bar 10 miles below White Bird, where Dan had been doing some mining. Then we went up the river a few miles above Riggins; there was mining in places the entire distance. I remarked to Dan that there must be considerable gold in the Salmon or there would not be so many people trying for it. He replied that they were all getting gold, that since mining began here, millions of dollars in gold had been taken out, and that there were millions left. We stopped at Lucile, 10 miles below Riggins, where some friends of Dan's had an operation. They had about 200 feet of sluice box they were shoveling into, and seemed to be doing all right. The gold was mostly fine, which signifies that it has traveled a long way. Only seldom did they get any coarse gold or nuggets.

Dan said that gold had been found in the Salmon River along its entire course, from where it empites into the Snake River above Lewiston east across the state over 350 miles to the town of Salmon, then 250 miles south to the Sawtooth Range of mountains which is its source. Dan told me that there was gold and salmon (fish) the entire 600 miles, and that he had prospected and fished a lot of it.

We returned to White Bird and left the boat for the Chrysler. On the way back to Grangeville Dan asked me what I thought of the Salmon River. I replied that I liked it, and asked what kind of set-up it would require to get in on the mining. He replied that it all depended on how much one wanted to get involved, that some miners have only a few dollars invested in sluice boxes and tools with some ground on lease, while others have fortunes invested in boats, barges, and equipment. He said that he had about $75,000 invested in barges, boats, and equipment, in addition to the mining ground that he would not put a price on. I asked him if he knew of anyone who might sell out. He said that he knew of a fellow who had been talking about

## Back to the Northwest

selling out, that the fellow had a boat and some good equipment, but he had no mining property and was working leased ground near Lucile. Dan said that he would see the party, and let me know the next day what he found out.

Dan was late the next day getting down to our usual meeting place, the "Idaho Club" where miners and businessmen gather. He didn't arrive until about 2 p.m. He said that he had driven to White Bird in the morning to take a machinist out to look at some work on one of his boats, and that he had decided to get a couple of his mining projects going while the water was so low. He has been surprised to see so many bars and islands exposed on our trip the previous day.

I asked him if he had contacted the man he told me about who had the placer mining outfit for sale. He replied that he had, but he was sure I would not be interested. At least, he would not recommend it. He said the fellow had about $15,000 worth of equipment that he wanted $25,000 for, which was all on leased ground. Of course, this was out. Then Dan told me something that I was really interested in. He said that after he got home last evening, a party called him from Riggins and told him that a new gold placer strike had been made on French Creek about 20 miles from there. This would be about 60 miles from Grangeville. I told him that was just what I was looking for, a new gold strike, and that I would be leaving in the morning and would contact him by mail or phone if I did not come back to Grangeville—and in the meantime for him to keep his eyes open for a good placer set-up some place on the Salmon River.

I was on the road to French Creek before daylight the next morning. I arrived early in Riggins for a big breakfast, the kind served only in mining camps. Here I inquired about a new gold strike on French Creek. I was told to go up the south side of Salmon River about 15 miles, then south on French Creek to the French Mining Company. I thought it was an odd name for a new gold strike. However, I didn't ask questions. I took off up Salmon River as directed, and about 15 miles I saw a sign pointing south with the words of "French Mining Co. 4 Miles." The road was very poor, and I thought that if it rained I might not get out, but I had to follow through. As I took off up the deep-rutted wagon road, another thought struck me and that was—if there were really a new gold strike up here, where was the stampede?

After driving a few miles, with my fingers crossed and praying that I would not get stuck, I came onto a large placer operation. I drove up to what looked like a bunk house. An old fellow came out dressed like "Buffalo Bill" and wanted to know what he could do for me. I replied that I was looking for the new gold strike. He asked, "The one we made the other day?" I answered yes, but I could see now that someone was mixed up, and it seemed to be me. So I said to him that I had been told that a new gold strike had been made on French Creek. He gave out a big laugh, and said that I had been the second fellow looking for the new gold strike. Then he explained:

The company had found an ancient channel about 30 feet above the present creek bed, and on the bedrock of the ancient channel they had hit some rich, coarse gold. It was a new, rich discovery for the company, but it was on ground that the company had owned for a long time. It was a new gold strike but not on open ground.

The old gentleman I had been talking to was a French-Canadian. He gave me his name, which I could not remember. He was manager of the French Mining Company and a fine fellow. He invited me into his office and showed me some gold, the likes of which I had not seen since leaving Alaska. It was coarse with a lot of nuggets in it. The manager told me the story about the new discovery and it sounded like a fairy tale. He said for years they had found coarse gold and nuggets in the creek bed that had been worked over, and that it appeared as if someone had spread the gold on the ground. Then one day he was panning beneath a gravel cliff when a nugget the size of a bird egg fell in front of him. He could hardly believe his eyes. Then some gravel fell off the cliff with gold among it. The following day they let a man down from the top of the cliff on a rope, and 30 feet above the present creek bed they discovered the bedrock of an ancient channel that ran back into the gravel cliff.

The manager took me up to see the new discovery. It was something in the nature of the ancient channel I found near Elk City, only this one had not been worked out. The old channel was exposed about 400 feet along the gravel cliff, and, of course, there was no way to estimate how wide it was. The old channel seemed to run in the same direction that French Creek did. The mining company was clearing off enough bedrock on the old channel to set up some sluice boxes. This would really be a miner's dream, with plenty of room for the tailings (gravel that had gone through the sluice boxes) and boulders which sometimes are a headache to get rid of. The water was going to be brought in from two miles above in wooden flumes to wash the gravel. It looked as if they had a bonanza. They had the gold and an ideal mining set-up. I thought to myself that I wanted to find just a little one like this.

The company had only 8 men working at this time, but was expected to enlarge their crew to 14 within a few days, when a large load of supplies and lumber for sluice boxes was expected in. All the crew were fine fellows. I met and talked with them when they came in for lunch. They seemed to enjoy the latest news which I tried to bring them up-to-date on. The manager remarked that if I wished to look around the rest of the day, that I would be welcome to be their guest for the night. This I thanked him for very much and told him that I would accept his hospitality, as I wanted to look the country over a little.

The manager told me that all of French Creek had been staked at one time, but a lot of it was open ground now. This area had been discovered in 1862, and as in most other discoveries, prospectors and stampeders covered the country like mad, putting up location notices in tobacco cans (usually Prince Albert) nailed on a post. They had 90 days to record their claims, but about 50 per cent of the locations were never recorded. Often the legal requirement of posting the claim (4 corner and line posts) was never completed. Even if all requirements of locating a claim were complied with, only a few held their claims legally by doing the assessment work required each year.

Because French Creek was short, I looked most of it over that same day. I found a lot of old workings but no gold. The old-timers did a good job of finding the gold. I came into camp in time to make the chowline for supper. (It was supper in those days; now it is dinner.) And what a supper! People who think miners live on beans and flapjacks should have seen this meal. Afterwards I gathered with the other fellows in the big bunk house to visit. I was surprised to see all the men in camp so far along in life. They all were past middle age. Many of them had been in Alaska, and, of course, these were interested in knowing how things were there now, as they had left Alaska long before I had. They were also interested in my recent travel of over 3,000 miles from Canada to Old Mexico. After about 4 hours of this, we all hit the hay.

The next morning I told the manager that I didn't want to impose on him, but I would like to look around until the late afternoon, at which time I would get back to Grangeville. He replied that I was welcome to stay as long as I wished. After an early breakfast I took off up French Creek for about three miles, then east out of French Creek some five miles to the mining district of Borgdorf; there was a trail all the way. At Borgdorff I saw some action. I came onto two outfits placer mining. One of them was quite a large layout with seven men working; the other had only two men, but both of them were cheap on their information. However, they did tell me there were other placer operations in the district, which I never found.

I spent most of my time at the old diggings looking for ancient channels and gold quartz ledges, as the formation looked very good for lode minerals. Also, no doubt the old-timers never looked for any gold-bearing ledges. I panned gold in several places, but the old-timers left only colors here. Not finding any-

## Back to the Northwest 159

thing that looked like an ancient channel or gold quartz ledge, I thought that I had better start back toward the French mine, as I had much unfamiliar country to go over. I made the trip back without any trouble and arrived at camp about dusk. I was asked to stay over at the camp another night, but I would not impose further by even staying for supper. I made an excuse by saying I had to get back to Riggins that night. Bidding this fine bunch of fellows goodbye, I headed the T-model down the road toward Salmon River, 4 miles away and all downhill.

When I reached the Salmon River, I found two miners who had just made camp. I pulled over near their camp and we had a little chat. They were going up on the south forks of the Salmon River about 40 miles away where they had a quartz mine, the first one I had heard of in the country, and I was interested. They showed me some white quartz that was studded with gold. I didn't know that there was anything in the country of this kind. Talking with the two miners, I could see that quartz mining in these parts had been overlooked. The miners told me that there was a trail over the mountains from here to the Borgdorf mining district, which was about 10 miles to the southeast, and also there was some placer mining out a few miles from the Salmon. It seemed that there was placer mining all over the country.

Bidding them goodbye, I made camp and a little supper, but nothing was as good as the previous evening. I hit the sleeping bag early. I had not been so tired in a long time. I went to bed not knowing what I was going to do the next day. I heard the two miners camped near me break camp and leave early. After I got up and fixed some breakfast, I decided to stay over here another day, as I liked this part of the country and thought that there were fortunes yet to be made in these old mining camps. After getting my pack loaded and a lunch, which I missed the previous day, I took out over the banks of the Salmon River toward Borgdorf. About 3 miles out on the trail I came across an old wagon road, and was surprised to see that it had recently been used.

I followed the road a couple of miles and came upon three men who had a placer operation going, which seemed to be somewhat more modern than others in the area. They had a screen-bottom hopper or container on the sluice boxes that the men shoveled into to catch the rocks and keep them from going into the sluice boxes. Beneath the riffles of the last sluice box they had burlap to catch the extra-fine gold, and they burned the burlap to recover the fine gold that it caught! They had only about 3 feet of overburden to remove from a smooth bedrock. Of course, the big pay is on bedrock, and the smoother it is the easier it is and the more gold that can be retrieved. The boys seemed to be doing all right. I could see coarse gold and nuggets in the riffles, but they didn't seem willing to give out any information more than could be seen, so I moved on.

I followed the road over a ridge about 3 miles to a little creek that had some old placer workings; several cabins were nearby. From the evidence there had been a good deal of work on this little creek, which would have had to produce a lot of gold to warrant all the work. I found some gravel banks in the creek and began to pan them. Once in a while I would get a good pan, then nothing for a few pans. I finally figured it out. There had been a narrow pay streak (like Yellow Creek in Alaska) and the miners who worked the creek missed some gold in some of the many bends that these pay streaks have; it was in these bends that I was getting the good pans. I had been so interested in panning gold I had forgotten to eat my lunch, and it was getting dark. I had taken out about half an ounce of gold. Going back to camp was out of the question, so I picked out one of the best cabins and retired for the night.

The cabin I selected to stay in had been taken over by field mice, chipmunks, and squirrels, and they were not very good housekeepers. I cleaned the cabin out the best I could, and ate my lunch for supper, which didn't fill the vacancy. There was a bed frame made out of tree limbs. I filled this with boughs, which made a pretty good bed but not a very warm one. I went to bed tired, but being the young, husky man I was in those days, I woke up full of pep and energy. For breakfast I had barbecued grouse. I always carried a 22 pistol, and from the number of grouse I had seen the previous day, I knew I would not have to look long before I got one. Not far from the cabin I got two, one for lunch. I cooked the grouse barbecue-style over an open fire and without salt or seasoning. I never tasted anything better. I cooked the second grouse for a cold lunch.

I panned about an hour the next morning, when I lost the pay streak altogether. I could not get a color for a distance of about 20 feet, then I picked up the pay streak again. The 20 feet of barren ground puzzled me. I kept trying to figure out what happened. Then I found out. It not only fooled me, it fooled the old-timers as well. There was a large boulder on bedrock at the edge of the stream that diverted the old channel and pay streak for the 20 feet.

Now I had a large amount of gold-bearing gravel to work, too much to pan, so I fixed up a couple of old sluice boxes I found at the diggings and fitted them with riffles and began to placer mine. I would pan once in a while to keep on the pay streak. I could see coarse gold and nuggets in the sluice boxes. The pay streak was narrow but rich, as it had not been disturbed. After I got around the large boulder, I had only about 15 feet of the virgin ground or pay streak to work, which I finished in the mid-afternoon, picking up little bits of gold here and there. After I worked the undisturbed pay streak, the creek was not very interesting, so I bid the little old rich creek goodbye and headed for the Salmon River and my camp. I missed the three miners going out that I saw coming in. In fact, I missed my camp on the Salmon River by about a mile.

When I finally got back to camp, I weighed the gold I had recovered. There were 4.6 ounces, which would be $680 at today's prices. I was paid less than $100 for it. While I was paid well for the few days I spent getting it, the thrill and satisfaction of finding the gold were worth more to me than the value of it. I was now tired, cold, and hungry. My first thought was to crawl into my sleeping bag, but I was too hungry for that; and driving to Grangeville sharing the road with the many deer in the country didn't seem to be a good idea. So I decided on something that I didn't argue with myself about, and that was to stay in Riggins overnight. So to Riggins I went and got myself a hot dinner, after which I took a room at the hotel. After a hot bath (very badly needed), I hit a good bed for a good night's sleep.

I arose the next morning as much confused as ever as to what I was going to do. However, the first thing on the agenda was to get some breakfast. I paid my hotel bill, the big sum of $1.25, then went to the Riggins' restaurant that every miner in this part of Idaho knew about. After breakfast I took off for Grangeville, and on the way I gave some thought to what I wanted to do. It was now the latter part of April. Miners who had placer claims were out working them, and mining property that was for lease had been contracted for. I was wondering if Dan Taylor had run onto anything for me during the five days I had been gone. I arrived back in Grangeville in the early morning, and at the rooming house where I had been staying there was a message from Dan. He wanted me to call him as soon as I arrived.

I called Dan's home and was informed by his wife that he had started one of his placer projects and would not be home until late afternoon. I asked her if she and Dan would have dinner with me at the club that evening. She replied that she was reasonably sure that they could, as she knew of no engagement that Dan had for the evening. I told her that I would be at the club during the afternoon and evening and for them to page me when they arrived. I went down to the club for lunch, visited, and played cards the balance of the afternoon. There were very few of the miners around. They were out working their claims, or were in other parts of Idaho in connection with mining.

About 7 o'clock Dan and his wife, Laura, arrived at the club. Dan had a grin on his face and said, "I guess I owe you an apology." He referred to the new gold strike on French Creek. I replied, "Not at all, " and I showed him the poke of gold I had

## Back to the Northwest 163

found on my trip. He looked surprised and said he understood that the strike on French Creek was on private-owned ground. Then I told him the story, that after I found out that the gold discovery was on the French Mining Company ground, I stayed over a few days and did some placer mining in the old Borgdorf mining district. He was amazed. During the course of our dinner, he told me what he had in mind for me.

He had opened up one of his mining projects near White Bird and was going to open up another one a few miles below Lucile. He said that the water was very low and that he could work ground that he could not get to other times of the year. He wanted me to go to work for him as a panner. This consisted of panning the gold out of the concentrates that is caught in the riffles. Dan explained, as I already knew, that this was a highly technical job, and for this reason he paid more for it than any other on the project. He further explained that the job required both skill and honesty, and that he knew of no one he could get except strangers. I remarked that I was a stranger to him, and he replied that he didn't think so; at least I was not a hungry miner and they were the ones who stole and kept on stealing.

I really didn't want to go to work for wages, especially not out in the sticks like this, but I wanted to learn more about placer mining on the Salmon River, and I liked Dan and wanted to keep in touch with him. I never asked him what he was paying for panning. I changed the subject by asking about the activity of mining on the Salmon at the present time. Dan said that everything was humming with activity because of the unusual low water. I asked if he had heard of any placer outfits for sale along the river. He replied that he had not, that everybody seemed to be making money now. Then he changed the subject back to my working for him; I could learn the technique and method of this type of mining.

We had finished our dinner and our third bottle of wine, when Dan fired his "Big Bertha" in his effort to induce me to go to work for him. He said that panning paid more than any other job on the project; that he would pay me $1 an hour, which was twice the wages of the other miners, and that my meals would be furnished me at camp, which was usually $1.50 per day. While I didn't need the money, I did need the experience and Dan's continued friendship. I felt like this was an offer "I couldn't refuse."

I told him that I would go to work for him. This seemed to please him very much. Now he would be relieved of the panning at White Bird and would open up some property he had a few miles below Lucile. The following morning he picked me and my bedroll up at my rooming house and we headed for White Bird, where we boarded one of his boats and went up the Salmon a few miles to his placer operation.

This operation was different from most of those on the river, as it was not on the banks of the river or on an island. It was on a strip of land that ran out from the bank to a higher piece of land that was an island when the water was high, but now would be considered a peninsula. This property was worked 24 hours a day, 3 eight-hour shifts, with 4 men to the shift. The work was being rushed while the water was low. Cleanup of the sluice boxes was made every morning. It took me 7 to 8 hours to pan the several hundred pounds of concentrates retrieved from the 24-hours' operation.

Most of the gold was very fine and hard to pan out of the concentrates without losing some of it. There were several hundred pounds of heavy black concentrates left after the gold was recovered from each day's concentrates, which I never knew what Dan did with. I often thought that these concentrates were very valuable from the way Dan treated them. There were also many gems recovered from the concentrates, such as fire opal, garnet, zircon, topaz, and others that I did not recognize. I turned them all over to Dan.

A few days after I started to work for him, he opened up the Lucile placer project, about 6 miles above the White Bird mine. This was a smaller operation with one 10-hour shift with 4 men, but they put out almost as much concentrate as the White Bird operation. Dan was supposed to pan the concentrates of the

Lucile mine, but he had business in Grangeville that kept him busy, so he asked me to pan the concentrates of both operations and use my car between operations—as they both could be reached without a boat at the present low-water level. I was putting in from 12 to 14-hour shifts, but Dan compensated me for the long hours and use of my car. I was making more money than I ever made in my life working for wages, but I was not too happy. While I had gained some knowledge of this type of mining, I wanted to get in business for myself.

I had worked for Dan about 2 months when the river began to rise. There had been an exceptionally heavy snowfall in the mountains during the winter and an early, warm spring, which made for high water in the Salmon River the latter part of May. Dan said that he was going to have to shut down until after the runoff, which would be from 3 to 4 weeks. I thought that this would be a good time to move on. I wanted something with more of a future to it, and perhaps more social life attached to it. I didn't know just how I was going to break the news to Dan that I was leaving. I didn't want to make up any alibi. I had always told him the truth. It was on a Sunday morning as I recall. I drove up to the Taylors' residence to tell Dan and Laura goodbye, and to say I was going to Portland for a while. Dan asked me to come back for the fall low-water mining, and as with all other good people I had met along life's path whom I didn't want to say a firm goodbye to—I told him I would try.

# CHAPTER 17

## *Leave Salmon River Area*

I was five days on my way to Portland, Oregon. I visited some mining activities in eastern Oregon, which I didn't like, as the worked-out mines and geological formation showed that the mineral values lay in the shallow oxide zone and had been worked out. Knocking around in Portland, I ran across a fellow by the name of Dale Yarney whom I had served with in the army. Dale told me that he was working on the Portland Street Cars and liked the work very much; that he had met a lot of interesting people. I looked around a few days trying to find a business to get into, any kind of a business (except show business), but to no avail. As I didn't want to go back to mining right away, I would have to get a job to keep from going buggy. I thought of the job that Dale had on the cars. It would be interesting work with the public, and I would familiarize myself with Portland.

I looked up Dale Yarney, who took me down to the employment office of the Street Car Company, where I hired on. It was at a time when the company was changing over from a 2-man operated car to a 1-man car. Where there had been a motorman to operate the car and a conductor to collect the fare, now one man did both. This meant that I had to break in for both jobs, which I did in a few days. I was assigned to the Piedmont car barns. In my two and a half years with the street cars, I can only recall a couple of instances that were out of the ordinary.

One of these was soon after I was okayed as a motorman. I was assigned a 2-car train on the St. Johns run, which had both a motorman and a conductor. We had just left the car barns headed for St. Johns with no passengers. Going north on

Greeley Street, which is downgrade, I opened up the controls and was traveling about 60 miles an hour when I suddenly realized there was a turn off Greeley onto Lombard. I put on the brakes, but hardly had time or distance enough to make the curve, so I put all controls in reverse, with the result that the front car was filled with smoke and flames. We made the curve, but I never knew how.

The conductor, who was an old-timer, came up in front and said, "Son, do you always make that corner like that?" I replied this was the first time I had made it like that and it would be the last time. I had the St. Johns run many times after this, but always remembered the downgrade on Greeley Street. I liked the run as it had much open country between the residences of Portland and the residences of St. Johns. Also there was less traffic and more time to visit with passengers who came up front. And the layover at the St. Johns terminal was longer than others, which gave us more time to visit.

I also recall an incident when I was the conductor. It was on what we call a "tripper," a single car with both motorman and conductor, operated to relieve the regular cars in peakload times, especially in the mornings. A friend of mine, Pete Becker, was the motorman. We had completed the morning run and were headed for the car barns going out Union Avenue. As we approached Alberta Street, where the track continued on Union Avenue and also turned east onto Alberta, the car was traveling at a fast speed. I wondered how Pete could know that the switch was closed. If it was open we were in deep trouble at the rate we were going. The next thing I knew we were out in a vacant lot with the car on its side. As I reconstruct the accident, when the car hit the open switch, it jumped the track, hit the curb, turned on its side, and skidded out into the vacant lot. I asked Pete later what he was thinking about. He said that he didn't get a stop bell from me, and he forgot about the switch. Fortunately, there were no passengers in the car, and the good Lord had his arms around Pete and me.

I met and made many friends in the two and a half years I spent on the cars, both with passengers whom I contacted and with employees I worked with on the cars and in the car barns. One, Fred Reed, became a life-long friends of mine and played an important part in my life in a later mining adventure. While I enjoyed meeting and making friends with people while on the cars, it was a vocation that I could not see a desirable future in. I think that when people lose interest in their work, they are doing their employer and themselves an injustice to continue their employment. I began to look around for something else to do or some place to go.

In the early fall of 1925, after leaving the cars, I opened a real estate office in the old Dekum Building at S.W. 3rd and Washington Street. I enjoyed good business for several months until a bad winter set in. I was alone in the office with the exception of a couple of fellows who worked part-time. Real estate at that time was not moving very well. I got into it mostly to try and find some kind of investment, such as putting out mortgage money, but after I viewed some property that bankers turned down for a loan—which I thought would be a safe investment— I began seriously to wonder if I knew enough about property values to go very far in the property loan business.

Some time after the first of the year, in 1926, I was listing property of Robert Hobbs for sale when I noticed a mining picture on his desk. I asked him if he had done any mining. He replied that he had. I asked him in what part of the country, and when he replied Idaho, I became interested. He became better known to me later on as Bob. It happened that Bob was also a policeman. He told me that he had been given a leave of absence the last few summers to work the placer property that his father had left him several years previously. As soon as I had completed the listing of his property for sale, I asked him to come into the office and we would talk mining. After two and a half years of uninteresting street-car work and a few months sitting in an office, I was ready for something with a little more excitement in it.

## Leave Salmon River Area

The winter dragged on, and the real estate business got worse. Bob came into the office once in a while as he was on the the Portland Vice Squad and didn't have a regular beat. He showed me some pictures of his placer property on Grimes Creek, about 20 miles north of Idaho City on the north edge of the Boise Basin; this had been one of the richest gold-mining districts in Idaho. He told me that the only experience he had had in placer mining was on the two claims that his father left him. In the several months during the last two summers that he had spent working his claims, he had only made expenses. Looking at the pictures he showed me, I could see why. He was shoveling gravel from a hillside into sluice boxes when he should have been using a giant in hydraulic mining. I told him that I would like to see his property and also the Boise Basin, which I had heard a lot about but had never visited.

## CHAPTER 18

## *Gold Mining, Boise Basin, Idaho*

It was then the first of March and Bob said that we could not get into the property until the middle of the month, at which time there might be some snow on the hillsides, but the creek bed would be clean. I told him that it was the hillsides I wanted to see, so we waited until the latter part of March to make the trip over there. I had graduated from the T-model Ford to a Chrysler sedan—that is, it was called a sedan but it had side curtains. We drove from Portland to Boise in one day and half a night. It was a long, rough drive in those days, with much of the highway—or just plain road—not paved.

We got into Boise late, and tired from our continued drive from Portland. When we told people that we had driven from Portland in one day, they looked at us as if they thought we were crazy. The next morning we drove over the crookedest 40 miles of road I think there is in Idaho, arriving in Idaho City with placer mines all around. It looked as though we were in a mining country. We were now only 20 miles from Bob's placer claims. We had our bedrolls and enough groceries to last a couple of days.

We arrived at Bob's cabin just about dusk, too late to look the place over, but I took several pans around the cabin and I got a few colors. The creek bed had been worked by Bob's father and others who owned the ground with him. Later, Bob's father purchased the claims from his partners, who thought that the claims were worked out. Fortunately, one of the claims ran up an incline, or kind of hillside, about 300 feet, or half the width of the claim, with a bench about half way up—an ideal piece of ground for hydraulic mining. I was anxious for the following day to arrive so I could look the claims over and also the country.

We were awakened the next morning by some noise up the creek just above our cabin. After breakfast, we investigated and found some miners installing sluice boxes near the creek on some property that joined Bob's claims. We were surprised to see this, as the creek had been worked out. We went up to where the men were working, and found out they were completing a hydraulic set-up that they had started the previous summer after Bob had left. Bob knew one of the men. He has tried to lease Bob's claims a year earlier, but he wanted to give Bob only 5% royalty (gross, which most all royalty is) with the lessor keeping the large nuggets. Now, I thought to myself, I know what I will have to come up with to get a lease on Bob's claims.

We went back to the cabin and got our gold pans, picks, and shovels, and started to pan the side hill slope of one of the claims. We started at the creek bed and panned up the slope about 300 feet, which was the rim of the creek and also the outside edge of Bob's claim. About 20 per cent of the time we got a good showing of gold but very little fine gold. Most of it was coarse, with occasionally a fair-sized nugget. Our panning showed that the solid formation was covered with overburden at various depths. There was no place that seemed richer than others, and there was no confined pay streak, which is often found in other placer-mining districts. It was somewhat different from the minieralization in the central north part of the state.

The next day I looked the two claims over while Bob did some fishing. He had rather fish than dig gold, and there were a lot of fish to catch; but as I recall, it was a little early to be legal. Only one of the claims would be workable that had a gradual sloping bank or incline from the creek to the formation rim. The other claim had a rock formation coming down to the creek bed on both sides.

Now, as I found out where the gold was and what part of the claims was workable, I began to look for water. I visited the fellows who had the hydraulic operation beyond Bob's claims, and they were taking the water out of Grimes Creek 4 miles above their workings and bringing it down to their ground in a wooden flume. This is not only expensive, but time consuming. I had quite a talk with the man in charge of this operation. He said he had a lease on the ground. I got some valuable information from him regarding the type of bedrock, the amount of overburden, and even the amount of recoverable gold. He was a nice fellow, and I found out later he was also named Bob; the last name was Burns.

Bob (who had been fishing) and I arrived at the cabin about the same time. It was nearly dusk. He had a nice string of trout and I had some nice samples of gold, but his results looked better than mine because I was hungry. Bob asked me what I thought of the claims. I replied that one could be worked and that it had a good gold showing, but there was a water problem. I asked him where he intended to get his water. He replied that he thought it could be taken out of Grimes Creek above where Burns got his water. I told him that this might be feasible, but 5 miles is a long way to bring water in a wooden flume. Besides, the expense and time would be a factor. This Bob agreed.

He wanted to go back to Portland the third day, but I had an idea about the water that I wanted to check into, which I never mentioned to Bob. The idea was to siphon the water out of a small stream near Grimes Creek. I took my surveying instrument and walked over the rim of Grimes Creek 300 feet from the creek bed, then upstream along the rim about 1,000 feet, then dropped down 200 feet into a small creek that had quite a bit of water. My instrument showed that from the small creek to the lower end of Bob's one placer claim, a distance of 3,200 feet, there was a 380-foot drop. This was after siphoning the water out of the small creek, over the rim, and down into Grimes Creek. I was amazed when I figured out what could be done in this situation. I had worked it out on a small scale once before. I got the idea many years ago from an irrigation project in Arizona.

I returned to the cabin in the early afternoon and did some heavy figuring. It was just a calculated guess of what the ground would yield. From my sampling and information I got from Burns, I figured the value would be around 40 to 60 cents a yard for everything that went through the sluice boxes, which would be all material from the surface to bedrock—rich ground for a hydraulic operation.

Bob was wondering what all my figuring was about. I told him that I had worked out something that would surprise him, that I could bring water to his claims by siphon for about one-tenth of what it would cost by wooden flume, and in one-tenth the time. I told him that I wanted a lease on the one claim that could be worked, which would give me workable ground of 300 feet wide by 1,500 feet long. I knew what Bob had already turned down on a lease, so I told him that I would give him 10% gross royalty, and we would divide the nuggets, and the coarse and fine gold in proportion to the royalty of one to nine. This pleased him. He suggested that we go back to Portland and draw up a lease. He had already over-stayed his leave from the Police Department. I quickly put up location notices for two claims along the route that I was going to run the hose, and also on the little creek where I was going to take the water.

We took three days going back to Portland, driving only to Boise the first day after getting a late start from the cabin. Back in Portland we drew up a lease. I closed up my real estate office and traded the Chrysler in on a Dodge pickup. I had figured that I would need 3,200 feet of 4-inch hose, which would give me drop, and water force enough, to operate a 2-inch giant, and in places on the claim two 2-inch giants. In addition to the hose and giants, I would need giant holders, or stands, sluice boxes and riffles; then I would be in business. As I wanted about 500 feet of new hose near the giants where the pressure would be the greatest, I purchased it in Portland. With this and some other supplies I headed for Boise, where I wanted to find out how much used equipment I could pick up.

In Boise I was surprised to find so much used equipment for sale, as well as so many "used miners" wanting work. I put an ad in the local paper for both, and needed a secretary to answer the replies. I was fortunate in hiring a couple of miners who had worked in the Boise Basin and knew mining equipment and whee to find it, other than from the dealers in Boise. We soon located 2,700 feet of 4-inch hose, a 2-inch giant with stand, and some heavy iron grids to eliminate large rocks and boulders from the sluice boxes, but could locate only 50 feet of sluice boxes that were good enough to set up. We then secured enough lumber in Boise to build another 50 feet of sluice boxes and riffles for them. First we set up the 3,200 feet of siphon hose and were very happy when it worked like a charm. I was even surprised. However, we decided to use only one giant to give us more water force. It was so powerful at the end of the hose that it would knock a person down.

About the middle of May, 12 days after the two miners and I left Boise, we had the giant going and gravel being washed through the sluice boxes at a cost at that time of $4,250. From here on, I spared no expense in putting the gravel through the sluice boxes. I saw that I could use two more men to move rock and boulders and also keep the sluice boxes lined up and tailings shoveled away, so I went into Boise and got two more miners and an old fellow for cook. We were really moving the gravel, about three times as much as Burns was up the creek from us, with three times as many men.

I had the show place of Boise Basin. Miners came from all over Idaho to see it. I was told that only one siphon operation similar to mine was operating in the state, and it was not too successful because of tailing trouble. I had ideal ground for this type of operation. The entire 300 by 1,500 feet had a gradual slope to the creek bed, where we rolled the large rocks and boulders, and also provided a space for the tailings. As we started at the

## Gold Mining, Boise Basin, Idaho

bottom and worked up the incline or slope, we never ran out of tailing space, which is a miner's dream.

A man would work the giant only an hour and then be relieved by one of the other men, whose place he would take. This way a man would be on the giant only a little over 2 hours during the 10-hour day we worked, which was about all the daylight we had at this time of year. I did all the panning of the concentrates from the riffles, from which we retrieved about 300 pounds every other day. After each pan-out, or cleanup, I would have two of the men sign the weight slip giving the amount of gold recovered. This was for two reasons: one was so Bob would know I was honest with him, and the other one was in case we got robbed. Bob would come over every ten days to collect his royalty of 10% gross of the cleanup, which usually ran from 300 to 400 ounces for the 10-days' run. About every other time Bob came over, I would meet him in Boise to save him the extra 60-mile drive. It also gave me a chance to deposit my gold.

I had the concentrates assayed, but unlike the Salmon River concentrates, they carried very little value and no gems at all. The first few months we did a lot of work. We moved more ground and washed more gravel than any operation in the Boise Basin. The water had been plentiful and we had good pressure. We had worked the lower 200 feet of the claim where we had the best water pressure and where the best values were. As we got to the upper 100 feet of the claim, we lost some water pressure, and the values were not so good. About this time one of the men got sick and another one had to go home, so my crew was cut in half. I spent much of my time looking for another piece of hydraulic ground like I had, but no luck. About every miner in the Boise Basin was looking for the same thing. There were several other siphon projects started up in the Boise Basin during the summer, but very few were successful. Many things had to be just right to have the ideal siphon operation that I had.

As we got higher up the incline on the claim, the gold got finer and there was less of it. By the first of October I was cleaning up every 15 days and getting only 60 ounces of gold—4 ounces a day—which would hardly pay me to operate. Pure, refined gold was $20.67 per ounce, but the gold that we were getting, like most placer gold, was so alloyed that we got only $16 or $17 an ounce for it. After I paid Bob the royalty and wages to the 3 hired men, I was about breaking even, yet it had been a profitable and exciting venture for me. For the 6 months that we operated with the one giant, we had taken out over 4,500 ounces of gold, valued at close to $74,000, at the price of gold at that time. Today, at the world market price of gold, it would be worth over $810,000.

Soon after the middle of October, I closed the operation, selling the sluice boxes and a few other supplies to Bob Burns. His property did not lie right to use my siphon set-up. I stored the hose and giants in Idaho City, hoping that some day I would find another bonanza in the state. In addition to taking a large amount of gold with me out of Idaho, I left a memory with the old-timers, and a history for the future generation about the stranger that came into the Boise Basin with a screwy idea and left with a fortune. During the 7 months I had been in Boise Basin I had come to like it and like the people whom I met there, but it held no future for me now, so I would move on—to where the good Lord only knew. I even stayed an extra day in Idaho City, and for what I don't know.

## CHAPTER 19

## *Joined the Portland Police Department*

The following day I headed toward Portland, hoping that I would find something interesting before I got there. I stopped a day each in Baker and John Day, but I found nothing new since my visit to these places several years earlier. So, I drove on to Portland. In the next few days I visited my good friends of the street-car days, Fred Reed and Dale Yarney. Fred had had a serious accident and had been in the hospital for some time. Dale was still on the cars, but getting ready to leave.

After a week in Portland and a visit to Vancouver, Washington, I got restless and began to figure on some other place to go. I had traded the Dodge pickup in on a new Packard, which was in a higher class than most cars in those days and was a wonderful machine. It was far ahead of any car I had ever owned or ridden in. I had decided to drive down through California on my way to Phoenix, Arizona, to visit my folks and enjoy some of the fine weather they have down there. However, I made one mistake: I decided to pay Bob Hobbs a visit before I left.

When I arrived at Bob's home, he asked, "Where have you been?" He had been trying to get in touch with me for several days. I asked him what he had, another gold mine? He replied no, but something more interesting—"I want to make a policeman out of you." I asked, very astonished, "Why me?" Bob explained that 10 new policemen would be put on the force, and the examination was going to be held within two weeks. Then he gave me a sales talk about how interesting the work was, and what a chance for advancement there was in law enforcement. He said that not all policemen wore uniforms, that men in the detective division, special police, the vice squad, and special investigators did not. For further inducement he explained that the work was civil service, which was non-political. Because I was about ready to settle down to something steady, I told Bob that I would give it a try.

For the next two weeks I studies the questions that Bob thought would be asked at the examination. I had talked to people I knew regarding police work, and they all seemed to thing that it would be a good vocation. By the time the examination was held I was enthusiastic about being a policeman. There were supposed to be about 25 men taking the examination for 10 jobs that were to be filled. We were told that there would be a written examination, a strict physical examination, and a requirement to run 100 yards in 10 seconds. The last two tests were right down my alley, as I had been training all summer for them.

The examination was held in the old Civic Auditorium. Instead of there being 25 taking the examination, about 40 showed up. Most of the men were tense and some afraid that they would not pass the examination. I wanted to pass, but I wasn't losing any sleep over it. When the examination was over, I figured that I had passed. One can tell pretty well if he has the right answers. I was sure I had passed the physical, and knew that I had made the 100 yards in 10 seconds. A few days passed, though, and I began to wonder if I was going south or going to be a policeman. Then I received a notice that I had passed the examination and was to appear at the Police Station at S.W. 2nd and Oak Street on December 20, 1926, to be sworn in as a patrolman for the City of Portland, Oregon.

I was very proud of being a policeman. At that time they were called the City's Finest. There were about 300 men on the force when I went on. My first assignment was to the Record Bureau commanded by Lt. Harry Niles. (Note: I will hereafter use assumed names when referring to some individuals, except those mentioned in news clippings in this story.) I liked Harry Niles from the start. He was from my home state of Oklahoma. He was a very capable officer, and as honest as they come. I found out something about the operation of the Police Bureau while in the Record Bureau, as all the officers' reports came to the Bureau to be filed. I had worked in the Record Bureau about 6 months when an order came through transferring me to the Vice Squad. Both Lt. Niles and I were very much disappointed.

# CHAPTER 20

## *On the Vice Squad*

Bob Hobbs, who was on the Vice Squad, was working on the day shift. New on the job, I was put on the night shift. I asked Bob what I was getting into, but he didn't want to talk about the job, other than to say I would be assigned a partner or put on a squad; then I would learn what it was all about. I was assigned to what was called the "Raiders Squad" by men in the department. It was headed by a young, tough Irish fellow by the name of Casey O'Hara. He not only put fear in the underworld, but he put fear in the men who worked under him. He had everyone understand that he was "head of the squad." There were six of us in the Raiders Squad.

What made the Vice Squad work so "hot" and stand out as different from other police duty was that we were in the Prohibition period. It was illegal for a person to have in his possession, transport, or sell any intoxicating liquors, and, of course, all the money made in this kind of traffic would be made by the underworld, which meant a bigger, prosperous, and more violent underworld. Our duty, or I might say purpose and authority handed down from "higher ups," was to serve search warrants (obtained by plainclothes officers) on places selling whiskey, wine, and beer; on those operating stills and brewing beer and wine; also to raid gambling places and keep "street walkers" off the street so the sporting houses (Tenderloin district) could make enough money to "pay off." There was crime in Portland, but it was regulated. We didn't have a Chicago, New York, or Detroit.

The enclosed news clippings will give some idea of my work and activity during the three years I was on the Portland Vice Squad. However, I will mention briefly the different crimes we

## On the Vice Squad 181

were contending with. If I described in detail all my activity while on the Vice Squad, it would take more than this book to cover it. Prohibition itself was a problem, and it also created problems in other law enforcement.

This law, Prohibition, that made it a crime to possess whiskey, wine, and beer, was and will always be the most unfair, the most unpopular, and craziest law that the legislators ever enacted in Congress. I was in the position to know that the "so-called higher ups" got their liquor—and most of the time free—while the ordinary citizen got arrested, tried for a crime, and if convicted paid a fine or got a jail sentence—while someone else was sitting up in his office drinking confiscated whiskey. I still have a feeling of guilt for things that I was ordered to do while on the Vice Squad. I recall one instance that I was ordered to take some whiskey to a City Commissioner who had a summer home near Mt. Hood. I went to the Police Station and loaded my car with 11 quarts of bonded Scotch Whiskey and headed for Mt. Hood. Since I would be going the wrong way for an alibi, I kept my eyes peeled for Federal Agents.

As I left the station, I passed a Federal Agent who asked, "Where are you going, Marsh?" and I replied, "To set a little bait," (give whiskey to informers). This was just in case he knew I had the whiskey. Everything went well until I came to a turn in the old Mt. Hood Highway at Cherryville, when one of my rear tires blew, and getting the jack out of my car I broke a quart of Scotch. I had to do something, and do it fast, as a Federal Agent can smell Scotch a mile. I packed the 10 quarts of Scotch up a hillside and hid them under logs, brush, or anything I could find to conceal them. I fixed my tire and drove down to Alder Creek, a few miles away and waited until after dark to go back for the Scotch. On my return, I could find only 8 quarts. The other 2 quarts are probably still there and should now be good, aged Scotch. After I delivered the 8 quarts, I said to myself, "This is the last time I am going to act as a free bootlegger and a law violator at the same time." I made no more trips to Mt. Hood with liquor, but I still was obligated to hand out liquor to the big boys.

I had seen the law violated so much around the City Hall and by high-ranking officers at the Police Station that I took it for granted as a way of life. The higher authorities acted as if they were above obeying the Prohibition laws, and seemed to thing that the Vice Squad officers should accept the fact that they were. I have delivered many cases of liquor (a few quarts at a time) to the City Hall, whiskey that I took on raids with search warrants—otherwise confiscated and stored in the Police Station storeroom. It was always gone soon after the trial—and sometimes there was not enough liquor left for evidence. It was disheartening to go out there and enforce the law by arresting and jailing people for possession of whiskey which I took away from them, then find it was drunk by the City Hall crowd and their friends. Surprisingly enough, as a result of my disagreeing on how the Vice Squad was run, I was appointed commander of the squad, and at the same time was in charge of the Mayor's secret police. (The newspaper clippings at the conclusion of the Vice Squad story, under the heading of "MARSH GETS JOB," will explain this.)

No doubt you have heard that people cry "frame-up" or "false arrest" after they have been arrested. In my 20 years of police work, I know of only one "frame-up," or "entrapment" (also illegal according to the law). There was a small Taxi Cab Company owned and operated by a Floyd McReynolds on S.W. Washington Street. This cab company also handled a little illegal liquor. Someone got a search warrant out for the company. My squad and I served the warrant and found some moonshine in the company office. We had no sooner reported back to the Station than Capt. Irwin, in charge of the Traffic Department, sent an officer by the name of Brown to McReynolds' office and pulled his Cab license off the wall, putting McReynolds out of business as of that moment. The City Council revoked McReynolds' license at their next meeting.

In about three weeks, McReynolds' case came before a jury trial. I don't recall whether it was because someone at the Station drank the evidence or if it was one of those unpredictable jury trials, but the jury was out only about 2 minutes before brining in a verdict of not guilty. This really put McReynolds in the driver's seat. He not only would get paid for loss of business, but he had a juicy damage suit against Capt. Irwin, the City Council, and the multi-million-dollar City of Portland. The one mostly to blame was Capt. Irwin, who started the whole mess by pulling McReynolds' license. My men working under me and myself were in the clear, as we only served a warrant that someone else swore to.

Meantime, I had been transferred out of the Vice Squad. Shortly after the transfer, Capt. Irwin came to me and said, "Marsh, you have got to get McReynolds for me." He further stated, that he had been to the chief and also the City Hall, and that I was going to be put on special duty to do the job. I told the Captain that I was now out of the Vice Squad and didn't want any part of it any more. I then turned and walked away. I was at the time working out of the St. Johns Precinct. When I came to work that evening I had a note in my box from the Chief of Police asking me to report to his office.

The next morning I was in Chief Jenkins' office. I had a great deal of respect for Leon Jenkins. I think that he was a very honest Chief, and if he ever did anything out of line, it was because it was forced on him by City Hall. Chief Jenkins had a very different approach from Capt. Irwin. When I came into his office he said, "Floyd, sit down. I want to talk to you." Then he passed a box of cigars over to me and invited me to have one. He said, "I am in a spot. That fool Capt. Irwin pulled a boner which also put the city in a spot, and I wish you would help us out." But he was quick to say,

I don't want you to do anything illegal. We know that McReynolds is still transporting liquor, but he is so clever that we can't get him, yet we think that with your know-how and connections with the liquor element that you can."

The Chief's approach for me to do the job was far different than I had expected. I was ready to help now. When I came into the office, I was ready to turn in my badge. Now I asked the Chief what he wanted me to do. He replied that we had to get McReynolds convicted of a crime, preferably a liquor charge, and that we not only had to get his company on a criminal conviction, but we would have to get McReynolds himself personally involved. The Chief asked me if I thought that I could do the job. I replied, not myself personally, but I could get men that would do anything except commit murder.

I could tell from talking to the Chief that the City Council was really worried, and I would have let them worry for a while if it had not been for the Chief; but I knew everything would come down on his head. The Chief told me that I could have whatever I needed in money and men to do the job. I thanked him for the confidence that he put in me. I was starting to leave his office when he asked, "What about the money for expenses on the job?" I laughed and replied, "That sounds too much like Chicago," and added that the expense wouldn't be much and that I would turn in the expense account when I was through.

I went to work on the job immediately. I called a couple of special plainclothes officers by the names of Roy Cox and John Seeley. They knew all the tricks. I told them the story and also told them that McReynolds had to be personally involved. Cox commented that this would take some figuring, but that they could do it. This fellow Cox should have been named "Fox." He was the cleverest operator I have ever known. He said that he knew how McReynolds worked his cabs and drivers, and that he and Seeley would have him in a few days.

Cox also said that he and Seeley needed a place to work out of, near 6th and Hall. I told them that they could use my apartment in the Nixon Apartments at Hall and Broadway. It was just before midnight on a Saturday night that Cox, Seeley, and myself went up to my apartment. After we were there a short while, Cox brought in another man whom I had never

## On the Vice Squad 185

met. After a few phone calls, the two special officers and the stranger hurriedly left. In about 20 minutes I received a phone call from Cox. He said that he was at the Police Station and that they had arrested McReynolds with a gallon of moonshine in his cab. I could hardly believe what I was being told. I wondered how they ever got McReynolds in a cab with a gallon of moonshine.

I went down to the station immediately, and sure enough on the docket were the words, "Floyd McReynolds arrested for transporting and possession on intoxicating liquor." Of course, I wanted to know how this was all brought about, so I had Cox give me the whole story. And this is the first time it has been told in almost 45 years. Cox said that he set McReynolds up this way. He knew McReynolds had only 2 drivers, and that McReynolds himself always took the third call, so what they were doing in my apartment was putting in two calls to McReynolds' office for a cab, which were false calls to get the cabs out.

Cox knew that now McReynolds would take the next call, so he immediately put in a call to 6th and Hall, where there was a well-known bootlegging place operated by Sadie Martin. McReynolds knew this place and what to expect there. It was a good-paying business, taking customers to and from the place. Cox had a person planted there with a gallon of moonshine, to take McReynolds' cab, which he did, while Cox and Seeley were nearby in a special police car. When McReynolds pulled out with his passenger (planted by Cox), the two special officers ran him into the curb. At the same time the special passenger jumped out of the cab on the opposite side of the police car and ran in between two buildings leaving the gallon of moonshine in the cab. When the two special officers walked up to the cab, McReynolds was surprised to find himself and a gallon of moonshine in the cab alone.

In a way my conscience was clear; I did not do the planning. But I felt kind of guilty in knowing that some kind of trickery was going on. This case proves how unfair a jury trial can be. In McReynolds's first trial, when he was guilty beyond a doubt, the jury acquitted him in two minutes, and in the second trial he was innocent by law, according to arrest procedure, while he was judged guilty by a jury. The law says that a criminal can be trapped, but not entrapped. McReynolds was entrapped and it was wrong. I was in the Chief's office the next morning and told him that I wanted a month's leave of absence, which I was granted. However, I did not leave to get out of testifying in the case, as I did not have an actual part in the arrest. Now after 45 years I still believe that McReynolds was entrapped. While I did not approve of the way we saved the City of Portland, the City Council, and many others, I also never approved of Prohibition.

Prohibition was not only an unjust law, but the way it was enforced on some people was a crime—for example, on the Italian people. It is their way of life to have wine with their meals, and a large number of families make wine and store it in their basement for home use. I have seen officers go into basements of these homes with sledge hammers and axes and smash barrels of wine and let it run down the drain, then take these poor people to court. Many of them didn't have the money to pay their fines, as this was during the depression years. They were then sent to jail, often leaving a large family at home, while the big rum-runner who was making a fortune was handing out protection money and bonded whiskey to the authorities, and continuing in business.

The poor working class of the Italian people, unable to pay off the authorities, were the ones arrested and prosecuted. This gave the publicity that showed Prohibition was being enforced. Here is an instance that is hard to believe: I was given a search warrant to serve on the residence of an Italian widow with three small children. In the basement I found a 10-gallon keg of wine she had made from grapes grown in her backyard. I let the widow stay home on her recognizance to appear in court the following day. Meantime, I received a call from her stating that one of her children was sick and that she would be unable to appear in court on this particular day. When the widow's case was called, I explained to the Court the circumstances, and the judge remarked that he would like to put the officer (meaning me) in jail for failing to enforce the Prohibition laws. Such instances hastened my departure from the Vice Squad and the enforcement of Prohibition.

Portland was a central distribution point for bonded liquor coming in from Canada as well as moonshine made in the woods nearby. There were 10 bonded whiskey dealers in Portland that I knew of, and there were at least 20 large and small stills being operated in Portland and vicinity. Also, there were at least 100 speakeasies (drinking places) where whiskey was sold by the gallon, bottle, and jigger (to be drunk there). There were also about 100 beer and wine parlors. About three-fourths of the above paid "hush money" protection in order to operate. At least $100,000 a month was paid out in protection money to authorities of Multnomah County and the City of Portland. This was in addition to cases of bonded whiskey and gallons of moonshine handed out, not only to City and County authorities, but to people of high social standing who could do a favor for a bootlegger or rum-runner in trouble.

"Gambling" was second in revenue to the underworld. While Prohibition had nothing to do with gambling directly, the money produced because of prohibition was funneled into the gambling racket. In the late 1920's there were about 40 gambling places operating in Portland. About two-thirds of these were operated by Chinese. Most all of them paid off. Some of them would try to sneak (not pay protection money), but their places would be raided and "busted up," and they soon got in line. There were about 50 lottery (referred to as Chinese lottery) ticket-marking places in Portland (the same as Keno now played in Nevada). These tickets were ususally played for 10 cents in those days, but ticket marketing was a big business. A great deal of money was made by the Chinese. They paid the man on the beat $10 per month, and the City Hall got theirs through two plainclothesmen who hung around the Station—who were there also to get their cut from the operation of other vice in the city.

The gambling pay-off in Portland was about $50,000 a month. The white men were poor "protection payers," but the Chinese were good payers. They were clever people; they make money in about everything they get into. One day a white gambling operator asked me why the Chinese gambling operators got so much "play" in their joints, and I told him that the white gamblers took 30 per cent of every dollar that went across their tables, while the Chinese were satisfied with 20 per cent. And I further told him, "When you fellows are raided, you make your customers pay their way, while the Chinese take care of their customers. Whether the Chinese are in a legal or illegal business, they incorporate and stick together, be it a gambling joint or a Chinese restaurant. They have one object in business, and that is to make money."

A "Tenderloin District" is one thing that goes with a boomtown or place where there is money; it is where girls of "easy virtue" abound. In the 1920's, when Portland was a boomtown from lumbering and logging, loggers came into town looking for action for the big money they made in the camps. And when they came to town, they came to spend money. As the 1930's approached, things seemed to slow down, and during the depression years the action in Portland lost steam. The boys who had come to Portland for a good time, now passed Portland up for other places that had more action. Women politicians killed Portland as a good-time town.

At one time there were 35 "sporting houses" with madams, and from 2 to 6 girls in each house. The city had a strict regulation on these houses. The girls were required to take a physical every so often, and the health certificate had to be displayed on the wall of the girl's room. Also, each house was required to take a pinch (arrest) every so often, in lieu of a license, and the resulting fine money would go into the City Treasury. In addition to this, each house paid some policemen on the beat from $5 to $10 each month, according to the girls they had. The two gentlemen that hung around the Police Station in civilian clothes collected for the City Hall. Over all, the "Tenderloin

## On the Vice Squad

District" paid about $20,000 a month for protection, in addition to the legal pinch they took every so often.

When a new madam came into town and opened up a new place, or bought out an established one, a "legitimate arrest" was always made. A new man from the Vice Squad would go to the house and get evidence for the arrest and conviction. Here is how the evidence was obtained: The new man, who posed as a "trick," would be put in a room and brought a girl by the madam. The girls would give him a price, which would be all the evidence necessary. I think that the City Statute defines this as, "one offering themselves for immoral purpose for a consideration." The evidence against the madam would be "bringing two persons together for immoral purpose."

When things got tough in the late 1920's, the madams were having a hard time making expenses. The girls were turning tricks for $1. It was sad to see beautiful young girls working in these houses. I talked to many of them. They were often from broken homes; others got started off in life on the wrong road, helped along by a slick-talking, smartly-dressed pimp. The depression had its effect on the underworld; Portland was no more a boomtown, where things happened that citizens of Portland would be shocked to know about.

Now, looking back on the activity of the Portland Vice Squad 45 years ago, some of its work was typical of the activity of the "Watergate" gang during the 1972 Presidential election. If I could remember clearly enough (and would dare to do so) to relate things that occurred in connection with the Vice Squad and how it was used for the benefit and convenience of the city authorities and political powers of Portland, it would not sound believable. I was on the Vice Squad and served as its leader during Portland's fabulous boom years. The work was interesting and exciting. I am glad I didn't miss it, but I would not want to go throuth that time again.

In concluding my experience on the Portland Vice Squad, I would like to say, in all fairness, that most of the men in the Portland Police Department were honest and efficient officers, and only a very few of them, as well as only a few City Hall officials, were corrupt—all of which fits into the category you can read about any day in the newspapers in any part of the country, counting the almost daily revelations of political and judicial corruptions that are being uncovered and prosecuted at all levels of government, from the policeman on the beat to the highest public officials of our land.

Following my experiences as head of the Portland Police Vice Squad, are some newspaper clippings, one of which states in bold letters,

"Marsh leaves for Arizona and will not be here to testify in Floyd McReynolds case." This is a typical case of how a newspaper can make a person look bad in order to get a little favorable news. I had no reason, no right, and no authority to testify in the McReynolds' case. You can see from my story that officers Roy Cox and John Seeley handled the whole thing. All the evidence I could give would be hearsay, which is not admissible in court. The newspapers had a hunch that I engineered the McReynolds' case but had no proof, and used my name because I had been in the limelight and my name would make better news.

As the McReynolds' case had been put over for some time (and I could not testify anyway), I decided to take a trip to Arixona for a few weeks before returning to my prowl-car beat. I was just about fed up with the Police Department and didn't know for sure whether I wanted any more of it or not. I told Chief Jenkins that I was ready to take my 30-day leave of absence, which I did, and left for Arizona.

Left: Floyd Marsh during his Vice Squad days.

Right: Floyd Marsh in Arizona after the McReynold case.

Floyd Marsh on the Portland Police Force in 1931.

## FRIDAY, SEPTEMBER 2, 1927.

## BEER RAID NETS MAN, 500 QUARTS

In one of the biggest hauls made in recent months by the vice squad of the police department, 500 quarts of beer were confiscated Thursday by Patrolmen Marsh and Cook and Federal Agents Green and Worden, late Thursday. The beer garden was located in a house at No. 232 North 15th street, alleged to be conducted by Charles Davis and his wife. The raid was conducted without search warrant.

Forty of the arrests were made on morals charges, 25 for possession of narcotics and 12 for gambling.

Total liquor confiscated during the month included 1601 pints of moonshine, 2026 quarts of beer, 87 pints of gin, 26 gallons of wine and 46 quarts of bonded whiskey. Three stills were taken 1787 gallons of mash and 3 automobiles were confiscated.

Narcotic raids netted 2000 grains of yenshee, 250 grains of opium and 6 opium smoking outfits.

## Patrolman Marsh Arrests Another Fighting Suspect

Patrolman Marsh, "stormy petrel" of the police vice squad, encountered another "tough one" Thursday when he arrested Tex Martin, 43, at the Amsden hotel, No. 268½ Third street.

Martin was approached in the hall of the hotel by Marsh, who asked to talk to the suspect a minute in his room. Martin said he would unlock the door. As he bent to insert the key, Martin turned and sent his right to the patrolman's jaw.

Marsh countered with a wood club to the head, and then, with the assistance of Patrolman Timm, was able to arrest Martin without further manhandling.

Charges of disorderly conduct and of possession of liquor were placed against Martin.

---

Some newspaper clippings from the Portland, Oregon, papers regarding the Author's activity while head of the Portland Police Vice Squad during the Prohibition days of 1927 and 1928.

**Author's Note:** The item, "Marsh Leaves for Arizona," implies misconduct of law enforcement on the part of Officer Marsh. However, the true facts of the McReynolds case are stated, beginning on page 183.

## MARSH GETS JOB

### Secret Police Head Also to Lead Vice Squad

Floyd Marsh, chief of the mayor's secret police, Monday also became squad leader of the police bureau vice division in a startling bureau shakeup affecting five other officers as well.

Chief of Police Jenkins declared that Marsh will still be answerable, as head of the mayor's so-called secret police, to Acting Mayor Pier, but that at the same time he will direct the bureau's raiding squad.

"He will hold both positions for the time being, anyway," said Chief Jenkins.

The surprise announcement directly controverts the declared city hall politics as it relates to the mayor's police.

That policy, the mayor and Hal White, his spokesman, have reiterated, is to employ the so-called secret police to check activities of bureau patrolmen, particularly those of the vice division.

# MARSH LEAVES FOR ARIZONA

## Policeman Will Not Be Here to Testify in His Case Against Taxi Man

Patrolman Floyd Marsh, erstwhile member of the police vice squad, who donned civilian clothes last Saturday night to engineer the second arrest of Floyd McReynolds on liquor charges, will not appear at the taxi proprietor's trial in municipal court Oct. 8, it became known Wednesday.

Marsh left for Phoenix, Ariz., at 10:15 p. m. Tuesday on his annual vacation, and is not scheduled to return until late this month.

He is generally recognized as the principal witness against McReynolds, and the city expected him to offer weighty testimony to refute the defendant's charge of frame-up.

### Tells of Injunction

Commenting on the injunction granted him Tuesday by Circuit Judge Tucker, restraining the city temporarily from interfering with his business, McReynolds declared he was confident his license to operate would be permanently restored.

He revealed that within two hours of his first arrest on Aug. 28, Traffic Officer Brown came to his offices at 4501½ Washington st. and ripped his licenses from the walls.

"I had not yet been tried," McReynolds said, "nor had the council given me a hearing. Brown had no more right to tear my licenses down at that time than he would have to shoot me. That incident, in itself, proved conclusively to me that the police department was out to 'get my skin'."

### Jury Acquits Him

A municipal court jury exonerated McReynolds subsequently after deliberating less than two minutes, although the city council in the meantime had ordered his license revoked. In that case McReynolds also charged he was framed.

Last Saturday night, the taxi man said, he received a mysterious call from Sixth and Hall sts.

"The party wanted me to drive over and get him, and that was unusual, because I never drive my cabs. Nevertheless, I went, and arriving there found a man carrying a large paper sack, waiting for me.

"I drove off with him, and within a few blocks a police car blocked my path. Here my passenger ducked out of the cab and disappeared into an alley, leaving the sack behind.

### Passenger Ignored

"I directed the officers' attention to my passenger, but they ignored him, and concerned themselves only with searching the car. They found the sack, of course, and in it was a gallon jug of moonshine.

"It was a frame-up—one of the most despicable ever attempted by police anywhere."

Police records disclose Marsh lives at Sixth and Hall sts., where McReynolds says his call originated.

---

# WOMAN DRINKS EVIDENCE

### Fainting Fit Staged for Purpose of Consuming Evidence.

A pint flask of whisky saved under great hazards as evidence from a raid staged by vice division workers on the residence of Mr. and Mrs. Israel Kohn, 185 East Fifteenth street, was almost consumed by Mrs. Kohn, who fainted in order to drink it up, the policemen reported. Despite her efforts, the officers saved a remnant of the pint as evidence to be used against Mr. and Mrs. Kohn, Israel Kohn, Jr., and Mike Miller, all charged with possession of liquor. Young Kohn was turned over to the juvenile authorities.

Israel Kohn Sr. poured out a gallon jug of moonshine whisky before he was stopped by Patrolman Marsh, who was in charge of the raid. He dumped all the liquor in the sink except one pint, which he gave to Israel Jr., who attempted to run from the house. He was collared by the patrolmen.

But not despairing of destroying the last pint of evidence, Mrs. Kohn fainted. Her husband and son said that the only way to revive her would be to give her some whisky. Patrolman Marsh risked part of the liquor to revive her, but when she asked for more he saw through the plot. The emergency physician was called, and reported her to be in excellent health.

## CHAPTER 21

### *Mining in Arizona*

While on the leave of absence in Arizona, I visited a number of mining projects. Most of them were very large copper mines with their own smelter, and what few small individually operated mines there were either sent their ore to the large company smelters or sold to an ore buyer. It looked as though it were hard for an individual to get in on the action.

Coming back to Portland, I reported for duty in the Police Department and was put to work on a prowl car out of the St. Johns precinct. The more I patrolled my district, the less I thought of the work. I had been back in Portland about a month when I met some people who owned an old copper mine 8 miles from Prescott, Arizona, on the White Spur road, which at that time was idle. I knew the location of the property quite well. My brother and I had hunted deer there several times. It was known as the old "Lucky Strike Mine." There were two 100-foot tunnels on the property and some shafts. Considerable work had been done on the property and several hundred tons of copper ore shipped to a smelter.

Knowing the history of copper mining in Arizona—that it usually increases in value with depth—I was interested in the old mine. After some dickering over the amount of royalties, I secured a lease on the property. I got another leave of absence from the Department, and with one of the owners of the property I again headed for Arizona, this time in a new Hupmobile. After three days of hard driving, we arrived at Prescott just before midnight. After a night's rest, we drove the 8 miles out to the Lucky Strike Mine. The mine had been shut down only 4 years, and the timber in the tunnels, shafts, and other works was in good shape. There was a large cookhouse and din-

## Mining in Arizona 195

ing hall, and 6 smaller buildings for men's quarters. At one time 20 men were employed at the Lucky Strike. After a few days of looking around and being shown all the lines and corners of the Lucky Strike property, Mr. John Hull, one of the owners who had come to Prescott with me, returned to Portland, and I proceeded to open up the old Lucky Strike Mine.

In Prescott I bought a new 1-ton truck and equipment enough to open up the mine. Because Prescott was in a mining district, I had no problem getting any kind of mining equipment needed. I started with only 4 miners to open up the mine, but later I had 8 miners and a cook on the payroll. There was one old miner by the name of Bill Beard who had a quartz prospect about a mile from the Lucky Strike. He had studied mining and geology at the School of Mines at Butte, Montana. He was my adviser and one of the finest old-timers I ever met. Bill and I looked the two tunnels over and decided not to open them up, as the ore we got out of them did not assay to be good shipping ore. Bill thought that there was better ore on the property, as there were 18 claims in the Lucky Strike group, and some of them had copper ore rich enough to ship.

The best prospect we found was up a little creek near the camp. The ledge was 5 feet wide and solid ground that didn't need timbering. We sank a shaft on the ledge and ran into ore 15 feet below the surave t hat assayed $115 a ton, with most of the values in copper. The other minerals were silver, lead, and zinc. On the 15-foot level we drifted both ways on the ledge. I employed more miners and began to ship ore to the Phelps-Dodge Smelter at Bisbee, Arizona. I shipped the ore out of Prescott by rail, which was quite expensive. The first carload of ore I shipped, that assayed $115 a ton in Prescott, netted me only $27.50 at the smelter. Of course, this was after the rail transportation and smelter charges were taken out, but I thought that this was way off. I got in touch with the smelter and asked them what had happened to values in the ore. I knew what the rail charges would be, and from what the smelter had charged for smeltering other ore, I should have at least $60 a ton net coming to me from the ore I sent them.

The buck was passed from one smelter official to another until it was the second day after my first call before I got someone to give me the cause of the low values. I was told that the compsote of the ore and complex of the minerals made the values hard to recover. In addition, there was penalty for the small amount of zinc, and due to the type of ore, a large amount of expensive flux had to be added. I didn't get much satisfaction from the smelter, other than they would try to give me a better return on the value of my ore. I soon got out two more cars of ore and sent them to Bisbee, with very little improvement in value over the first car. In the meantime I was contacted by an ore buyer in Prescott who told me he would buy my ore f.o.b. Prescott, saving me the shipping and smelter charges.

I asked him where he made his profit; he would have the expense of the smelter and transportation. He replied that he didn't ship the raw ore, that he ran the ore through a ball mill (reduction mill) at Prescott and shipped only the concentrates to the smelter, where the shipping and smelter charges were reduced about 80 per cent. This sounded good to me, so I hauled 10 ton of ore to his ball mill for a tryout, with the result that I received $53.25 net per ton for the ore, with only the expense of hauling the ore from the Lucky Strike to the ball mill about 9 miles.

We had shipped about 50 ton of ore to the ball mill when the values began to drop. Instead of the copper increasing in value with depth, the value decreased a little. We were now down 60 feet and a drift each way on the ledge 50 feet from the shaft, which meant that it would require some expensive machinery to continue operation where we were. Bill Beard said that he knew where there was a small gold vein on one of the claims on the Hassayampa River, where he thought the Hassayampa placer gold came from. After some time, Bill and I located the small gold ledge, which was partly covered by an old slide. After

## Mining in Arizona                                                    197

getting into the hillside about 10 feet, we found a rich 4-inch vein of free gold. It was small but it looked good. Crushing the quartz, we could pan a nice string of gold. This was on one of the Lucky Strike claims that was never worked, but some of the old-timers like Bill knew about it.

We took a ton of the ore to the buyer at Prescott. He said it would be ideal ore to recover the values from in the ball mill. He added that the free gold could be panned out of the residue which would be caught on the mineral concentrate tables; then the concentrates could be shipped to the smelter. This way, the gold could be recovered without running it through the smelter and taking the chance of someone going "south" with part of it. This ore had the advantage over the previous ore that we mined in that the silver and lead sulphides were in the form of galena, which is a good flux for smeltering, thereby reducing the smelter charges.

The 4-inch vein of gold quartz assayed $720 per ton, of which over $500 was in free gold. The ore buyer paid me $576 for a sample ton of ore, which was 80% of the value recovered; and he told me that he would pay me on this percentage for other ore delivered to his mill that had a large amount of recoverable free gold in it. Taking the ore out of this small vein was a slow process. We had only a 4-inch vein of ore in a 5-foot-wide tunnel to take it from, which meant for every ton of ore we retrieved from the 4-inch vein, we had to handle 14 tons of tunnel matter. However, the tunnel was easier and more convenient to mine than the shaft we had previously worked in. Also, waste disposal was easier.

We were hand-sorting from 3 to 4 ton of ore a day, which brought me a little better than $2,000 f.o.b. the ball mill at Prescott. This was the nearest thing to placer mining I knew of. We had worked the small gold vein a few days less than 5 weeks and had taken out over $50,000 in gold and concentrates when my good fortune began to run out. We had driven the tunnel back into the hillside out of the oxide zone into the sulphides and lost the gold values. And, of course, with the gold gone in a small vein like the one we were working on, you were out of business. We drifted another 20 feet in the tunnel following the vein but never picked up any more gold values, so we abandoned the little bonanza since we were getting deeper into the sulphides and were not likely to hit another oxide zone.

I let all the men go, with the exception of Bill Beard and another prospector-miner by the name of Joe Rilley. Then we three looked the 18 claims of the Lucky Strike Mining Company over thoroughly for about a week. There were several good copper deposits on the property, but I just couldn't get enthusiastic about copper the way I did when I first came to Prescott. After trying to find another gold deposit without success, we decided on St. Patrick's Day, March 17, 1930, to bid the old Lucky Strike Mine goodbye. After a few days in Phoenix and a visit with my mother and brothers, I headed north, back to Oregon.

Back in Portland the latter part of March, I had a couple of weeks left on my extended leave of absence from the Police Department, so I decided to visit my old friend, Bob Hobbs, but I was told that Bob got into some kind of a jam with the department and had moved to Boise, Idaho. As I wanted to go to Boise anyway, I got his address in the Idaho city and drove over there; but upon my arrival at the Boise address, I was informed that Bob had split up with his family and had joined the Merchant Marines. This was the last I ever heard of him.

While in Boise I inquired about placer mining in the state and learned that there was a lot of activity in the Boise Basin, which I would have liked to visit but didn't care for the drive. Back in Portland, I found waiting for me the unpleasant task of foreclosing on an apartment house that I had a mortgage on. After securing a manager to operate it, I reluctantly reported back for duty on the Portland Police force.

I was assigned duty in a prowl car at precinct No. 2, which was in the downtown area. This was a little better than being out in St. Johns. However, I still didn't like the work. I was put on the second night shift from 11 p.m. to 7 a.m. That was called the graveyard shift. There was very little action and no excitement at all in the work. For one like myself, who had been active and part of the action all my life, the work became increasingly uninteresting. I began to look for something more interesting, and I found it very shortly.

## CHAPTER 22

## *Building a Gold Dredge*

A canceled check I have shows that on January 20, 1932, I made an initial investment of $17,000 (a fortune at that time) in a gold dredge in California. That is, I went into partnership with a fellow by the name of Ed Chemmo to rebuild this dredge; a portion of it had been destroyed by fire several years previously. The hull and some of the machinery were in workable condition, but all the electric motors and controls needed replacement, in addition to the trommel screen and sluice troughs (to catch the gold). There was a great deal of this material readily available on the American and Feather rivers, which were old dredging areas in the vicinity of Marysville and Yuba City, a short distance from our operations.

The dredge we purchased, and were to rebuild, was located on the Trinity River near a little town by the name of Lewiston, 35 miles west of Redding, California. There were 240 acres in the tract of land covering one and a half miles of the Trinity River, and they belonged to Ed Chemmo. For many miles from Lewiston, both up and downstream on the Trinity River, there was continued placer mining. Six miles downstream from our operation, there was the Hook-and-Ladder Placer Mine, the largest hydraulic mine in the world, where the ground was so rich that a small town was moved to permit mining of the ground. About 8 miles upstream from us was the largest gold dredge ever built, The Esterbrook, which operated with 32 buckets on a conveyor line, each bucket holding 21 feet of material and dumping a bucket into the hopper of the dredge every 5 seconds. The Esterbrook was truly the king of placer mining. Several years before our appearance, the dredge had run into some cement gravel, and nothing works cement gravel. Since

## Building a Gold Dredge

cement hardens with age, the hardness of cement gravel which is several million years old is almost incredible. When the big dredge hit the cement gravel, it began to break up, and the owners shut it down to rust and decay in the wilderness of the Trinity Mountains. We were told that it cost a million dollars to set the dredge up, but it was too costly to dismantle and haul out of the rough country. However, it was said by the old-timers that the dredge amply paid for itself.

The Trinity was one of the richest gold-placer-yielding rivers in North America. It ranked alongside the American and Feather rivers in California, and the Yukon River in Canada and Alaska. I often thought what a "storehouse" of gold there must have been in the Trinity Mountains that the Trinity River ran through, and which is its source. The Trinity River has yielded millions of dollars worth of gold (at the old price of $20.67 per ounce) in its length of over 100 miles of placer mining. The entire area around Lewiston has always produced placer gold between Lewiston and Redding. There are several old mining camps, such as, Old Shasts, French Gulch, Whisky Creek, and many others that were at one time large-sized camps, but are now occupied by only a few snipers (gold panners) working in the various creeks. On my way to and from Redding I often picked these people up. I enjoyed talking to them. Some said they were doing well; others were just making enough for beans. However, on the average, most of them seemed to be making better than wages; that is, wages if one could get a job in those days. It was during the Depression in the early thirties.

We called our enterprise the Gold Bar Dredging Company, with only Ed Chemmo and myself in the company. Each of us put in $17,000 for an equal interest and each of us was issued 17 shares of stock at $1,000 value per share. We started with only 4 men and gradually added to the crew as the dredge advanced. We were fortunate in securing the services of a very capable dredge man and machinist by the name of Bob Setzer. He had been employed for many years as a dredge builder for the Yuba

Dredge Company and had built and operated his own gold dredge on the Trinity River about 50 miles below our operation. Bob and I made trips to Marysville and along the Feather River, where we obtained used parts from old dismantled dredges. Material we could not pick up used, we purchased from the Yuba Dredge Company in Yuba City. By the first of March we had the dredge looking good. However, there were controls, electric motors, and wiring, along with other expensive works that had to be done on the inside.

While we were purchasing material for the dredge at a very low price and had excellent labor at reasonable wages, I was very much surprised to find that we had run up against a problem that has ruined many enterprises—the lack of finances. Ed Chemmo was the treasurer of our company and wrote the checks. He lived about half the time in San Francisco and incurred expenses that I thought didn't belong with the building of the dredge. As I recall, it was on a weekend when Chemmo told me that there was not enough money in our bank account to pay the week's labor.

This was a shock to me. I couldn't imagine our spending $34,000 in 2 months with the way we were buying material. I suggested to Ed that we put in another $10,000 each, which should finish the dredge. This would make a total of $54,000 in the project. Ed told me when I went in with him on the dredge that it could be built for $34,000 or less. Ed and I then went over the books. There were a number of things that I didn't like about my partner's bookkeeping, in addition to some missing canceled checks. However, Ed finally came up with enough money to meet the week's payroll.

I had money to finish the dredge, but I wasn't going to build his equity up and let him go scot-free after taking me as he had. I immediately engaged an attorney and also an accountant in Redding to find out what I could do to save my investment. The attorney advised me to get control of our company if possible, and the accountant advised me to get the company books. This I knew would require a lengthy court action, by which time everything would be down the drain.

I had to figure out a fast and simple way to get control of our company. After talking with my attorney and accountant together, along with the information I got by looking over our books, I figured out a plan to pursue. I had spent the entire week in Redding in conference and running down illusive check that Chemmo had listed in his books. During the week I had $20,000 transferred to my Redding bank account. I was determined to finish the dredge, but not to give Ed Chemmo a free ride.

I arrived back at the dredge Friday afternoon. Saturday came and passed but no Ed Chemmo came with our checkbook to pay the men. This made me very angry. His disregard for me didn't bother me as much as his lack of concern for the men who worked for us. I told the men that they would be paid Monday for sure, and that the dredge would be finished; they could bet on that. The next morning I called Ed at his hotel in San Francisco and asked him to meet me the following day, Monday morning, at 10 a.m. in the district attorney's office in Redding and to bring all our company books. He wanted to know why I chose the district attorney's office. I replied that I thought it was as good a place as any to meet, and let it go at that. I wanted to give him something to sleep on during the night, so he would be easier to deal with the next day. I had no intention of doing anything in the district attorney's office except meet Ed there and go to my attorney's office next door.

Ed met me the following day at the appointed time in the district attorney's office. We then went next door to my attorney's office where Ed asked what this was all about. I asked him if we had any money in the bank. He replied no, that the company was broke. I said, "You know we have to raise some money and raise it today for this past week's wages." Chemmo remarked that all he had was stock in the Gold Bar Dredging Company. I am sure his idea at this time was that I would finance the finishing of the dredge to protect the money I had in it, but I had a different idea. I said that I was putting $10,000 in our company, and if he didn't have this amount to put in that he could sell some of his stock. He asked who would buy stock in our company. I told him that there was a man in Redding who would buy $10,000 worth of the stock. Ed thought that I was bluffing when he replied, "Produce the man."

I picked up the office phone and called a Mr. Fred Reed (who, of course, was a friend of mine) and asked him if he was still interested in the 10 shares of stock in the Gold Bar Dredging Company. He replied that he was. I told him to bring a $10,000 check to a particular attorney's office and the stock would be ready for him. Ed Chemmo had a puzzled look. I think that he just then realized what he was doing. I had him so confused when I asked him to meet me in the district attorney's office that he was just now gaining his senses. And now he realized that he would not only be taking a minority interest in the dredge, but he would be out as treasurer. The books would all be relinquished to me, and I would have complete control of the company. But there was no way he was going to get out of losing equal interest in the dredge. The district attorney's office was too close for that, and he knew it.

Fred Reed arrived and the attorney allowed us to use a room in his office for a stockholders' meeting. Reed handed me the $10,000 check made out to the company, but our attorney said that it would have to be done differently. He had Reed make the check out to Ed Chemmo and then had Ed endorse the check to the Gold Bar Dredging Company. Then Chemmo transferred 10 shares of his stock in the company to Fred Reed. During the meeting (which was cut and dried) Reed was elected secretary-treasurer and myself president. I asked Ed if the few books he had were all the company books there were. He replied they were. I informed Chemmo that his salary would be discontinued as of that day, and also told him that I was still checking on checks that he had put out in the company's name and that I expected him to make all checks good that were not put out in the interest of the company.

Bo and I at Mt. Hood just before we were married.

Left: Fred Reed, on the left, with Bo and the author on a sunny day in Portland.

Right: Floyd Marsh retrieves some meat for his hungry miners at the Lucky Strike mine in Arizona.

Whether this method I used in gaining control of the company was ethical or not, it certainly was the right thing to do; and when anything is right to me, it is ethical. For one thing, I saved the dredge and our company, and I even saved the money Ed Chemmo had in the dredge. With this extra $10,000 to get Ed Chemmo out, I was now in $37,000 on this mining adventure, so I had to make it work. I felt that it was a great gain to me to have Fred Reed with me and to have Ed Chemmo out. Reed was a very unusual man. He was very efficient and capable at whatever he attempted to do. He had a wonderful personality and was excellent in handling men. I employed him as general manager, and it was he who helped me pull the company out of the predicament that it was in. I felt that everything was in good hands with Fred at the dredge, so I spent more time traveling over the country getting material for the dredge.

It was on one of these trips to Portland at this time that I found the sweetest treasure of all. One evening while walking down Fourth Avenue, I saw through the window of a small malt shop the most beautiful little girl selling 10 cent milk shakes and 5 cent hot dogs. For the next few days I ate more hot dogs than I had in all my life, trying to find out the name of this girl, but all I could come up with was "Bo," which her customers called her. However, in my persuasive way, I finally got her up to the license bureau to put the name of Leona Calhoun on the dotted line. Ever since, she has been known as Mrs. Floyd Marsh—but she is still "Bo" to her friends and me.

After getting rid of Chemmo, we found that he had taken me for more than I suspected. We discovered bills that had been sent to himself that were irrelevant in building the dredge, in addition to canceled checks given for items for his personal use. On the other hand, Fred was a very capable bookkeeper. Two weeks after he took over the books, he found that Chemmo had fraudulently taken or embezzled more than $12,000 of the company funds. After verifying these frauds and misuse of company money, I contacted my attorney in Redding and was advised that I had a good embezzlement case against Chemmo. But to

## Building a Gold Dredge

put him behind bars would not build the dredge. I told Fred that I had reason to believe that Chemmo had money, and that he kept it in cash and gold nuggets in the Redding Bank. I had seen him go in and out of the bank with a small black bag, from which I had seen him display gold nuggets.

I told Fred that I had a plan to get some of the money, and maybe all of it, that Chemmo had taken from the company, and when I revealed the plan to him for him not to think I had been seeing too many outlaw movies. I told Fred that we would go to San Francisco and bring Chemmo back, and make him go into the bank and get the little black bag and reimburse the company for the $12,000 that he'd taken. Fred replied, "Fine if it works."

As I recall, it was a Friday morning that Fred and I left camp about 2 a.m. We arrived at the Oakland Ferry slip in time to get the 6 a.m. ferry to San Francisco. From the Ferry Building we drove directly to Chemmo's hotel. We went to his room without announcing ourselves. Ed was just getting up. He was very surprised to see us, and wanted to know what it was all about. I told him to get dressed and we would tell him. After he got dressed Fred and I entered his room and locked the door behind us.

Chemmo was pale and a little scared. He asked, "What are you going to do to me?" I replied, "That all depends." Then I laid the facts out before him. We produced faulty bills and canceled checks for items of his personal use, amounting to over $12,000 that he had taken the company for. Ed attempted a weak defense by saying part of the money was his, but I reminded him that once his or my original investment was in the company treasury it was company money. And I also told him that he jeopardized my investment when he used company money other than to build the dredge. I said that he was going to do something now in which he had no choice, and that was to go back to Redding with Fred and me. At Redding, though, he had a choice, either to go into the bank and get his little black bag and reimburse the company for the $12,000 he had embezzled, or to go to the district attorney's office and face a charge of embezzlement. Further, we had chose a weekday to make this trip so we could do business with the district attorney. After telling us that he had only a few hundred dollars in a lock box in the Redding Bank, he agreed to go with us, which pleased me, as I knew that he had more than a few hundred dollars in that little black bag in the Redding Bank, and I intended to get it. We left Ed's room and went to my car, which was parked at the curb alongside the hotel. At the car Ed looked around, saw some people on the sidewalk, and perhaps thought that I wouldn't do anything to him if he refused to go with us.

Of all the tight spots I have been in, handling murders, robbers, and criminals of every category, I have never lost my cool. But at this moment it wasn't Floyd Marsh standing in my shoes. There alongside my car on the streets of San Francisco I did the most foolish thing I have ever done in my life. I almost committed a murder. I reached in my pocket and pulled out a large pocketknife that I always carry. Opening it, I told Ed that I would lay all his guts right out there on the street if he refused to go with us. I meant it, and Ed could see in my eyes that I did.

Chemmo got in the car and I was relieved when we boarded the ferry for Oakland and were on our way to Redding. On our way back I got hold of myself and wondered what came over me to almost kill a man. I was angrier with Ed now than before because he almost got me into a lifetime of trouble by killing him. Then I told him that if he didn't square with me that I would not dirty my hands on him as I could get a man from the underworld to throw him in the bay (and I pointed toward San Francisco Bay) for $500. And that is just what I might have done if he had not gone absolutely straight with me on our other dealings.

We arrived in Redding just at noon. As I recall, my thinking was that there perhaps would be only a few people around the bank. As we drove up to it, Ed remarked that he would go in and get the black bag that I wanted. I replied, "No deal." I

## Building a Gold Dredge 209

didn't know if I would be allowed to go into the lock-box department with Ed or not, but I was going to give it a try. Ed still insisted that he go in alone.

I told him that if he went in the bank alone and didn't bring the black bag out with $12,000 in it, he was going across the street to the district attorney's office, and in addition to this he was going to get the bay treatment. Ed thought that I meant what I was telling him, and I did. He then asked me to come with him into the bank. I gathered up a handful of papers as though we were on a business deal, and we went into the lockbox department of the bank. The little black bag was in his box. After examining the box for other values, we returned to the car with the long-sought "little black bag."

Upon examining the bag we found $3,000 in Government Bonds, $2,000 in cash, and a lot of gold nuggets. Ed said there was about $3,000 worth. Seeing that we had him over a barrel, he wanted to work out a deal with us. He said he would cash the Government Bonds and give us the $3,000, in addition to the $2,000 in cash, and also half the gold nuggets. He pointed out that he owned half of the $12,000 we claimed he'd taken from the company, and that I only owned half. He figured that $6,000 should cover his obligation. I replied that his figures would be correct if I was personally getting the $6,000, but that the money was going back in the company, of which he still owned a large interest. However, it seemed that Ed's offer was the best way out for both him and me.

We could use the money to finish the dredge, and his doing "time" would not benefit anyone. So we settled on his figures. He gave us the $2,000 cash, and the $3,000 from the Government Bonds. The gold weighed out to a little over $3,000 worth. We made out a deposit slip for a little over $6,500 and had Ed watch us deposit it in the account of the Gold Bar Dredging Company. This gave us about $26,000 to finish the dredge. With this money and a capable fellow like Fred Reed with me, I felt very confident that we would soon have a gold dredge going.

Front end of dredge before conveyor bucket line had been installed.

Stern of the dredge—which was 65 feet long and 40 feet wide—showing long gravel stacker in the center with riffles (to catch the gold) on each side.

## Building a Gold Dredge 211

With all this behind us and more money to work with, Fred and I poured on the coal. Besides, I now had an increased desire for the dredge to succeed because of my new bride, Bo. We were spending our honeymoon in a tent at camp instead of a swanky hotel in Hawaii—Bo being with me to help me endure the long hours I was spending at the dredge. We increased the crew to 16 men, of four different trades: carpenters, plumbers, electricians and machinists. Then we had a drilling crew testing ground to be dredged, and a truck crew hauling material to the dredge and supplies to camp. My brother Pete was hired to cook. He had lost one of his legs when a young boy, but this didn't dampen his joyful nature or his desire to be useful. He kept the camp in a jolly mood with his stories, jokes, and good humor. Pete was the brother next younger to me in age, and I often wished that I had been born with his cheerful philosophy. He lived as though he truly enjoyed life, good or bad, though, he never had an extra dollar. Pete passed on several years ago, broke but happy.

We wanted to float the dredge by July 1, and once afloat, we hoped to start digging. As we progressed, sightseers, salesmen, promoters, and "what-have-you" appeared at the dredge. Many, we knew, were sent by Ed Chemmo, trying to sell his remaining shares in the company. In fact, some would tell us that they had come to look the dredge over in view of purchasing Ed's stock. Some were interested in an investment of only $1,000, meaning that we could have as many as seven new shareholders—which would be a nuisance. And what questions these prospective shareholders would ask! I had one "stock" line for all of them. I would tell them that mining was a gamble; and I would also tell them what Harold's Club in Reno tells its customers, and that is, "If you can't afford to lose, don't play."

About the first of July, Chemmo came out to the camp and said he would like to look at the dredge. I told him, being a stockholder, that he was certainly welcome to do so. After looking the dredge over, Ed remarked that he had been offering his shares too cheap. He wanted to know what the book value of our stock was. I said that of late we had purchased more material for the dredge than we previously thought would be necessary, and had employed more technical labor as the dredge advanced; also that the over-all cost of $60,000 that I once thought would build the dredge seemed now to fall short from $8,000 to $10,000. This would put the book value of the original 34 shares to over $2,000 per share.

Ed Chemmo then told me what his visit to the dredge was for. He said he had a very good prospect in Portland that he wanted to bring to the dredge in a few days. He said that this prospect wanted all his stock, which was 7 shares. This pleased me very much as one more stockholder would be better than seven. Ed told me all about his new prospect, and asked me to help him make the deal. He said the man was a retired logging operator, and was a financially and responsible businessman by the name of Alf Olin. Ed made an appointment with me when he could bring the prospect to see the dredge, as he was sure Olin would want to talk with me. As I recall, for some reason Olin wanted to arrive at the dredge on a Sunday afternoon. We made the appointment for the following Sunday, which was only a few days away.

After Chemmo left, I got busy figuring out the material and labor cost to complete the dredge, as this fellow Olin seemed to be a person I might want to have a large interest in the dredge. After figuring a safe margin on the material and labor to finish the dredge, I found the total came to a little less than $8,000 beyond what we now had. I had an insurance agent come out to the dredge and give me an estimate of the value we could insure the dredge for, and I was surprised when he told me that the figure would be in the neighborhood of $80,000. I was pleased for two reasons at this figure. One was, it showed we did a good job economically in building the dredge; it would also be a good talking point in selling Ed's interest to Olin, in case I liked him—and it wouldn't take much for him to be a better business associate than Chemmo. I was going to be the one who made the sale or killed it.

## Building a Gold Dredge 213

On the following Sunday, Ed arrived in camp with Alf Olin, Olin's son Herb, and another party. They got there about 2 o'clock in the afternoon. After a few remarks about the weather, we walked over to the dredge. On our way, Olin remarked,
"Perhaps you wondered why I wanted to come on a Sunday afternoon." I replied that I did, and for a bit of humor, I said it didn't interfere with our church service, as we attended in the forenoon. Then Olin told us why. One reason was that by leaving Portland in the early morning he would arrive at our camp in the early afternoon, and he wanted to visit the dredge on a Sunday when there would be no men working so he could get a good view of everything. I replied that that was a good, logical reason. After spending about two hours at the dredge, we returned to camp for one of Pete's good Sunday dinners. This particular Sunday it was "chicken and dumplin's."

After dinner Olin and his party wanted to meet with just Fred and me, to go over the books and get an early history of our company, as well as prospects for the future. The first thing Olin wanted to know was why Chemmo was selling his entire interest. I told him about Chemmo's activity in the company and why he was not involved in the operation any more. As to why he was selling his stock, I didn't know, unless it was that he needed the money, as I thought Ed had confidence that the dredge would make money. Olin wanted to know when we expected to complete the dredge, and if the money we now had in the treasury would be enough to finish the job.

I replied that I hoped to start the dredge digging about the first of July, and that my estimate at this time was that we would need about $8,000 more than we now had in our treasury to finish the job. He asked me by what means I intended to raise the money. I told him that I myself had the money to finish the job, but as we were a stock company we would have to borrow the money on the company's assets, which would be no problem.

I assured Olin that the dredge would be built, that I already had the finances lined up. I showed him the $140,000 insurance estimate I had been promised on the dredge when finished. This somewhat attested to the value we had in it. The estimate was raised from an $80,000 estimate we had received earlier. After we went over the books and gave Olin a picture of what lay ahead for us, he seemed pleased and bid us goodnight, and we all hit the hay long past midnight.

The next morning Olin asked me to walk over our ground with him and show him the boundary lines, which I did, and also showed him drill test holes and ground that carried gold value enough to dredge. After another viewing of the dredge, Olin and his party left with Ed Chemmo for Redding, stating that they would be back in the late afternoon or evening. I knew then that we would soon have a new stockholder, and this pleased all of us. It was late in the afternoon when Ed returned from Redding with his party, and as I suspected, a deal had been made.

Olin handed me 7 shares of the Gold Bar Dredging Company stock registered to Ed Chemmo and assigned over to him, and asked me to have it transferred to the name of Alf H. Olin. This I very happily asked Fred Reed to do. I never learned exactly what Ed got for his stock, but he later told a certain party that he made a "bundle" on the deal; but to me, he never said "thank you."

Olin was now in a hurry to get back to Portland and wished to drive part way that evening, so after having dinner with us, and with his stock tucked in his pocket, he and his party headed toward Portland. He seemed to be a very happy man, saying that he would return in about a week and bring his son, Herb, back, who had already made arrangements with Fred to work on the dredge. This particular evening, now over 44 years ago, was the last time I saw or heard of Ed Chemmo. I never missed him; however, I will never forget him.

After this deal was over, everything progressed smoothly. We were now two weeks away from the target date of July 1, to start the dredge. We were also out of money. I furnished a friend of mine $8,000, who in turn loaned it to the company, as

Fred B. Reed, superintendent of Gold Bar Dredging Corporation.

Conveyor bucket line on the dredge dumping in the hopper.

Bo and I at the dredge.

I was advised by my attorney to finance the finishing of the dredge this way. A week before our digging date, we floated the dredge to pick out any bugs that might be in it. Everything seemed to be in order with the exception of a couple of electrical parts that we hurriedly had sent out from Yuba City. We planned to operate the dredge 24 hours a day. This meant 3 shifts and 3 crews. To find 3 good dredge operators to handle the digging bucket-line was not going to be easy.

Bob Setzer, who had been with us since we started the dredge, was an old dredge master and a good one. He could pick and train dredge oprators for us, and he knew when a man was handling the controls right. Fred Reed's son, Elton, had been with us through the construction of the dredge. Bob liked Elton; he said he was a good machinist, steady and reliable, and that he would make a good dredge operator. (Elton Reed later became dredge master and in charge of some of the largest U.S. Government suction dredges on the West Coast.) We secured two other operators from Marysville. Bob stated that he himself would work the relief shift, in addition to overseeing the general operation of the dredge. This about fixed us up for an operation crew. The oilers and riffle attendants could be taken from our construction crew.

We had a modern-sized dredge, 65 feet long by 40 feet wide, with a digging ladder of 42 heavy steel buckets weighing 300 pounds and holding 10 square feet of material each, with 16 buckets a minute dumping into the dredge hopper. We could handle a lot of gold-bearing gravel in 24 hours. We had our ground all drilled and plotted out where we were going to dredge. The dredge digs its own pond to float in, so we didn't necessarily have to follow the river channel if there was ground that tested richer elsewhere. However, the ground must be level so the dredge can dig a pond to bedrock. It is on bedrock that the best gold values are found, and especially the largest nuggets. About 6 inches of bedrock is dug up and run through the dredge in order to get the gold in the crevices.

Floyd Marsh in control house of the dredge. Large bull wheels at right give one an idea of the size of the machinery.

Bo, right, on bridge of dredge with friends.

## CHAPTER 23

## *Start to Dredge Gold*

We had the big celebration set for July 1, to start the dredge out, but some trouble developed in the electric wiring that set us back a couple of days. However, during the two days no one seemed bored or complained. While Prohibition was still in force, there were many cheers in evidence. Olin had his family and friends at the camp, and there were many friends of employees there also. I had some friends down from Portland and out from Redding. It was a big week for me. I had worked hard and long for it, and I will never forget the thrill and satisfaction of seeing the big, endless bucket-line turn over, dumping gold-bearing gravel into the dredge hopper and going through the trommel screen and out over the gold-retrieving riffles. The first week of July, 1932, will always be a memorable week to me for a great accomplishment.

As I recall, the dredge starting digging about 4 p.m., July 3. My wife Bo broke a bottle of champagne over the bow, and a big "Hurrah" went up from everyone. Pete had fixed a big turkey dinner at 2 p.m. that day, so everyone stood around the dredge during the evening and watched it work. Needless to say, very few of us slept any that night. In fact, I slept on the dredge for the next two nights. Everything worked beautifully. We happened to start out in some rich ground that tested good. We could see the coarse gold in the upper riffles. About midnight I had Bob shut the dredge down and everyone looked the riffles over and retrieved a good-sized nugget for a souvenir. At today's gold price this would have been quite a loss to the company, but 43 years ago, with gold values at $20 per troy ounce, it didn't amount to much.

## Start to Dredge Gold

After an exciting night around a big bonfire watching the dredge operate, we answered Pete's call about 7 a.m. for breakfast. Most of the guests slept the greater part of the day. I took a nap in the forenoon and made a trip to Redding in the afternoon. As I drove back to camp from Redding, I picked up some snipers who were panning the creeks crossing the highway. They, not knowing me, of course, excitingly told me about the large new gold dredge that was starting up on the Trinity at Lewiston. Our dredge was the talk of the countryside. Once we started operating we had no trouble getting experienced technical help. We always had a list on file of dredge operators, oilers, and tradesmen of every profession.

We had operated only a couple days when we discovered that we were losing some fine gold. By panning the tail end of the riffles we found that a considerable amount of fine gold was going out with the tailings. We could figure only two reasons for this. Either the riffles were filling up and the fine gold was flowing over them, or we needed quicksilver in the riffles to catch the fine gold. We had intended to clean up only about once a week, but with the trouble of losing some fine gold, we decided to make a clean-up after the first 3 days. This first clean-up was exciting as we didn't know what to expect. After we had operated for a while, we had a pretty good idea what the clean-up would be. We had run 3 days and 4 nights, with 3 hours out for repairs, giving us about 80 hours of operation. We cleaned up from the riffles 82 troy ounces of gold, and the concentrates yielded 4 ounces of gold.

This was not too bad, but on the other hand it was not too good either. With our gold testing a little over $18 per troy ounce in value—which put our 80-hour run at $1,568—we didn't have much surplus for uncalculated shutdowns, mishaps, and other misfortunes. Our actual operation expense was a little over $350 for the 3 shifts in the 24 hours. We knew that we had lost some fine gold in this first run, but we didn't know just how much, so for the next run we put a 55-pound flash of quicksilver in the riffles, after which we could not pan any fine gold at the tail end of the riffles. So, it looked as if we had put an end to the fine-gold loss.

However, on the next run we found other trouble. We shut down for 12 hours for a quick trip to Yuba City for parts to a broken water pump. After getting replacements and repairing the pump, we continued on our second run. We ran for 6 days this time before we shut down for a clean-up, and to our most pleasant surprise we had a whale of a clean-up. I don't recall the exact amount of gold, but the receipts were something over $8,000 from the riffles and over $500 in value in gold and other minerals from the concentrates. We knew now that we had been losing a lot of fine gold that was going out over the riffles into the tailings.

There was one problem in using quicksilver to catch the gold, which was several hours work; this was to retort the quicksilver from the gold. However, it paid off, as a 55-pound flash of quicksilver that we used in every run cost only $85, and we retrieved about half of it through the retort process.

A problem we had not figured on was getting honest men to attend the riffles. We fired 4 men the first 3 weeks for taking nuggets from the upper riffles where we did not use quicksilver. It was only the upper riffles section that caught the nuggets where the theft problem was. I placed a heavy screen over the sluice trough that held these riffles. I locked the screen in place and gave the key to the dredge operator so the riffles would be accessible in case of overflow or clogging of the sluice trough.

Locking the riffles that caught the nuggets seemed to solve our nugget-theft problem. Then one day Pete remarked to me that there must be a lot of gold around the dredge. I asked him why, and he replied that he was finding gold in the lunch box of one of the men. I got the name of the man, who was a night riffle tender. When this gentleman brought his lunch box in the next morning, I examined it and found gold attached to quicksilver in the inside lining. This particular fellow had been a placer miner and knew how to retort the quicksilver from the

## Start to Dredge Gold

gold, which was an act only an experienced placer miner would know how to perform. Needless to say, we let this fellow go.

In my many years of police work, of course, I never ran up against anything like this. I didn't know exactly what to do other than employ a bonded watchman. I contacted the Burns Detective Agency and got the price of a watchman for the late night shift where the theft had occurred. This was not only expensive, but it would be embarrassing. An idea struck me to try a ruse before putting on a watchman. So, the next men we hired to attend the riffles on the night shift were told what the situation had been, that within the last 3 weeks we had fired 4 riffle tenders for taking gold out of the riffles, and now we had installed a device in the dredge that would detect any thief, and it was a device that would hold up as testimony in court. Now, in addition to being fired from our employment, the riffle tender would be turned over to the district attorney to be prosecuted for theft. This was a long shot, but it worked. After this we had some traps set, and even unlocked the riffles that caught the large nuggets. I don't think we ever lost another bit of gold.

After a few 6-day-run clean-ups, which were consistent in value, we set our clean-up period to every 10 days, which ran from $8,000 to $9,000 for each clean-up. This, with the smelter returns of $1,000 to $1,200 for the concentrates, made a profitable operation. Bo and I were living high, taking in shows and night clubs every week-end in San Francisco, and a trip to Portland every once in a while. Fred Reed and his son, Elton, were doing a good job overseeing the dredge operation. I was at the dredge now only at clean-up time. My wife and I were making up for the long months we had spent at camp while building the dredge.

Our August clean-ups came to over $30,000 and we were shut down for 4 days for repairs. We had run into some hard bedrock, which was giving us trouble, and for some reason or other experienced labor, especially machinist and dredge operators, was demanding higher wages and was harder to find. When our next 10-day period came to clean up, we had run only 9 days as

Left: Three gold bars from our last clean-up that weighed 800 ounces, for which we received $15,000. On today's market it would be worth more than $135,000.

Right: Fred Reed in front of our office at the dredge.

Camp at the dredge at left is where Bo and I lived. Next on the right are: Office, Fred Reed's cabin, Elton Reed's and his wife's cabin, then the Olin's cabin where Herb lived.

we had been down one day for repairs. However, we cleaned up anyway, and it was one of our best, with over $13,000 in gold from the riffles and over $1,200 values in the concentrates, which came to about $15,000 for the 9-day run. This was about 80% profit. At this time we had the dredge more than paid for and a good bank surplus, However, there was trouble awaiting us ahead that we could not foresee.

About half way through the next 10-day run we ran into some rough, hard diorite bedrock which broke our conveyor bucket-line. After a day repairing it and getting it to operating again, we ran into some real trouble. The lower tumbler of the conveyor bucket-line went out. It was something we could not repair on the job. It weighed about 4 tons. It had to be loaded on a special truck and hauled to Yuba City for repairs. While shut down, we made a clean-up on the few days' run which was 4 days and 5 nights; this came to a little over $5,000.

The values were holding up well, if we could only shake the hard luck or get into some different kind of bedrock.

When we got the tumbler back and installed in the dredge, we had been shut down 5 days, which meant 120 operating hours and a lot of gold when taking it out at the rate that we were. The repair charges and camp expense for the 5 days cost us over $12,000. This was quite a setback for us, in addition to the expense. We had lost valuable working time, as we were working against time to get over as much ground as we could before the bad winter weather set in. Then there would be the high water in the spring.

The next 6-days' run put us to the first of October. We had just a fair clean-up of a little over $8,000 for gold recovered and concentrates values from the smelter. The bedrock was so rough we were not getting all the gold, and we were afraid to dig deeper into the bedrock because of destruction to the machinery. As we were running under a much slower bell and putting a lot less material through the dredge, we decided to run for two weeks between clean-ups. This would save some time, as we put in about a day to a clean-up and the dredge had to be shut down. Our first clean-up in October was just an ordinary one as to value. Of the two weeks we intended to run for the clean-up we were shut down two nights and a day for repairs. We recovered $10,000 in values of gold in the riffles and smelter returns of concentrates values.

On the last couple of visits to the dredge, Olin seemed to be displeased about something. He had come to camp especially for the last two clean-ups, and to my surprise he asked me if I ever thought of selling my interest in the dredge. I could not imagine what was eating on him. After he left for Portland on this last trip, I heard through the grapevine that his son, Herb, who was one of the dredge operators, was not getting along with Bob Setzer, the dredge master, and thought that he could do a better job himself.

While I told Olin I had given no thought to selling my interest in the dredge, I had turned over the thought several times in the back of my head that I was now tied down too much at the dredge, and in order to look after my interest, I had to look after everyone else's. I could get out at a good profit as I was sitting in the driver's seat. I had built a good dredge that was making money, and, too, I had controlling interest—and I had put myself on at a good salary. But I had no idea what I should ask Olin for my interest, above, of course, what I had in the dredge—all of which had been returned to me.

I realized that the price of everything had increased since we built the dredge. And we had made many improvements since we had the dredge appraised and fire insurance put on it for $140,000. Then we had the dredge reappraised and fire insurance raised to $235,000, and I remarked to the insurance representative that I doubted the dredge could be rebuilt for this amount. However, I was more concerned about break-downs and mechanical trouble than I was about fire. Now I had some idea of what to ask Olin for my interest, and I had some concrete proof of what value the dredge carried.

Since the last clean-up we had been shut down several times, sometimes for a day. The rough, hard bedrock continued to plague us. We had run only 6 days during the 10 days since the last clean-up, but we decided on a clean-up as the riffles showed good gold value. To my surprise, Olin was at the dredge, and for the 6-day run we had a very good clean-up of large bright nuggets. It was the best clean-up for a short run that we had experienced. Gold in the riffles came to a little over $9,000, with good values in the concentrates. Olin seemed to be very enthusiastic about our gold recovery, and he didn't ask about the break-downs and trouble we had been running into lately. I was glad that he didn't as I could not lie to him, and I didn't want to tell him the truth.

I waited for him to bring up the subject of buying my interest, and he did after we completed and weighed the clean-up. He asked me if I had given any further thought to selling. (Trying not to show it, I had given a lot of thought to selling—with winter fast approaching and more frequent break-downs.) I replied that I had given it some thought, at the same time trying to act reluctant in order to get as good a deal as possible, since this seemed to be one chance in a lifetime. I remarked that I held controlling interest, which made my stock more valuable than any of the other stock in the corporation. Olin replied that he realized this, and for that reason he was ready to offer me a good deal. Before I could reply, he said that he had some property in Portland that was worth a quarter of a million dollars that he would trade in on the dredge.

This last remark from Olin about floored me. I knew I had to make some kind of reply. After taking a deep breath and trying not to look surprised, I said that this kind of property would carry a large tax burden. His reply to this really left me groggy. He said this was income property; the income would make the taxes seem insignificant. He said it was a brick apartment house with an income at this time of $5,000 per month, with only 60 per cent occupied. My feeling was to say—let us start for Portland this very moment, but I had to play it cool. I said I might be interested, but could not get to Portland for a few days. As this was in the middle of the week, Olin wanted to know if I could get to Portland by the following Monday. I told him that I thought I could (in fact, I knew I could).

It was just 4 days until the following Monday and a long 4 days it was. The more I thought of the deal, the more I liked it. I was just praying that we would not have any serious breakdowns until we could get some kind of deal going. The day before I left for Portland, we were down half a day with a broken conveyor bucket-line. The bedrock was not getting any easier to work, and we had one dredge operator who just didn't know how to work hard bedrock. The dredge master, Bob Setzer, told me he would stay with this particular dredge operator all he could while I was in Portland. I had sort of built myself up to thinking I would get a good deal, but when I saw this 5-story brick apartment with 265 apartments I wondered if I was dreaming.

I just could not believe what I was looking at. I checked the apartment house street number to be sure I had the right one. And, in addition to the apartment house, I was to get a half block of vacant business property nearby. I got in touch with Olin and got permission to have an appraiser look at the property. The appraiser and I spent half a day going through the apartment house, and getting values on other like apartments in this vicinity and on vacant land in the area.

The appraiser had a high regard to property in this particular part of Portland. He told me that values on property here had risen quite rapidly during the last few years. He said that the Olin apartment house would have been valued at about $200,000 a few years ago, but at this time he would appraise the property at $245,000 (valued at over a million dollars today).

Needless to say, I was very excited about making the deal, but knowing Olin as I did, I realized that I had to handle him with kid gloves. I didn't want to go right back to him with an acceptance. After visiting some friends and seeing my attorney, I called Olin, only to find he had been quite ill and that it would be several days before he could see me. I had now been away from the dredge almost two weeks, during which there had been breakdowns several days, making about a 10- or 11-day run for a clean-up. I thought it advisable to return to the dredge for a clean-up, which I expected to be a good one that might take Olin's mind off our troublesome breakdowns.

Arriving back at camp, I found the dredge down with a minor conveyor bucket-line break which would take only a short time to repair. As I arrived at camp late in the day, I told the night crew to take the night off. They could do the repair work the next day while we made the clean-up—and what a clean-up! The 11-day run produced over 800 ounces of coarse gold. With the smelter returns for the concentrates we had over a $15,000 clean-up. This would be power in my hands in dealing with Olin. I waited a few days to call Olin to inquire how he was getting along, but more so to find out if he was able to resume talks on our deal. He told me that he was feeling good and for me to return to Portland within the next few days. Of course, I told him of our last big clean-up; he replied that he had heard about it from his son, Herb.

After a few days I returned to Portland. I contacted my attorney and we set up an appointment with Olin and his attorney. I told my attorney that I had Olin's property appraised and that there was ample value there to cover my investment in the dredge by about three-fold, and far in excess of the entire value of the dredge at this time. But I had decided to ask for $25,000 in addition to Olin's property for my interest, and this I thought that I could get. However, I would forego the $25,000 cash in order to get a quick deal. My attorney said he thought this was a good strategy and that I might just get the extra cash in the deal. I told my attorney that I wanted something to bargain with in order to get a quick deal as time was against me, that our break-downs were occurring more frequently and winter was fast approaching.

When we met the next day, Olin produced a good balance sheet of what the apartment house was bringing in, with only 60 per cent occupied. This, with the property increasing in value, made the deal much more favorable than I expected. Olin's attorney made the first remark regarding it. He said,

"Now, Mr. Marsh, as you have looked the property over and had it appraised, what comments have you got on the deal." I replied (with tongue in cheek) that I would have to have $25,000 in cash in addition to the apartment house and the vacant property, that had been suggested by Olin.

For a few seconds no one said a word. Then Olin broke the silence by a remark that he would like to visit the dredge again, that he wanted to take another look at some things and have a talk with his son, Herb. I was not prepared for this, which I did not expect. I had been sure that Olin would make me a counter-offer, which I was going to grab, but this he did not do. So I had to abide by his latest suggestion.

The next few days dragged on. The weather began to get colder. Snow covered the Trinity Mountains around our camp. It was now the first part of December. As I recall the date, it was on a week-end, the 10th of December, 1932. I remarked to Bo that we should go to San Francisco for the week-end and take in a couple of shows. She replied that she thought this was an excellent idea. As we drove down the mountain road from our camp on the Trinity River, I remarked that we were now in the blue chips, that we would soon be the owners of a large, valuable brick apartment house that would bring in a good income for the rest of our lives, and that we could just travel and enjoy ourselves. We soon arrived in Oakland, where we took the ferry across the bay to San Francisco. After registering in our hotel and having dinner, we selected a show to go to.

I don't recall just what was playing at the show, but I will never forget the message that greeted us upon our return to the hotel. It was from Fred Reed, my superintendent at the dredge, and it wasn't pleasant to read. The message said there had been a fire on the dredge. I immediately got in touch with Fred, who informed me that he didn't know the full extent of damage other than that some large motors and transformers were destroyed. As there was nothing I could do on this particular night, I instructed Fred to get in touch with the insurance adjusters the first thing the next day and said that I would return to camp early the following morning.

What greeted me at camp the next day was not a pretty sight. The wheelhouse, several large motors and transformers, and also part of the big hopper had burned and fallen through the upper deck, and with other burnt material covered the inside of the dredge hull. It was hard to assess the damage until some cleaning up was done. The insurance adjusters were right on the job. I called Olin and asked him to sit in with me at our meeting with the insurance adjusters. Olin didn't want any part of rebuilding the dredge. He said that he was just a stockholder and the insurance company should rebuild the dredge. This made me feel very bad to think that I had made him a lot of money in the dredge, and now to protect my interest I had to pull his chestnuts out of the fire.

After we figured out what was burnt and damaged, Fred Reed, Bob Setzer, and I met with the insurance adjusters 5 days after the fire. The adjusters had been at the dredge every day since the fire, figuring the damages (and to their advantage I learned later). They seemed to know the price of every piece of equipment we had put in the dredge. This didn't bother me as I knew they were obligated to replace the dredge. But they caught me off balance and much surprised when they gave us a figure of $55,000 to replace the dredge. This really had me dazed, as this was almost as much as it cost us to build the dredge. I asked the adjusters to allow Reed, Setzer, and myself a little conference, which they did. After a few minutes we decided to grab the offer, and to this day I can visualize the adjusters' pleasant expression, and I was soon to find out why.

I learned later what a big mistake we had made. Not wanting to go through building the dredge again, I contacted a dredge builder in Yuba City and had him come to camp and give us an estimate on putting the dredge back in working condition with warranted material. The contractor was at the dredge the better part of two days and gave me the shock of my life when he presented me with a bid of $95,000 to rebuild the dredge. I thought that the man was stark mad, and almost told him so. Dismissing this fellow, I contacted another contractor at Marysville a few miles away, and after little over half a day at the dredge he gave me a bid of $96,000 to repair the dredge.

I thought now that maybe I was the one who was stark mad, or had been asleep the last year and didn't know what had been going on. So I had a little talk with this last contractor and told him what it cost us to build the dredge, and asked him why the rebuilding of the dredge was so high. He cited many things that I had not taken into consideration. One was that the dredge now was in a rough place to get equipment into. A truck road of over a mile would have to be built to the dredge in order to get equipment in. Also, used equipment available to me when I built the dredge was no longer available, and new equipment had risen greatly in price, as well as labor.

Now, this gave me a different picture to look at. With the money in our treasury, together with the insurance money (the latter was promptly and willingly paid), we could rebuild the dredge. However, to rebuild the dredge to protect my interest would be carrying Olin along on my shoulders. Still, I wanted the dredge rebuilt as I had secured the land from Ed Chemmo that the dredge was on, and I had been getting royalties which had been good. Therefore, I wanted the dredge rebuilt and to continue to operate.

I had previously been approached by a Mr. E.W. Elrod of Portland, who had offered me a good price for my interest in the dredge. Now my thoughts turned to him. I contacted Elrod and told him the story. He immediately came to Redding, where I met him and drove him out to camp. After we looked the dredge over, we went through the books and figured our assets. We were in better condition than I realized. With company money in the bank, together with the insurance money, we had a ready cash worth of a little over $100,000, which seemed to be very pleasing to Elrod.

## Start to Dredge Gold

I told Elrod to make me an offer whereby he would replace me, one in which he would have controlling interest in the dredge and would be elected president with a plus of $100,000 in the treasury. After taking another look at the dredge and the 240 acres of land under lease (from me), Elrod made me an offer of $75,000 for my interest. I wanted to put my hand out and say "Lay it there," but I used a little more diplomacy. I told Elrod that I would accept his offer as I had other projects to devote my time to. And in addition to the $75,000, I expected to realize a good revenue in royalties from my ground that the dredge was to work.

Elrod and I drove to Redding and consummated our deal. Returning to camp, I had to take one last look at the project that for a year I had my heart and mind so engrossed in that I could think of nothing else.

As I stood on the banks of the dredge pond looking down on the once-proud dredge that now lay in black ruins, I had mixed emotions. I was leaving something that had been so close to me that it seemed to be a part of myself. Yet, I now felt free, like a man who had been released from jail. Walking back to camp, I thought of the many ventures I had been in and how I had grabbed a little fortune from some of them, and how someday I was going to hit the big one.

And Floyd Marsh did hit the big one. He went on to become rich and famous in a business that was the largest of its kind in the world. However, to him the past "20 Years As A Soldier of Fortune" were worth more to him than all the fame and wealth he accomplished during the rest of his fabulous life. And now in this year of 1976, he wants to thank the Lord for a good life, and offer thanks for the wonderful 77 years that the Lord has tolerated him.

"I appreciate the fact that very few men have enjoyed the exciting and adventurous life that I have; my adventures resemble those of a real Horatio Alger. In addition to making three

Leona "Bo" Calhoun just before she became Mrs. Floyd R. Marsh.

Floyd R. Marsh just before his marriage to Bo.

fortunes (most of which have been spent and enjoyed), I have narrowly missed several, such as the big oil discovery on the North Slope of Alaska (missed by only two hours), which would have been worth millions to me; and a big oil project in California that would have meant a lifetime of wealth—but these are now of no concern to me.

"As I approach the sunset of life, which is inevitable, and it nears the western horizon, I am thankful for a wonderful life and the fine family that have been afforded me—a life that has been full of *real living*, where I have met and cultivated the friendship of many wonderful people. It is the love of my family and friends that I will take with me; the gold I will leave here. I have often remarked to friends that if life were to be lived over again, and I had a choice, I would not change one thing.

"At the end of every day I am thankful that I am healthy and alive, and I offer a prayer for those less fortunate. And every morning I am appreciative of this, another day."—Floyd Marsh

# Index

## — A —

Airplanes visit Alaska, 62
Alaska arrival, 40
Alaska interior hike, 41, 42, 44
Alaska range, trip through, 52, 56, 57
Armistice signed, 35
Atwater, Mrs., had her baby, 104

## — B —

Blue, Perry, 49, 52, 54, 65
Bo and I, trips to Portland and San Francisco, 221, 228, 229
Bo, my dearest treasure, 206, 211
Boise Basin, placer mining, 109, 176
Borgdorf mining district, 159, 161
Break-up of rivers and streams, 48, 122, 124
Broad Pass, 40, 41, 76, 108
Buffalo Bill "101" Wild West Show, 20
Bundy, Leo, 87

## — C —

Cabin on the claims, 9
California gold fields, 5-7, 151
Caribou carried away, 53
Cash asked for kills deal, 228
Chemmo brought back to Redding, 205, 207, 208, 209
Chemmo, Ed, 200-214
Chemmo embezzled company funds, 206
Church service in Cripple Creek, 16
Clegg, Cecil H., 19, 59, 62, 70, 110
Clifton, Arizona, 2
Copper mines at Santa Rita, 147, 148
Copper ore produced, 195, 196
Corporation control changes, 202-204
Cripple Creek, 9, 21
Cripple Creek return, 23
Cross, Larry, foot frozen, 112-119

## — D —

Deposit, $50,000, Seattle bank, 139
Diamond City, 64
Dog killing case in court, 97
Dog team with Jake, 63
Dredge floated, and start to dig gold, 217
Dredge insured for $235,000, 224
Dredge replacement bid shocking, 229-230
Dredge sold to Elrod, 231

## — E —

Elk City, Idaho, 152
Elrod, E.W., 230, 231

## — F —

Family visit to Phoenix, 146, 147
Fight on the high seas, 137
Fine gold being lost, 219
Fire at the dredge, 228-230
Fire damage settlement too small, 229, 230
First clean-up, 219
First mining adventure, 2
First night at the cabin, 10
Flu epidemic at Healy, 44, 45
Flat, Alaska, 88
Fortune lost by unwise move, 228
Fort Worden, Washington, 25
Foster, Wilbur, 6, 8
French Creek gold strike, 155-158
Frisco Creek, Arizona, 2, 3

## — G —

Geese shooting almost fatal, 124
Gold Bar Dredging Corp., 201-231
Gold carried out in lunch box, 220
Gold dredge at Marysville, Calif., 5
Gold dredging of Gold Bar Dredging Corp. starts, 218
Gold quartz found at Two Boy mine, 16-18
Gold on Oregon beaches, 32
Gold quartz sold, 21
Gold snipping on Yellow Creek, 50

Gold strike, quartz, on Yellow
  Creek, The Oklahoma, 56, 67
Government Railroad, 41, 47, 59,
  107, 108
Grain harvest in Kansas, 20
Grangeville, Idaho, 153
Green, Dr. W.F., 73, 87, 112-119
Green Creek, Alaska, 52, 53, 68
Greene, Captain, 84, 130-132,
  135-136

— H —

Hart, Sam, files suit, 97, 99, 103
Hassayampa gold, 195-198
Healy, Alaska, 46
Higgins, Ralph, 2
Holy Cross departure, 91
Holy Cross trip, 88, 92
Holy Cross welcome, 89
Honesty best policy, 6
Hospital Corps, 26
Hydraulic syphon mining, 174-176

— I —

Iditarod, Alaska, 80, 88, 89
Insurance adjusters' meeting, 229

— J —

Joe, Old, 78, 105, 106
Joined Army, 25
Joined Portland Police
  Department, 178-193

— K —

Kantishna, Alaska, 47-58, 65-68
Kantishna trip over the trail,
  63-65
Kirkenoff, Mary, 61, 71, 73, 109,
  132
Knight's roadhouse a heaven, 70
Kuskokwim River, 84, 120-124,
  129, 132

— L —

Lake, Dr., 44, 45, 46
Lake, Johnnie, 68
Lang, Herbert, 4
Last and most valuable clean-up,
  227
Leave for Bethel, 129
Leave Kantishna, 68
Lemon, Dr. Oliver, 26

Lewiston, California, 200-201, 219
Little black bag, 207-209
Little Mint mine bid goodbye, 4
Little Mint mine, 3
Log cabin on Yellow Creek, 47, 60
Loomis, L.B., 84, 87
Lost on the pass, 78
Lost prospectors, 57
Louie, "Two-step," 42, 43
Lucky Lue claims sold, 134

— M —

Maddox, Lew, 99-103
Marriage plans changed, 110
Mary replaced with death letter,
  132
Mary sick in Nenana, 109
Mayor's secret police, 182
McCoy brothers, 12
McGrath arrival, 84, 85
McGrath bid farewell, 134
McGrath return brings anxiety, 94
McMullen, Pete, U.S. Marshal, 84,
  86, 88-93, 99-108
McReynolds, Floyd case, 183-186
Midnight sun, 99-103
Mining at "Two Boy" mine, 15
Mines, placer, start operating, 122
Money shortage, 202-206
Moose Creek, 49, 65

— N —

Nenana, Alaska, 46, 59, 60, 71, 73,
  108, 111
New gold strikes at Cripple Creek,
  11-12
Newspaper clippings, 192, 193
Night journey back to McGrath,
  111-113
Now a policeman, 178, 179
Nuggets stolen from riffles, 220

— O —

Olin, Alf, 212-220, 230
Olin buys stock, 214
Olin, Donald (U.S. Marshal),
  107-111
Olin, Herb, 213-227
Oklahoma, The, rich, then fails,
  66-67
Oklahoma, The, sold, 68
Operation successful, 117-119

Orofino, Idaho, 143-145
Oroville, California, 6, 151
Owens, Harry, 46, 108

— P —

Partnership formed, 8
Pass, on the great divide, 78
Pete, the cook, 211, 213, 218
Placer mining, Oroville, 5, 6
Proposed to Mary, 71
Property offered by Olin unbelievable, 226
Prospecting trip pays off, 125-129

— Q —

Quicksilver, used for fine gold, 219

— R —

Railroad a welcome sight, 59
Real estate business, 168-169
Reed buys stock, 204
Reed, Elton, 216, 221
Reed, Fred, general manager, 206, 221, 229-230
Released from the Army, 57
Resigned as U.S. Commissioner, 134
Ritter, Jack, 49, 52, 54, 65, 68
Return to Yellow Creek, 53
Rich strike on Lucky Lue Creek, 127-129
Roadhouses in Alaska, 42, 105-106
Rough bedrock troublesome, 225

— S —

Salmon River, Idaho, 153-165
Sampling Wilbur's claims, 11-14
Seattle departure for Alaska, 41
Serious breakdowns at dredge, 223
Setzer, Bob, 201-229
Sick on Yellow Creek, 54
Snow and rock slide disaster, 19
Souvenir given everyone, 218
Special train, 70
Spruce Division, 28, 36
States, return on M.S. Anvil, 135-138
Street car operator, 166-168
Sunday service at the mine, 4
Syphon mining operation unique, 172-176

— T —

Takotna River, 23, 24, 94-96
Tanana River, 46-48
Taylor, Dan, 153-155, 162-165
Theater business, 140-142
Tim, the beach miner, 32-34
Tom, my first mining adviser, 2-4
Tooth-pulling episode, 94-96
Trail into McGrath long and bitter, 74-76
Transferred to Fort Wright, Wash., 36
Trapping and shooting ducks, 47, 60
Trinity Mountains, 201, 228
Trinity River, 201-219
Trip to the railroad, 104-111
Two Boy Mining Co., 15

— U —

Unknown glacier and river, 55
U.S. Commissioner, appointment, 72-73
U.S. Commissioner's office taken, 86

— V —

Vancouver Barracks again, 56
Vice pay-off, 187-189
Vice Squad assignment, 180, 193
Vice Squad, in charge, 182
Visited picture studios, 38
Visited with my folks, 5, 38

— W —

Waldport, Oregon, 29, 31-34
War declared, 27
Wilbur killed in action, 37
Wilbur, with 165th, moves out, 66
Wilson, Herbert, U.S. Commissioner, Kantishna, 49, 50
Wolves, following Pete and I, 92-93

— Y —

Yellow Creek, 50-56, 62
Yuba City, California, 202, 216, 221
Yuba Dredge Company, 202, 229

## The Author

Floyd Marsh was born in the Indian Territory in 1898 (near Elk City) nine years before it became the State of Oklahoma. When he was three years old, his father took up a homestead in the sand hills in the northwest part of the Territory, about 40 miles north of Elk City, where the family lived for five years in semi-poverty. At the end of this time the family (there was now five boys) moved back to Elk City, and raised cotton on a rented farm.

Floyd was fifteen years old when his father died, just a mixed-up kid with an unfinished education and a desire for adventure and traveling. After some time on an Arizona cow ranch, he worked in the copper and gold mines in Arizona, California, and Colorado. Then came a year of roaming over the country with a partner. During this time he rode in the famous Buffalo Bill's 101 Wild West Show at Denver, Colorado, and worked in the grain harvest in Kansas. He served in the Army in the First World War; after the Armistice was signed and the smoke had cleared away, he went to Alaska where he did find adventure, gold and romance.

This young boy was so adventurous and daring in the mining camps, and while traveling over the frozen trails, that he became known throughout the Territory as the "Alaska Kid." He had been in Alaska less than two years when he became U.S. Commissioner in the Fourth District. After three years in Alaska he returned to the States with a fortune in gold; he had made two rich gold strikes while in the Far North. Returning to the States in 1923, he engaged in gold mining in Idaho, where he took out another fortune in gold.

In 1926, Author Marsh joined the Portland Police Department. Disappointed, disgusted and not approving of how he was required to enforce the prohibition and vice laws with favoritism, he desired to return to the more pleasant and enjoyable endeavor of his gold-mining days.

In 1932, he built a gold dredge on the Trinity River in California. It was about this time that this roving gold miner made the greatest discovery of his fabulous life, and that was a sweet little girl by the name of "Bo," whom he found working in a 10-cent malt shop in Portland, Oregon—where they still live. She took the place of his long-lost love in Alaska. Together they enjoy a wonderful family of two sons and a daughter and a number of admirable grandchildren.